"Poverty is a recurring theme of Christian wisdom: it's a defining concern in Jesus' teaching, a central principle in Franciscan spirituality, and a core issue in liberation theology. But I imagine many of us might pair admiration for the poverty of saints like Mother Teresa with an equally firm desire to avoid poverty for ourselves! Susan Pitchford writes with clarity and insight, and in *The Paradox of Poverty* she draws a number of surprising connections and conclusions to help us form a nuanced understanding of poverty, and to recognize why it remains an important touchstone for both nurturing our inner lives and giving shape to our collective mission. If you want to appreciate both the power and the tensions beneath 'Blessed are the poor,' this book is a wonderful resource."

—Carl McColman, author of *Read the Bible Like a Mystic* and *Eternal Heart*

"A wise old Franciscan friar once said that we moderns have forgotten the secret to a life in God, namely, that 'God is powerless and we keep looking for God where there is power.' But, as Susan Pitchford beautifully explains in these pages, this powerlessness of God is paradoxically the real power, the power of the poverty of God who did not cling to divinity but emptied himself by becoming human and dying on a cross. Those who enter into God through the portal of that seemingly powerless poverty are those whom Jesus calls 'the poor in spirit.' Why Jesus does so and why he also calls them 'blessed' are at the heart of Pitchford's fascinating book. It is the story of how and when the powerlessness of poverty becomes the power of God in us. I found *The Paradox of Poverty* a profound and moving read."

—Murray Bodo, OFM, author of *Francis: The Journey and the Dream*

“Susan Pitchford’s beautiful new book could not be more perfectly timed. In a world where division and doubt seem to be gaining the upper hand, she calls us back to our belovedness and to the countercultural paths of surrender, spiritual poverty, and devotion that lead us ever deeper into the heart of God.”

—Mary DeTurris Poust, writer, retreat leader, and spiritual director

The Paradox of Poverty

Why Are the Poor in Spirit "Blessed"?

Susan R. Pitchford

LITURGICAL PRESS
Collegeville, Minnesota

litpress.org

Cover design by David Drummond. Cover art: *Saint Francis in Meditation* by Francisco de Zurbarán. Wikimedia Commons (public domain).

Printed in the United States of America.

Library of Congress Cataloging-in-Publication Data

Names: Pitchford, Susan author
Title: The paradox of poverty : why are the poor in spirit "blessed"? / Susan R. Pitchford.
Description: Collegeville, Minnesota : Liturgical Press, [2025] | Includes bibliographical references. | Summary: "In The Paradox of Poverty, Susan Pitchford examines the ways in which followers of Christ have understood "poverty of spirit," and the traditions that have formed around their attempts to follow Jesus on this radical path. The Paradox of Poverty looks at some of the wisdom traditions that have formed this understanding: the scriptures, the desert mothers and fathers, the Franciscans, Liberation theologians, the 12 Step movement, and more"— Provided by publisher.
Identifiers: LCCN 2025009764 (print) | LCCN 2025009765 (ebook) | ISBN 9798400802102 trade paperback | ISBN 9798400802119 epub
Subjects: LCSH: Poverty—Religious aspects—Christianity | Spiritual life—Catholic Church | Christian life—Catholic authors | BISAC: RELIGION / Christian Theology / Ethics | RELIGION / Christian Living / Social Issues
Classification: LCC BV4647.P6 P58 2025 (print) | LCC BV4647.P6 (ebook) | DDC 248.4/7—dc23/eng/20250515
LC record available at https://lccn.loc.gov/2025009764
LC ebook record available at https://lccn.loc.gov/2025009765

For Mary Ellen Bryngelson, the freest person I know,
with love and gratitude for all you've been to me.
Your soul is a well-watered garden.

Contents

Acknowledgments

I'd like to begin by thanking Sister Laura Swan, OSB, for encouraging me to bring more of myself as a sociologist to my work. She also moved this book forward by convincing the sisters at St. Benedict's Monastery in St. Joseph, Minnesota, to put me up for five weeks in their Spirituality Center or *Studium*, where they offer to creatives the famous Benedictine hospitality. It was a joyful and unforgettable experience.

I'm also greatly indebted to my global Franciscan community, The Third Order, Society of St. Francis, for teaching me to love poverty in the way of Saints Francis and Clare. The humility, love, and joy that the two saints of Assisi embodied are alive and well in their spiritual descendants today. It's a privilege and a joy to be numbered among them.

Epiphany Parish in Seattle has been my home since 2015, and has been a place for my soul to thrive. I'm especially grateful to the Reverend Doyt L. Conn Jr., Epiphany's rector, for providing me office space: a lovely little hermitage and "room of my own" where I can think, pray, and write.

Finally, as always, my deepest debt is to my husband, Bob Crutchfield, who supports me in everything and taught me to celebrate each small victory on the way to the goal. What would my life be without you?

Introduction

The Poor Are God's Beloved

The whole Christian life is a life in which . . . the more we progress, the poorer we get so that the man who has progressed most, is totally poor—he has to depend directly on God. He's got nothing left in himself.

Thomas Merton, *Conjectures of a Guilty Bystander*

"Blessed are the poor in spirit," Jesus said, "for theirs is the kingdom of heaven" (Matt 5:3). It was the opening line in his most famous and important sermon, the manifesto of his movement. In a move reminiscent of Moses, Jesus ascends to a high place[1] and gives his listeners a new law, the terms of life in his kingdom: how they are to live, and what makes for a "blessed" or "happy" (*makarios* in Greek) life. This is not a "law" in the sense of "Be poor in spirit or I'll smite you," but something more akin to the law of gravity: "Do X and Y will follow." Some of the subsequent *beatitudes*—calling "blessed" those who mourn and those who are rejected and persecuted—are really just elaborations on being

1. Though in Luke's gospel, it's not a "mount" but a "plain."

poor in spirit. So this poverty, this spiritual diminishment and destitution, is the recipe Jesus gives for happiness.

And we nod in our pews and say, "Yes, I almost know that by heart; isn't it poetic and lovely?" Unless we're getting past the familiarity of these words and really listening. In that case, we're likely to sit up a little straighter and ask ourselves, with all piety and reverence: "What is he, nuts?"

Who defines happiness this way? Grief and loss, being misunderstood and marginalized, the subject of gossip and mockery, even unjust accusations and whatever consequences may follow them? *That* is the way to be happy? Hungering and thirsting for something and never being fully satisfied. Putting yourself between adversaries, at the risk of having both of them turn on you. Showing mercy to others sounds nice enough, until Jesus gets around to saying that those "others" include our enemies, those who have hurt us the most, even when those wounds may not yet have healed. A listener could be forgiven, perhaps, for reacting to this message with shock and incredulity, even wondering—as Jesus' own family sometimes did—if he might have loosened his grip on reality.

Over the centuries, however, those who've heard Jesus have learned the truth of his promise that we will find the greatest happiness, our deepest fulfillment—the kingdom of heaven, in fact, our blessedness and our belovedness—in the things that seem to impoverish our souls. In this book, I will be examining the ways in which followers of Christ have understood "poverty of spirit" and the traditions that have formed around their attempts to follow Jesus on this radical path. Let's begin with a quick look at one of the most well-known and powerful traditions, one which we'll return to study later in much greater depth.

Franciscan Poverty

Francis of Assisi is one of the most well-known and beloved saints in Christian history. But before he renounced the things of this world and shifted his focus upward, he was one of a band of young men who liked to party late into the night, knocking back the wine, singing songs, and no doubt annoying the good people of the town. Francis particularly enjoyed treating his friends to food and drink, and putting it on his father's tab. And as long as the charming and popular Francis seemed headed to take his place in his prosperous father's cloth business, his parents were happy to indulge him.

But there came a night when Francis, out once again with his buddies, stopped abruptly in the street. He stood there in a kind of daze, and when the guys started teasing him—"Francis, are you in love?" "Francis, are you thinking of getting married?"—he replied that he was indeed in love and was going to wed the most beautiful and noble bride ever seen. That bride turned out to be the Lady Poverty, the chosen companion of Christ throughout his earthly life. Francis, figuring he wasn't likely to do better than Jesus, remained faithful to her to the end of his days.

Meanwhile, Francis had caught the eye of another beautiful and noble lady of the town, Chiara Offreduccio. Clare's story is often eclipsed by that of Francis, but she was a strong, smart, and politically savvy woman who knew her own mind well enough to flee home at age seventeen to become part of Francis' movement, and never look back. The church didn't know what to make of a community of women who insisted on renouncing not only personal possessions but even community property—of living, that is, with no means of support at all. Church authorities, including the pope himself, tried to persuade Clare to accept gifts of land and live a more conventional religious life. But Clare stood her ground and demanded what she called the "privilege of poverty." She demanded it, and she got it.

Can Poverty Be Holy?

Poverty as a privilege, as a noble lady . . . it all sounds kind of medieval and charming, the sort of thing you'd commemorate with a birdbath in your garden. But most of us, when we think of poverty, don't use that kind of language. We tend to see poverty as something wholly negative, and in a certain way, we're right.

Francis and Clare of Assisi were devoted to *holy* poverty, which is quite a different thing from the unholy poverty of deprivation that comes from selfishness and greed, the starving of the poor to feed the voracious appetites of the rich.

Holy poverty is different from all externally imposed forms of vulnerability and marginalization. Refugees; the enslaved; targets of racism, sexism, and violence of all kinds; plus the mentally and physically diseased and disabled—those who "suffer in body, mind, or spirit"[2]—are all experiencing a kind of poverty. The critical difference lies in whether poverty is thrust upon us against our will or whether it's chosen voluntarily, or at least, when it comes to us involuntarily, we embrace it for the love of God. So any and all of these forms of poverty can become holy in the hands of those who suffer them, depending on how they suffer them. But they remain unholy for those who inflict them upon others, as well as those who fail to oppose them.

This is especially true for religious people, those who are called by God's name. When those who've been taught the ways of God withhold justice and compassion from the poor, even their piety reproaches them. Through the prophet Isaiah, God demands, *Who asked you to come before me with this worship? Get out of my house. I can't endure the coexistence of worship with iniquity*:

> Your new moons and your appointed festivals my soul hates;
> they have become a burden to me,
> I am weary of bearing them.
> When you stretch out your hands,
> I will hide my eyes from you;
> even though you make many prayers,
> I will not listen;
> your hands are full of blood.

2. Episcopal Church, *The Book of Common Prayer and Administration of the Sacraments and Other Rites and Ceremonies of the Church: Together with the Psalter or Psalms of David According to the Use of the Episcopal Church* (Seabury Press, 1979), 389.

Wash yourselves; make yourselves clean;
remove the evil of your doings from before my eyes;
cease to do evil,
learn to do good;
seek justice,
rescue the oppressed,
defend the orphan,
plead for the widow. (Isa 1:14-17)

For nearly thirty centuries, we have known that there is no blessing on those who create, manipulate, or simply fail to see the needs of the poor—especially if they claim to be following God's commandments. So how can poverty be holy?

This is important, and I don't want to be misunderstood. I'm a sociologist, and I take poverty, and all the personal and social problems that come with it, very seriously. I've no wish to minimize or trivialize the disgrace represented by a society's unwillingness to care for its vulnerable members, or for the strangers who come seeking sanctuary or just a better shot at life. And I don't want to spiritualize away real, concrete suffering of any kind, economic or otherwise. Renouncing worldly wealth, status, and power is the luxury of those who have the time and leisure to reflect on the spiritual implications of their possessions, not those who spend every waking moment scratching at the earth so their children won't starve. Francis and Clare both came from very affluent families. They'd had a chance to see how empty the offerings of the world can be; they'd tasted them in abundance. And it was the rich man whom Jesus challenged to give everything away (Matt 19:16-22), not the blind beggar (John 9:1-11).

To the blind, the lame, the lepers, the deaf, the poor, and the dead, Jesus brings good news (Matt 11:4-5), and promises them both earth and heaven (Matt 5:3-5). "Woe unto you!" is a message reserved for the rich and powerful (Matt 23:1-36; Luke 13:10-16). So to those who are struggling now to eke out a living in a society that is increasingly hostile to the poor, my message would be this: We, society as a whole, and the church in particular, will be judged by how we treat you, whether with justice and compassion or callous indifference. If we haven't responded to your suffering in genuine love, *active* love, I believe we will pay a terrible price.

But this book is not addressed to the practical needs and concerns of the 10 percent of the world's population living on less than two dollars a day[3] or the 1.1 million asylum seekers who arrived in Europe in 2023 alone[4]—not to mention the victims of forced migration elsewhere in the world. And it's not about those who live in modern slavery, or in the midst of conflict, epidemics, racism and inequality of all kinds. The material needs and concerns of such people are critically important, and are at the heart of most of the courses I taught throughout my career. If I accomplished nothing else in my years of teaching, at least I made a few generations of college students take a long, serious look at the suffering of those on the margins, learn how they got there, what their lives are like, and why there is so little change.

What Is Poverty of Spirit?

In this book I want to take a greatly expanded view of poverty. In the gospels, we have two accounts of the Beatitudes, that manifesto of the Jesus movement (Matt 5:1-11 and Luke 6:20-22), in which the Lord describes the things that make for joy. In Luke's version he blesses the poor, full stop, while in Matthew's version he blesses the poor *in spirit*. In both, the "kingdom of heaven" is promised. I think we have these two versions for a reason. We know that there is a special place in God's heart for those who are poor in the sense of material need, and it's important to hear

3. The World Bank Group, "Poverty," April 11, 2018, accessed April 17, 2018, https://www.worldbank.org/en/topic/poverty/overview.

4. Sarah Marsh, "Asylum Seekers in EU at Highest Level Since 2015/16 Crisis," *Reuters*, February 28, 2024, accessed August 13, 2024, https://www.reuters.com/world/europe/asylum-applications-eu-highest-level-since-201516-crisis-2024-02-28/.

Jesus say so. But for Jesus to bless the "poor in spirit" tells us that there are forms of poverty that aren't all about our bank account. Not all problems can be solved with money, after all. Rich people commit suicide too.

So for the purposes of this book, I will define poverty of spirit as *any experience that diminishes us, that suggests that we need something or someone we don't have.* Anything that challenges our sense of self-sufficiency, satisfaction, and control, that makes us feel "less than" or "not enough" to be comfortable with ourselves and our lives.

Using this broad definition, there are so many ways to be poor: a loveless marriage, job burnout, living with depression or chronic fatigue or pain and needing four times the strength to do things other people do without thinking about them. Having a shattered self-image, losing your faith, living or working or worshiping with people who drive you crazy. Burying a spouse, a parent, a child. Contemplating their burying you one day. A lifetime of dealing with racism or the aftermath of sexual assault. Living with addiction, shame, and regret. There are so many ways to be wounded, and each of these wounds is our poverty. Sometimes we keep them well bandaged and out of sight, and other times they form puddles of blood on the floor. Weakness, disability, imposter syndrome. Being trapped in feelings of inadequacy, doubt, guilt, and grief—it's all poverty, and Jesus said that in all of it, we are *blessed.*

This is a book about why that seemingly insane statement makes sense. In Luke's gospel, when the risen Jesus appeared to the disciples, "they were startled and terrified" (Luke 24:37). And why wouldn't they be? Not only had they never seen anything like this, but having denied and abandoned their Master in his hour of greatest need, they had good reason to think that if Jesus had indeed come back, they were in deep trouble. But what does he say? "Peace be with you." This was not just the Jewish version of "Have a nice day." To wish someone "peace" was to wish them complete blessedness, utter well-being.

And what does he do next? *He shows them his wounds.* "Why are you frightened, and why do doubts arise in your hearts? Look at my hands and my feet; see that it is I myself. Touch me and see . . ." (Luke 24:38-39). They fear his deity, but he approaches them with his humanity—his wounded humanity, still visible in his risen body. He shows them the consequences of the poverty he chose and embraced for their sake. As the great hymn in Philippians puts it, although God, Jesus "emptied himself, taking the form of a slave, being born in human likeness" and submitted to death, "even death on a cross" (Phil 2:7-8), which is about as gruesome and undignified a death as human ingenuity has ever devised.

Jesus entered the poverty of the human condition by choice, and in entering it, sanctified it. We don't usually go into places of poverty by choice, but because, as Jesus foretold of Peter, we've been girded and taken where we don't want to go (see John 21:18). But Jesus has gone to all the dark and empty places by choice, precisely so that he could meet us in them. Of his own life, he says: "No one takes it from me, but I lay it down of my own accord. I have the power to lay it down, and I have the power to take it up again" (John 10:18). Being God, of course he had that power. But to use it to *choose* to become human, to live a hard life and suffer a terrible death? To be almighty and choose to enter the world helpless, as an infant, and to leave it helpless, bound to a cross? That is a paradox indeed—the same kind of confounding paradox that calls the poor in spirit "blessed."

"For Theirs Is the Kingdom of Heaven"

What is this "blessedness" that Jesus promises to the poor in spirit? We can assume that it's something fundamental, since Jesus doesn't just include it in his sermon; he leads with it. It's the very first point he makes, or at least, the first point the gospel writers record. The Greek word *makarios* means "happy," yes, but this can hardly be the superficial kind of happiness we think of in relation to pleasing life circumstances. How could it be, when Jesus associates it with exactly the opposite?

So much has been written and preached about what Jesus meant when he announced the "kingdom of heaven" (or, in Luke's gospel, the "kingdom of God"). Nothing this important is going to be simple; the "kingdom" has enough facets and implications to keep us all busy until Jesus returns. But I think we can get at the heart of it with some assurance.

All kingdoms reflect, to some extent, the nature and priorities of the monarchs who rule them. In some ways, that "reflection" is quite concrete, as when coins are minted that bear the king's or queen's image. In other ways, it is the monarch's values that are held up to the realm, perhaps whether to hold fast to tradition or to modernize. In God's kingdom, we have a concrete reflection of God in the incarnation of Jesus, who came and showed us exactly what God is like. As Jesus told Philip, "Whoever has seen me has seen the Father" (John 14:9).

And what God is like is love. "God is love," Scripture tells us (1 John 4:8). In the Trinity, Christians see God as relational, and the relationship between the three Persons is love—such a powerful and perfect love that the Three are One. That is God's nature, and this is why Jesus is able to summarize the whole of the law into the commandments to love God and love our neighbor. Love is who God is, and love is God's priority, at all times and everywhere. Certainly in God's kingdom, love is the principle that guides our actions toward one another. But what about our relationship with God? God loves us; whether we know it or not, whether we welcome it or not; God has loved us since before we were born. Before the world was made, God knew us and loved us. Life is about returning that love to God and learning to share it with others.

But before we can do that, we have to learn to trust in God's love for us, because as long as we're not secure in our belovedness, we'll be too driven by our own ego and its needs to love others as Jesus called us to. Abject, overweening, or somewhere in between, a fragile or broken ego is not a place from which to love people with the freedom and generosity God wants for us. We need a place to stand, a place that gives us enough confidence and strength to lay aside our own agendas and focus on the other. That place is our belovedness in God: the certainty that we are cherished and that nothing we do can change that.

This can be such a hard thing to learn. When life is treating us well, we may get self-congratulatory and forget God altogether. Or we may consider ourselves "blessed" in a superficial way that is likely to collapse when the good times end. And when bad times come, we so often think that God has abandoned us, is disappointed or even angry with us. Life impoverishes our spirit, and the idea that we're "blessed" and possess "the kingdom" sounds like a bad joke.

But in fact it's a paradox, and there's only one way to meet this paradox, which is to know our utter, absolute belovedness. We were created by Love, in love, and for love. We are infinitely loved by an infinitely powerful God who *is* love, who knows everything about us and cherishes us in spite of—or perhaps, because of—it all. Jesus blessed the poor in spirit because poverty brings us to the end of our own resources, and, if we look to God at that point, we may be ready to learn how deeply we are loved. Not for what we have or what we've done, but because we are God's. Then we will possess the kingdom, where everyone is known to bear the image of God, to have dignity, to be loved. Then we will be blessed indeed. But we don't have to wait passively for it: the more deeply we learn these lessons, the more we begin to live in the kingdom now.

Let's be clear about one thing, though. God does not inflict suffering upon us; suffering is a natural consequence of living in a broken world. But God will always find a way to use our wounds to draw us in, to hold us close, to name us "Beloved." As God's own beloved Son, Jesus voluntarily and humbly entered into suffering and death, and rose from them in power, to bring us home. In the meantime, he offers us his wounds as a place to bring our own, uniting our suffering to his, and, in that union, finding our most transcendent joy.

The Transformation of Poverty

There's a divine alchemy that turns poverty into joy, but it doesn't tend to happen all at once. For me it's been a series of stages, and I'd like to tell you a little of that story. I'm inclined to see most spiritual stage theories as thinly veiled autobiography: even the series of inner mansions in Teresa of Avila's celebrated *Interior Castle* should probably be read as her own story of spiritual growth, rather than a prescription for all people at all times. Still, when you're on a journey, it can be helpful to have signposts to see that you're on an actual path and not lost in the wilderness. So here's my growing experience and understanding of poverty. If it resonates, great. If not, ask God and I'm confident you'll be given your own sense of direction.

I've written elsewhere[5] that the sin of pride comes in two flavors: thinking too much of myself or thinking too little of myself ("overweening" or "abject," as I noted above). In each case, my *self* is at the center: I have created a little solar system, made myself the star, and set everything else in orbit around me. My own form of pride tends to assume the merciless self-critic version, so when God tries to shake me out of it, the message is not so much "You ain't all that" as "Stop abusing my child."

Early on in this process, when my inner critic lashed out at me with accusations of inadequacy, I just agreed with her and felt predictably miserable. But as I kept praying and trying to observe some of the basic disciplines of the Christian life, despite knowing I was a complete fraud, eventually there came a turning point, a kind of hinge moment. I stopped praying "Lord, I feel worthless" and started praying, "Lord, I feel my poverty right now." It was analogous to the internal change that happens when you go from seeing misfortunes as unfair impositions on your right to live a happy and successful life and instead begin to think of them as the cross you bear as you follow Christ. In other words, what was once just meaningless suffering began to acquire meaning, to take on spiritual significance.

But there was another hinge moment, a point when poverty took on a deeper spiritual significance. In her exquisite little book

5. Susan R. Pitchford, *The Sacred Gaze: Contemplation and the Healing of the Self* (Collegeville, MN: Liturgical Press, 2014).

Sacred Heart: Gateway to God, Wendy M. Wright traces the historical development of devotion to the wounds and heart of Christ, which we'll examine in chapter 4. She notes that it wasn't until the High Middle Ages that a focus on the humanity of Jesus took hold, providing a context for attention to his wounds. It was a time of spiritual revival throughout Europe, which saw the rise of great religious movements: the Franciscans, the Dominicans, the Beguines, and others. The spirituality of the age contained a great deal of imaginative energy and lush, vivid imagery brought to prayer.

"Medieval Christianity," Wright tells us, "was affective, participatory, and somatic."[6] Meditation on the wounds of Christ could be an emotionally intense and intimate experience, and the wound in his side was particularly significant:

> The opened side was still the gateway through which salvation poured. It was . . . a portal through which one could enter. The side wound was the entryway to God's most secret life. It was, devotionally speaking, only a short step inward from the side wound to the heart. That organ was to become the supreme symbol of the loving intimacy between creator and creatures. Medieval Christians moved deeper and deeper into the body through the side wound into the divine-human heart . . . [and] medieval mystics who desired union sought intimacy inside the refuge of the wound.[7]

The second hinge moment was when I came to understand that *poverty is the side wound*.[8] It is the way into the heart of Christ, and every experience we have of being poured out, of "emptying ourself" as Jesus did, every painful episode of diminishment, is

6. Wendy M. Wright, *Sacred Heart: Gateway to God* (Maryknoll, NY: Orbis, 2001), 20.

7. Wright, *Sacred Heart*, 20.

8. In putting it this emphatically, I don't wish to imply that there aren't other ways to see or even mystically enter into the wounds of Christ. But this one is particularly powerful to me, as it was to the medieval believers Wright describes.

part of the process of paring away the excesses of ego, making us small enough to enter that wound. How I understand my poverty makes all the difference, and this second step is the shift from a cry of pain—"I feel my poverty!"—to a sense of being honored by an invitation to go deeper, to know a little more as I am known. It's the difference between bearing my poverty like a cross and wearing it like a crown—though sometimes, to be sure, like a crown of thorns.

This, I believe, accounts for the mysterious and passionate attachment of Francis and Clare, and many others like them, to poverty. Poverty is not an end in itself, any more than the crucifixion was an end in itself. God did not become incarnate in the person of Jesus just so he could suffer a cruel and unjust death. And although they didn't always make it explicit, I don't believe Francis and Clare were in love with poverty for its own sake. I believe they cherished poverty because of a shared intuition that poverty is a shortcut into the heart of God. Francis was no masochist, and although self-inflicted suffering was popular in his day, it was a thing he tended to discourage.[9] But he and Clare found, as others have before and since, that by kicking other supports out from under us, poverty drops us straight into the arms of God.

So holy poverty is the means, but the end is love: to love God, and to know our belovedness in return. In short, it's possessing the kingdom. But—and I want to be very clear about this—poverty cannot be holy unless two preconditions are met. First, we must learn to see the face of Christ in our poor neighbor. As St. John Chrysostom is credited with saying, "If you cannot find Christ in the beggar at the church door, you will not find him in the chalice." Or, I would add, in your own poverty. However seemingly deep and mystical an experience we might have in connection with our

9. At the famous "Chapter of the Mats," a gathering just outside Assisi of Franciscans from around Europe, it was brought to Francis' attention that many of the brothers were suffering terribly because of devices worn to inflict pain. They were having trouble attending even to their prayers. Francis ordered that the instruments of penance be rounded up and left on the ground.

own pain, if it's disconnected from the pain of our neighbor, it's an illusion, a self-indulgent spiritual joyride and nothing more.

Second, as I suggested earlier, we must respond to the poverty of Christ in that neighbor with concrete, positive action. If we are doing nothing to relieve the suffering of the poor, then nothing I have to say about the power of interior poverty applies. Nothing we might suffer can have spiritual content if our hearts are closed to those around us.

But if our hearts are open, if we choose to see our poverty as a cord that may take us where we don't want to go but connects us to the rest of humankind, and to Christ in them, then our poverty becomes holy. Then it has the ability to take us deeper and deeper into our belovedness, that of all of humankind and, indeed, all of creation. In the rest of this book, I want to explore how that happens, drawing on some of the great mystical and theological traditions that have linked holy poverty to our profound belovedness in God. In his powerful book *Man's Search for Meaning*, Viktor Frankl said that life can take away from us everything but the last freedom: the freedom to choose how we respond to suffering we have not chosen. Asceticism is poverty that's chosen, but most of us probably find that life offers us plenty of trouble without going out looking for it. What's up to us is whether we go through life filled with bitterness and resentment or seeing our suffering for what it truly is: an invitation to enter deeply into the heart of God and find our refuge there in God's kingdom, our belovedness, and our joy.

In the chapters to come, we'll look at a set of movements within the church that have grappled with the paradox of poverty—poverty broadly defined. These movements run from the ancient to the medieval eras and continue into our own time. Many of them focus on the personal experience of poverty, but two chapters will consider collective forms of poverty: that is, the impoverishment of people based on their group membership. Finally, we'll consider a contemporary movement that began in church circles but has expanded well beyond them into the general culture. In these ways, I hope to give a broad survey of how people across time and space, on both individual and corporate levels, have made sense of Jesus' strange and challenging words.

We'll start in the next chapter with an overview of the church's history of understanding—or not—poverty of spirit. At times poverty has been prized, but for much of its history, the church has succumbed to the seduction of worldly wealth, power, and prestige. In our own time, the Prosperity Gospel movement shows us just how far that seduction can go. Yet there have always been those prophets of poverty who've called us back to the original vision. In chapter 2 we'll look at how poverty is treated in the Scriptures. Chapter 3 examines the Franciscan movement, in which poverty is a core value. Chapter 4 will take us into the history of devotion to the Sacred Heart, which began early and evolved through the Middle Ages and into the modern era. This tradition explicitly links poverty—especially understood as our woundedness—to our place in the heart of Christ as his beloved.

Next we'll look at two collective experiences of poverty. Chapter 5 focuses on gender and uses the medieval community of nuns at Helfta, in Germany, to show that when society tries to silence the voices of women, the Spirit finds ways to amplify them. Chapter 6 focuses on racism as another form of collective poverty. While nothing can ever make the unspeakable suffering of African Americans and others "worthwhile," the gift Black Liberation and Womanist theologians have brought to the church is nothing short of the authentic gospel. It's a gospel that, as did Isaiah and Jesus centuries before, focuses on the poor, the captives, and the oppressed. A gospel without this concern, as preached by many white churches—deliberately or unwittingly—is not an authentic gospel. Black theologians who have wrestled with the tragic and unholy poverty of their history have mercifully restored the true gospel to their own people, and to all of us as well.

In chapter 7, we'll examine a completely modern tradition of poverty: that of the 12-step movement. In Alcoholics Anonymous (AA) and other 12-step programs, poverty is exactly where the healing begins: Step 1 is admitting one's powerlessness over the object of their addiction. The subsequent steps admit that a Higher Power of some kind is absolutely required if the addicted person is ever to be restored to wholeness. AA is a tradition that Richard Rohr has called close to the "marrow of the gospel."[10] It insists simultaneously on our poverty and our belovedness. As such, while controversial in some quarters (and we'll look at those controversies), AA offers a model for understanding that link that has become a powerful cultural and religious influence in our own time. Finally, in chapter 8, we'll draw the threads together and see with greater clarity why Jesus promised the kingdom of heaven to the poor in spirit.

And now, as Francis of Assisi said, let us begin, for up to now we have done very little.

10. Richard Rohr, *Breathing Under Water: Spirituality and the Twelve Steps* (Cincinnati, OH: Franciscan Media, 2011).

PART ONE

Poverty, the Institutional Church, and What Might Have Been

Chapter 1

An Unholy Trinity

Power, Wealth, and a Compromised Church

Contrary to being a disaster, the exilic experiences of loss and marginalization are what are needed to restore the church to its evangelistic place. On the margins of society the church will once again find its God-given voice to speak to the dominant culture in subversive ways, resisting the powers and principalities, standing against the seduction of the status quo.

Elaine Heath, *The Mystic Way of Evangelism*

Christianity began as a fringy little movement on the geopolitical edge of the Roman Empire. Small, mostly poor, and without worldly power, Christian communities were always vulnerable to persecution. Nearly all of the saints of the first few centuries were martyrs, which were never in short supply.

Rome was normally tolerant of foreign religions, content to let residents of conquered regions keep their gods and carry on with their customary worship. In a polytheistic society, this tolerance is an easy, popular, and low-cost policy: at a well-populated table, there's always room for one more. It's monotheism that creates a problem: a religion that claims its god is the only one, and that the others don't really exist—or worse, might actually be demons—makes it impossible to "live and let live." The Jewish people had forced this issue long before the Christians came along, and had suffered for it. But Judaism is not an evangelizing religion, and their numbers were usually small enough to pose no threat.

Christianity was a proselytizing religion, however, and was growing fast. With a twenty-first-century consumerist mindset, it's easy for us to think, "Well, so what? Let the people make their choices." But in the ancient world, effective propitiation of the gods could make the difference between famine and plenty, between plague and health, between war and peace. So when a religion comes along that doesn't honor the traditional gods, it poses a threat something akin to what we would call national security. Rebel religious movements threatened societies in the ancient world in the way that terrorism threatens us today.

So it's not that officials in the Empire were unusually bloodthirsty or intolerant—for the times, anyway. They just wanted peace, order, and prosperity as much as we do. And when something went wrong, say an earthquake or a drought or a losing military campaign, with science still centuries in the future, they had to find explanations elsewhere. Christians, who'd refused to give the gods their due, seemed a pretty likely source of the trouble.

Because of this, most of the persecution of Christians in those early centuries was local and sporadic throughout the Empire, in response to local and sporadic problems. Some emperors were more anti-Christian than others; Nero famously used Christians as living torches to light up his parties. But it wasn't until the emperor Diocletian came along that the campaign against Christians became both vicious and systematic.

Diocletian assumed the purple in 285 CE, a time when the overstretched Empire was having both internal and external problems. Invasions of rivals from the north and east put constant pressure on an army that was charged with maintaining the *pax romana* across an impossibly extended territory. Constant war and recurrent famines caused severe inflation, and the frequent assassination of emperors by rival factions created political instability. All of this had people wondering: had the gods deserted Rome? And if so, who was to blame for this fall from divine favor?

As a practical matter, it was particularly easy to pin the Empire's troubles on the Christians. Christianity was an urban religion: from the beginning, preachers like St. Paul had gone from city to city to carry the gospel. It was a sensible strategy in a time without mass communication. You'd want to speak your message to as large a crowd as possible, the kind of crowd that would gather in a city's forum to hear the latest news.

An urban base made the church visible. Furthermore, with the numbers of Christians growing in the cities, they had begun to need larger buildings in which to meet. The homes of members, even the wealthy ones, eventually became too small to hold services for these expanding communities. So they began to build new structures, or modify old ones, to serve the purpose.

But it wasn't only the physical structures that put these communities at risk. As the church grew, it developed an institutional leadership structure with bishops, presbyters/priests, and deacons, which started to look like a rival seat of power. Together, all these things meant that if you wanted to curb Christians' enthusiasm by making an example of their leaders, they weren't hard to find.

Diocletian found them—lots of them. Church leaders were enslaved, imprisoned, and executed in their thousands, while Christian Scriptures were seized and burned. Diocletian was frantic to create stability in his empire through religious uniformity, and although the church's leaders were most at risk, all Christians were eventually required to offer sacrifice to the gods of Rome. The penalty for refusing was immediate execution.

Diocletian mainly persecuted Christians in the east, in places like Antioch and Alexandria. His co-emperors in the west were less zealous to stamp out the faith, and Christians in places like Gaul, Britannia, and Spain were left in comparative peace. Still, in Diocletian's "Great Persecution," it's estimated that over twenty thousand Christians were killed. To put that into context, it's worth remembering that the ancient city of Rome only had roughly a million inhabitants at its peak. Corinth, a smaller but still important city that is well known to readers of the New Testament, had a population of about ninety thousand in 400 BCE. So twenty thousand is a lot of souls, a lot of blood to have on your hands. Today, as a reminder that living well is the best revenge, the Baths of Diocletian in Rome have been rebuilt according to a design by Michelangelo and turned into a church: the Basilica of St. Mary of the Angels and Martyrs.

The Blessing—and Curse—of Constantine

By the turn of the fourth century CE, a battle-weary church was ready for a break, which came in the form of the emperor Constantine. Constantine's reign was a hinge moment in Christian history: it changed everything, in ways that were immediately welcome but proved a mixed blessing in the long run. It's been said that at the beginning of the fourth century, you could be killed for being a Christian, but by the end of the century, you could be killed for *not* being a Christian—or even for being the wrong kind of Christian. It was this century in which the church throughout the Empire tasted freedom and imperial favor for the first time, but also learned to turn the sword against its own enemies. The speed at which the fringy little movement begun by Christ and based on love betrayed its basic principles—and its founder—was breathtaking.

But we're getting ahead of the story. In the middle of his campaign to wipe out Christianity, Diocletian retired as emperor and a war of succession ensued. A crucial battle took place at the Milvian Bridge, but it's what happened before the battle that was decisive. Tradition has it that the night before, Constantine was worried about his chances because his rival Maxentius had the bigger army. Constantine sought help from the gods, and had a dream—or perhaps a vision—in which he saw the sign of the cross—or perhaps the Chi-Rho—and was told, "*In hoc signo vinces*" ("By this sign you will conquer"). So Constantine had the crosses—or Chi-Rhos—put on the shields of his soldiers, and the next day, though outnumbered, they won easily. This victory secured Constantine's position as sole and undisputed ruler of the western Empire.

At least, that's the story. Naturally, we don't really know for sure what happened, but we do know that after his victory at the Milvian Bridge, Constantine started to favor Christianity. It began with the Edict of Milan, which Constantine passed with the eastern emperor Licinius in 313. This made Christianity and other outlaw religions legal (making it the official religion of the Empire would come a couple of emperors later), and Constantine gave Christianity increasingly favored status as he began the long journey of his own conversion.

Among Constantine's pro-Christian reforms was the abolition of crucifixion throughout the Empire—good news for Christians and many others. Also abolished was facial branding, on the grounds that to disfigure a human being was to mar the image of God. Bishops were given legal status as magistrates, a source of power that was unheard of before this time. Sunday was declared a day of rest, and gladiatorial games were prohibited, which was not the same thing as being eradicated, but the intention was good. Church property that had been confiscated under prior emperors was restored, money was contributed to the church's treasuries, church building projects were undertaken, and existing structures (such as the Lateran Palace in Rome) were handed over to the church.

It was a stunning reversal: with a Christian emperor, the church's troubles would be over. Except that the church was about to discover that Constantine's reforms created a whole new type of trouble. Having backed the church, Constantine worked to ensure that it would prosper. This included not only meddling in its business, but also providing resources to support it. Confiscated money and property were restored. Funding was suddenly available to build worship spaces, to provide lavish residences for important church leaders (especially the bishop of Rome), even for his own mother to carry out an expedition to the Holy Land to identify the places where important events in the life of Christ took place.

It's hard to imagine what it must have been like for a blood-stained church crying out *How long, O Lord?* to suddenly find itself enjoying this kind of imperial patronage. It must have seemed like the next best thing to the Second Coming itself. It's true that after Constantine there was a brief moment in 361 when the emperor Julian came to the throne and tried to reinstate paganism throughout the Empire. While Julian is known to history as "the Apostate," he likely was never a Christian to begin with. In any case, determined as he was, he only reigned for two years, so there was little he could do. Christianity had already triumphed, and while paganism lingered on in the Empire, especially in the hinterlands, it was clear that anyone who aspired to any kind of position in society had better accept the Christian faith.

And that was where Constantine's reforms caused a new kind of trouble for the church. Before them, the church's membership consisted of those who'd joined it in spite of the risk, in spite of the personal cost. It was a battered church, but a relatively pure one when no one would join for anything less than an unshakeable personal conviction. But once the emperor and his court were Christian? Once being a Christian became important to one's career and social standing? No longer did one embrace poverty along with the poor Christ. Where the potential costs of believing had previously kept out all but the most ardently devoted, now the rewards of affiliating brought people flooding into the church whose motives were anything but pure, whose spirits were anything but poor.

While most Christians were undoubtedly breathing sighs of relief when the persecutions ended, there were some who foresaw that an easy faith would be a compromised faith. The risk of martyrdom—better still, *actual* martyrdom—had been a way of confirming to oneself and others that one was fully committed to the way of Christ. This was how saints were made: in the early centuries of the church, nearly all the saints were martyrs. After the Edict of Milan, it became tough to find someone to kill you for your Christian faith. So how does a person live who is still willing to embrace the most extreme poverty for Jesus' sake? Many of them found their answer in the desert.

Seeking Poverty in the Desert

In Egypt, by the second half of the third century, there were already people living on the edges of cities, on the fringe of society. We don't know much about them, but some of them seem to have lived lives of material poverty and spent their days mostly in solitude and prayer. Escape to the desert wasn't new: it had been a traditional Roman way of evading one's family, taxes, and the law in general. What was new was the motivation: those hermits who would become known as the "desert fathers and mothers" fled the cities to the wilderness because they wanted a life of total spiritual commitment. They saw the desert as a place to clear away the clutter of urban life, with the chaos and confusion it creates, and to focus entirely on God. They understood that the desert would be a place of struggle, where they would do battle with temptations, distractions, boredom, and demons of all kinds—not to mention their own egos. But they also understood this to be the path that would lead them, finally, to freedom and peace.

The desert has meant many things to many people, in different times and places. But ultimately the desert is a place of *poverty*: it's a place where all of our supports get kicked out from under us. It's a place where all the costumes and props that have enabled us to cling to the illusion of our self-sufficient personas get stripped away, torn by merciless winds and bleached by an unforgiving sun. The desert leaves us naked, reveals who we really are. There are no privacy hedges in the desert, no places to hide. Once the desert is done with us, our mortality and dependence, our contingency and our poverty, are undeniable. And that is just when we begin to live into the full abundance that Jesus promised.

In this section, I'd like to introduce some of the desert fathers (*abbas*) and mothers (*ammas*) who fled the comforts and distractions of the cities precisely in order to subject themselves to this process of stripping away. These early hermits, monks, and nuns deliberately sought out the poverty of the desert, and the wisdom they gained there was collected in sets of sayings that reveal what mysterious, strange, and delightful characters they were.

Let's begin with the most famous of them. In 269, in a small town in Egypt, there lived a young man named Antony. He'd come from a wealthy family, but by his late teens, he had already lost both his parents. So he was trying on his own to discern the course of his life. He went to church one day, and on that day the gospel reading happened to be the one where Jesus meets the rich young man. He asks Jesus the same questions that have been worrying Antony: what constitutes a life pleasing to God? How can I inherit eternal life—the one thing my parents could not leave me? Jesus tells him to observe the commandments, but the man is already there; what else can he do? Jesus replies: "If you wish to be perfect, go, sell your possessions, and give the money to the poor, and you will have treasure in heaven; then come, follow me" (Matt 19:21).

Antony, identifying with that other rich young man, heard Jesus' words as a personal message for himself. But unlike the man in the gospel, Antony decided to follow Jesus' counsel. It took him a while, but he eventually sold off most of his inheritance, making provision for a sister his parents had left in his charge. Then he joined the men living on the periphery of his town. Eventually, though, Antony sought greater solitude and moved farther and farther into the desert. He lived almost entirely alone for several years, with very little human contact.

We can thank Bishop Athanasius of Alexandria, by the way, for the information we have about Antony's life, as they were contemporaries and Athanasius wrote a biography of the saint. Some of Antony's letters and sayings, recorded by others (Antony himself was most likely illiterate), have also survived. But if we knew nothing else about Antony's way of life, it was certainly good for his health: he lived in the desert for 87 years, and died in 356 at the age of 105. Notice that his life (251–356 CE) spans the transition from the persecution of Christians to their legal tolerance and imperial favor. So Antony experienced in his own lifetime the influx into the church of converts with mixed motives and the cooling off to lukewarmness that came with it.

Antony went to the desert for solitude and lived there a life of isolation and extreme asceticism. Yet as word began to circulate of a holy hermit living in the wilderness, people began to follow him out there. There were pilgrims, there were tourists, but there were also devout men who came for spiritual direction or to live near him, emulating his way of life. In short, despite his best efforts to be alone, Antony found himself with disciples, who urged him to become their leader. He finally accepted this role and spent a few years figuring out how to do the desert life in community. This was a move from what would come to be called "eremitic" to "cenobitic" monasticism, that is, from living in solitude as a hermit (eremitic) to living with other monks in community (cenobitic).

It was a later monk, Pachomius (292–348), who is credited with developing the cenobitic form of monasticism, but Antony and others, men and women, were already experimenting with different configurations. Some lived in solitude but met occasionally for the Eucharist, some lived in hermitages but came together regularly for meals and fellowship, while others built complexes in which groups of monks or nuns lived together. Pachomius was the first to write a rule for monks living in community, and as monasticism spread throughout the Middle East and before long to Europe, every community's rule would be the core set of principles by which it would live. A couple of centuries after Antony and Pachomius (in 516), St. Benedict of Nursia, Italy, would write his famous Rule which would govern monastic communities of both men and women throughout Europe. The Rule of St. Benedict is still serving this function today, and because it is such a wise and far-seeing document, even today it guides many lives lived within and outside of monastic settings.

While Antony was not the first of the desert hermits, his move to the desert is often seen as part of the beginning of the monastic movement. The words "monk" and "monastic," incidentally, come from the Greek word for "one," "alone"; even in community, those living a monastic life seek regular time for solitary prayer. And while the beginnings of monasticism preceded the Edict of Milan, certainly the expansion of this movement, and of its geographic reach, coincided with the increasing wealth and safety of the church and church membership. It's hard to escape the conclusion that the move into the desert was a direct response to a church growing fat and lax, a church offering cheap discipleship. In religion, as elsewhere, you get what you pay for. A costless Christianity that avoids the cross and goes straight for resurrection—or settles for worldly comfort—is a distortion the desert hermits were eager to reject. If martyrdom would no longer come from the sword, it would have to be found elsewhere.

The word *martyr* simply means "witness," and there's a tradition that distinguishes three types of martyrdom: red, green, and white. Red martyrdom is the kind we're all familiar with, in which the martyr dies violently for their faith. White martyrdom is that of the person who leaves home and loved ones behind, on pilgrimage or some other holy pursuit, and who may never return. Antony and the other desert hermits could be characterized as white martyrs, but they were certainly green martyrs—namely, those who lived lives of such heroic asceticism that they could say, with St. Paul, "I die daily" (1 Cor 15:31, New King James Version [NKJV]).

Consider the asceticism of these desert hermits. Not only did they get by on little in the way of food and other necessities of the body, but they also endured long fasts from the sacraments, as not everyone had a priest nearby. Further, there were temptations of every kind, but one of the fiercest they faced was *acedia*, which is a complex word meaning boredom, listlessness, spiritual sloth, restlessness, and a host of other interior torments. They called it the "noonday demon," and Rowan Williams offers a chilling and all-too-familiar account:

> The morning is wearing on, getting hotter and stickier; there is still a long time to go before eating or any other break in the routine. Hours spent plaiting reeds for making baskets

> have left you feeling numb and bored. Is there any progress at all to be seen? Or is this life as featureless as the sand around you? Surely making progress would be more possible elsewhere; after all, in this dead landscape you have no chance to share what you discover, even if you do finally manage to discover something. And then, this must be a selfish life: surely there's one of the brothers who'd like a visit, who needs something? And wouldn't I be more useful in the city, anyway? That's where the real need is, and I could supply it so effectively! Anywhere but here, anywhere but now . . .[1]

Williams goes on to comment that "You don't have to be a hermit to appreciate all this; anyone who lives with a routine will recognize the symptoms instantly."[2] It's so easy to fantasize about how much more "useful" and "effective" I could be somewhere else, doing something else, with someone else.

But it's a trap. Amma Syncletica explains why:

> If you are living in a monastic community, do not go to another place: it will do you a great deal of harm. If a bird abandons the eggs she has been sitting on, she prevents them hatching; and in the same way the monk or nun will grow cold and their faith will perish if they go around from one place to another.[3]

The thing about moving around from one place to the next is that it allows you, as Rowan Williams explains, "to distract yourself in the usual way, by self-dramatizing and fantasy."[4] If I'm lamenting the fact that my life is making no big splash in the world, if I'm laboring away in obscurity at something that often seems not just exhausting but pointless, there are two paths in front of me. I can

1. Rowan Williams, *Silence and Honey Cakes: The Wisdom of the Desert* (Oxford: Lion, 2003), 83.
2. Williams, *Silence and Honey Cakes*, 84.
3. Quoted in Williams, 82.
4. Williams, 83.

accept my own insignificance, in the world's terms, and know that my significance lies only in what God sees in me. In other words, I can embrace the poverty of my situation and come away with genuine humility. Or I can entertain fantasies of how much more productive and appreciated I'd be in some other line of work, in some other place, with some other colleagues. I can imagine how much more my opinions would be valued, how I could actually be the hero the comic strip "Chickweed Lane" used to call "Superlative Girl," and swoop down and save the world.

But this is not what the world needs. The world already has a savior. This kind of fantasy is just what my ego needs, to prop itself up when the poverty of the desert threatens it with real conversion. The other thing my ego craves is distraction—the very thing these ancient ascetics went to the desert to escape. Entertainment, daydreams, fantasies: distractions of every kind keep at bay the terror of sitting alone with myself, with the boredom, the repetition, and the overwhelmingly prosaic nature of my life.

Moving is one answer to this: going off in search of the next city, the next lover, the next church, the next vocation, are, as Williams says, the spiritual equivalent of drinking saltwater.[5] However extreme and even understandable your thirst, this is not the way to deal with it. The seductive nature of moving has been recognized across the ages, not only by the desert hermits: as a Benedictine sister reminded me just the other day, St. Benedict had very little use for monks who moved around from one monastery to another. Calling them *gyrovagues* (those who "wander" [*vagus*] in "circles" [*gyro*]), Benedict thought them undisciplined and sketchy, and Benedictines have always taken a vow of stability.

Eventually the Franciscans and other mendicant orders would make a case for the religious road trip. But the insight Benedict shared with the early desert hermits was that the more you wander, the less you leave behind the distractions and confusion that drove

5. Williams, 97.

you to the desert in the first place. Each time you move, you're just picking them up all over again. When we're on the move, we can keep fixing our attention on the next shiny object. We aren't forced to sit still and deal with unpleasant realities, least of all about ourselves. Sitting quietly alone for an hour, with no distractions, is the hardest thing, as the philosopher Blaise Pascal said. I've challenged many groups of students to try it, and not one has come back saying they did. Being alone with myself is a kind of poverty, one that threatens to reveal too much, one which I'll do almost anything to avoid. This is why Abba Moses famously said, "Go, sit in your cell, and your cell will teach you everything."[6]

Remaining in our cell, whatever our "cell" is (a job we'd rather leave, a spouse we'd rather leave, a friendship grown boring, even the utter monotony of the daily routines of body maintenance), will teach us things about ourself that we cannot learn while in perpetual motion and flight. It's not that there's not a time to move on (a toxic workplace, an abusive spouse); it's that the choice between "staying" and "fleeing" (two chapters of Williams' book) calls for discernment. And the answer to the temptation to flee that is born out of denial and illusion lies in the advice one of the elders gave to a younger hermit: "Go. Sit in your cell and *give your body in pledge to the walls*."[7]

Pledging ourself to the place or situation where we are—at least until we have good reason to believe it's time to move on—means embracing the poverty of the self and our current circumstances. It means choosing to face them with a willingness to take a good look at what our desire to flee says about our spiritual state. The desert hermits knew the value both of fleeing and of staying: of fleeing a world in which Christian affiliation had become a means to comfort and advancement, and then of staying in a place that would relentlessly reveal the true state of their own soul.

6. Williams, 82.

7. Williams, 89; original emphasis.

Pledging oneself to the cell of the boring and mundane was of utmost importance to the desert hermits, but another famous story suggests that this is a means to an end, not the end itself:

> Abba Lot went to see Abba Joseph and said to him, "Abba, as far as I can I say my little office, I fast a little, I pray and meditate, I live in peace and, again as far as I can, I purify my thoughts. What else can I do to become holy?" Then the old man stood up and stretched his hands toward heaven. His fingers came like ten lamps of flame, and he said to him, "Why not become fire?"[8]

The collected sayings of the desert fathers and mothers don't dwell much on our belovedness in the eyes of God, but this story shows that asceticism is never for its own sake. Desert time, whether literal or figurative, changes a person. To be sure, it does that by exposing things that form obstacles to drawing closer to God, but what is the point of that if we don't in fact draw closer to God? And the reason for drawing closer is indeed so that we can "become fire," so that we can catch a spark from our God who, as Hebrews reminds us, is "a consuming fire" (Heb 12:29). Ultimately, the goal is to become so conformed to Christ that we ourselves become fire, ablaze with a powerful, passionate love that warms and illumines the world.

The church since the time of Constantine has been through plenty of changes, but human nature doesn't change much, nor do the temptations that beguile us. In our own time, we have seen a tendency in some quarters of the church to associate discipleship with worldly wealth, status, and power—despite Jesus' specific warnings to the contrary. Today, this tendency is organized explicitly as a theology known by various names, including "Word of Faith," "Name It and Claim It," and "Prosperity Gospel." It is the basis of a movement that has made millions for its proponents and

8. My paraphrase.

taught adherents that if they'll recite the right formulas, believe the right ways, and donate lots of money, God will bless them with health, wealth, and every kind of victory over adversity.

The Prosperity Gospel is the logical conclusion (or at least, a long logical extension) of the marriage of Christianity with the world that began during the reign of Constantine. It was exactly this worldly compromise that the early monastics went to the desert to escape. The notion that one can follow Christ in comfort and ease is a far cry from the relentless demands of desert asceticism: the need to master the desires of the body and face the realities of psyche and soul don't feature much in prosperity preaching. And while the teaching that goes under the name "Prosperity Gospel" explicitly promises worldly blessings to those who follow, there are subtler versions that pervade preaching and teaching throughout the church today. (There's even a secular version of this in Western culture: the expectation that our success or failure in life is in our own hands, all our illusions of meritocracy and control that allow us to blame those who struggle for their misfortunes.) The result is a church that speaks too little of poverty, too little of its link to the blessedness Jesus promised. This is one of the foremost heresies present in the church today, and as it's a direct challenge to Jesus' teaching on poverty, it deserves our attention.

The Prosperity Gospel: Blessed Are the Not-Poor

The roots of the "Prosperity Gospel" movement are buried deep in American soil.[9] This belief system, according to historian Kate Bowler, weaves together three strands in US intellectual and religious history. First, the Pentecostal tradition, with its emphasis on supernatural manifestations of divine power, especially healing, plus its tent revivals, provided both a message and a medium with which to convey it. Pentecostalism teaches that salvation is to be

9. In this section, I am deeply indebted to Kate Bowler's seminal work *Blessed: A History of the American Prosperity Gospel* (New York: Oxford University Press, 2013).

followed by "baptism in the Holy Spirit," which will be accompanied by supernatural gifts including speaking in tongues, prophecy, and healing. This form of Christianity was and continues to be foundational to the Prosperity Gospel movement.

A second strand is "New Thought," a nineteenth-century movement that taught, among other things, that physical disease is a product of faulty thinking. Mesmerism, or hypnosis as developed by Franz Anton Mesmer, was part of this movement, and New Thought itself was indebted to the First Church of Christ, Scientist (Christian Science) founded by Mary Baker Eddy. New Thought attracted not only Christians, but also many people who did not identify as Christians, including Ralph Waldo Emerson and William James. Some adherents of New Thought even took it in the direction of the occult. What these diverse forms of New Thought have in common is that in each of them, all manner of sickness and death was seen as the result of mental errors. So believers or practitioners could straighten out their thinking and overcome their maladies with what William James called "the religion of healthy-mindedness."[10] Ultimately, the New Thought concept of the "mind cure" would contribute as well to the nascent field of psychotherapy.

Pastor and evangelist E. W. Kenyon (1867–1948) was no fan of New Thought, as he considered it too abstract and not true to Christian doctrine, nor was he a Pentecostal. Yet he did bring some of the principles of New Thought into Pentecostal awareness. Kenyon preached that sanctified believers have great power over illness and other adverse circumstances. This power was attached to the "Word," a multivalent concept that included the Scriptures and Christ himself, as most Christians believe, but added the spoken word. The latter, in the form of "positive confessions," was said to contain spiritual power.

This idea would ultimately find its way into the wider culture, in self-help and popular psychology, which recommend using affirmations and visualization to create "empowerment" and personal

10. Quoted in Bowler, *Blessed*, 14.

fulfillment. Norman Vincent Peale's *The Power of Positive Thinking*, which advocates these techniques, sold two-and-a-half million copies in the first four years after publication, and has continued to sell since.[11] But Kenyon and other early prosperity preachers were the first to teach that speech has power, so speaking one's goal in what Kenyon called a "confession" is expected to make that goal a reality. Kenyon taught that believers had been given "Power of Attorney" by God, and had both the power and the "legal" right to make *demands* on God, who was bound to honor them. As Bowler observes, "The Holy Spirit became merely an assistant as Kenyon gave the credit for casting out demons, speaking in tongues, and curing disease to the rightful use of the name of Jesus."[12]

The third strand in the fabric of the Prosperity Gospel, which made it fit so naturally into the American religious landscape, is its "can-do" approach to life's adversities and its link between material success and God's favor.[13] This link was classically explored in the work of the German sociologist Max Weber, *The Protestant Ethic and the Spirit of Capitalism*. Weber argued that a Calvinist emphasis on predestination (technically, "double predestination") meant that individuals were assigned by God to the elect or the damned, and there was little one could do about it. But one could look for signs that one was part of the elect, and prominent among these signs was material prosperity. This gave people an incentive to work hard and spend little, which would increase the chance that they'd at least look like they were destined for salvation. (There's a little confusion here between correlation and causation.) A whole

11. James A. Cosby, *Devil's Music, Holy Rollers and Hillbillies: How America Gave Birth to Rock and Roll* (Jefferson, NC: McFarland, 2016), 26.

12. Quoted in Bowler, *Blessed*, 20.

13. See Tara Isabella Burton, "The Prosperity Gospel, Explained: Why Joel Osteen Believes That Prayer Can Make You Rich," *Vox*, September 1, 2017, accessed August 9, 2022, https://www.vox.com/identities/2017/9/1/15951874/prosperity-gospel-explained-why-joel-osteen-believes-prayer-can-make-you-rich-trump.

lot of people thinking and working along these lines, Weber suggested, would be a fine way to build up a capitalist system.

Weber's argument traced an important way by which material success began to take on moral significance. Moreover, the celebration of individualism and rags-to-riches stories embedded in American culture added further moral meaning to material success or failure. The popular view of the United States as a meritocracy and a land of equal opportunity implies that anyone who fails to prosper either lacks talent or the willingness to put it to work. For those mired in poverty, this adds insult to injury: not only do they suffer material deprivation, but also the stigma that goes with it.

It's not hard to understand why, in a largely Protestant society with substantial inequality in which poverty is a sign of moral failure, the message that God desires to bless the faithful with health and material prosperity would be eagerly received. As the Baptist lawyer and preacher Russell H. Conwell (1843–1925) thundered in his "Acres of Diamonds" sermon, "I say you ought to be rich; you have no right to be poor!"[14] Nobody much wants to be poor, to begin with. But when it's our Christian duty to be rich, most of us will sit up and take notice. So it's no surprise that today, after more than a century of hearing this message, survey data show that two-thirds of American Christians believe that God desires people to prosper, and 43 percent of Christians believe that the faithful are blessed with health and wealth.[15] It's also no surprise that the Prosperity Gospel movement has seen explosive growth, especially since the turn of the millennium, in the global South.[16] People anywhere struggling with poverty and disease are going to welcome a message that marries supernatural deliverance with the personal power to set it in motion.

14. Quoted in Burton, "Prosperity Gospel, Explained," 32.

15. Burton, 6.

16. Philip Jenkins, *The Next Christendom: The Coming of Global Christianity* (New York: Oxford University Press, 2011).

Cast of Characters

Granville Oral Roberts[17] (1915–2009) was a pioneer of the Prosperity Gospel movement. Born into a poor Pentecostal Holiness family in rural Oklahoma, Roberts at age seventeen nearly died from tuberculosis. He finally recovered and finished high school, but after two years of college, he left without a degree. At age twenty, he married Evelyn Lutman, and they would have four children, only one of whom survived their father.

By age eighteen, Roberts was already preaching in the Pentecostal Holiness church, but his message changed when he came across a Bible verse he'd never noticed before: "Beloved, I wish above all things that thou mayest prosper and be in health, even as thy soul prospereth" (3 John 2, King James Version [KJV]). On the strength of this verse, he began to preach that wealth was acceptable with God, and health a blessing God wanted to give. It was only a month later that Roberts was said to have cured a woman whose hand had been unusable for 38 years.

Apart from his founding of a hospital and a university, what made Roberts' ministry so important is that his emphasis on physical and financial prosperity was conveyed not only through tent meetings, but also through radio and mass mailings. As one of the earliest televangelists, Roberts would provide a template that later preachers would use to build television empires. And while Roberts never fell prey to the sex scandals that would bring down many of his successors, neither was he always a model of dignity and decorum. He enjoyed wearing fancy suits and diamond jewelry which, his *Guardian* obituary alleges, his staff airbrushed out of publicity photos. As his ministry made him increasingly wealthy, he acquired multiple luxury cars and holiday homes.

But Roberts' most memorable fundraising stunt was when, in 1987, he declared that if he didn't raise another $4.5 million for his

17. I have drawn the details of Oral Roberts' life from his obituary in the December 15, 2009, online issue of *The Guardian*, accessed August 11, 2022, https://www.theguardian.com/world/2009/dec/15/oral-roberts-obituary.

hospital in short order, "God will call me home." He then retreated into solitude and emerged on the deadline to say that the money was in. All the same, his hospital eventually closed, and he had to curtail his personal spending, selling off some property. For a religious figure to essentially hold himself hostage and demand money made him "a figure of ridicule"[18] and began the decline of a ministry that had raised hundreds of millions of dollars and made him a religious celebrity.

Roberts went into semi-retirement in 1992 and died in 2009 at the age of 91. His ministry brought the Prosperity Gospel into the Christian mainstream: he said the opening prayer at a Billy Graham crusade in 1950, which conferred an aura of respectability despite reports of people dying during his healing meetings. A spokesman for the ministry pointed out that, with so many sick people present, it was only to be expected that a few would die.[19] Roberts also shared in the controversy Graham attracted by insisting, during the era of segregation, that audience members of all races sit side by side. But it was his phenomenally successful methods of spreading the message of health and wealth that made him one of the true innovators of the Prosperity Gospel movement.

Once the pairing of discipleship and wealth became acceptable, it seemed there was no limit to the gaudiness and greed of prosperity preachers. "The lack of money is the root of all evil," proclaimed Reverend Ike, inverting the actual Scripture, which says that the *love* of money is the root of all evil. Reverend Ike, born Frederick J. Eikerenkoetter (1935–2009), assured his listeners, mostly African Americans who, like him, had come to the urban North during the Great Migration, that "You can't lose with the stuff I use." With his flashy jewelry and clothes, his appearance made the promise

18. William Lobdell, "Oral Roberts Dies at 91: Televangelist Was Pioneer Preacher of the 'Prosperity Gospel,'" *Los Angeles Times*, December 15, 2009, accessed August 11, 2022, https://www.latimes.com/local/obituaries/la-me-oral-roberts16-2009dec16-story.html.

19. Lobdell, "Oral Roberts Dies at 91."

that much more compelling, in spite of his message being in direct contradiction to the Scriptures.

The 1980s ushered in what Bowler has called the "golden age of televangelism."[20] The growth of megachurches with tens of thousands of members and hundreds of thousands of viewers was part of a larger conservative Christian movement gathering steam at this time. This movement included fundamentalists, charismatics, and evangelical and Pentecostal churches, a small but growing minority of which were led by ministers preaching prosperity theology.[21] As Ronald Reagan declared that it was "morning in America," popular optimism fueled a "bigger is better" mindset, and the church growth movement was well underway. But it wasn't just churches. Following the model of the earlier radio evangelists, prosperity preachers worked to establish global television networks. One of the most memorable teams to head a television ministry was the ultimate prosperity power couple, Jim and Tammy Faye Bakker.

James Orsen Bakker was born in 1940 in Muskegon, Michigan, to Raleigh and Furnia ("Furn") Bakker. The youngest of four children, Jim's birth reduced his mother to tears, as she'd wanted a girl. Furn was an emotionally distant mother, and Raleigh accepted the religion of his father, who was an exceptionally joyless Pentecostal evangelist. Fortunately for young Jim, Furn's parents lived next door and his grandmother doted on him, offering the unconditional love and warmth the boy craved.

The family lived in cramped quarters in a working-class neighborhood until Jim was seven years old, when they moved up to a large house in a much nicer part of town. Although they were comfortable and others remembered Jim as a happy kid, in his 1976 autobiography, Bakker remembered his house and personal possessions as shabby, and his younger self as wracked with insecurity and shame. Nevertheless, young Jim partnered with a

20. Bowler, *Blessed*, 104.

21. Bowler, 101.

neighbor boy to sell fruit, flowers, and anything else they could get their hands on. They did well, and Jim polished his sales skills by practicing in front of a mirror and into a tape recorder.

Bakker attended an Assemblies of God Bible college in Minneapolis, where he met Tammy Faye LaValley (1942–2007). Tammy Faye was born in International Falls, Minnesota, to Rachel and Carl LaValley. Both were Pentecostal preachers, but soon after Tammy Faye's birth, they divorced, and Rachel became disenchanted with the church. Not Tammy, however: "At 10, she found God, falling flat on her back in an Assemblies of God church and speaking in tongues; at 16, she discovered make-up. The two have never left her."[22] Jim and Tammy were married in 1961; they would eventually have two children, but first they began a traveling ministry in which Jim preached and Tammy Faye sang.

In 1966, the Bakkers began working with Pat Robertson at the Christian Broadcasting Network. Successful shows they established included "The 700 Club," "The PTL Show," and "The Jim and Tammy Show." Another major project was Heritage USA, a Christian theme park on 2,300 acres near Fort Mill, South Carolina. The compound included a water park, campground, chapel (the "Upper Room"), skating rink, conference facilities, an amphitheater where passion plays were staged, and a residential complex. It opened in 1978, and by 1986 it was taking in nearly six million visitors per year.[23]

Critics mocked Tammy Faye's over-the-top hair, makeup, and clothing, as well as both Bakkers' tendencies to grow maudlin when soliciting donations. Jim once announced on the air that they'd failed to reach a fundraising goal and burst into tears. The

22. Leslie Camhi, "At 10 She Found God. At 16 She Found Make-Up. And the Two Have Never Left Her," *Guardian*, August 10, 2000, accessed August 12, 2022, https://www.theguardian.com/film/2000/aug/04/culture.features2.

23. Tim Funk, "Jim Bakker's Theme Park Was Like a Christian Disneyland. Here's What Happened to It," *Charlotte Observer*, March 20, 2018, accessed September 19, 2024, https://www.charlotteobserver.com/living/religion/article205362719.html.

phones lit up and the donations poured in. Tammy seemed to weep at anything and everything, dabbing at her mascara while trusting in Jesus. And Jesus seemed to be coming through—to the tune of over a million dollars a week. As the Bakkers' lifestyle grew more lavish, the criticism grew more brutal: one particularly memorable episode was when the press revealed that the Bakkers' dog had an air-conditioned doghouse. (I've heard that this went unoccupied because the dog didn't care for the noise made by the AC. I cannot, however, substantiate this rumor.)

And then the empire came crashing down. The first sign of trouble was in 1979, when the Federal Communications Commission (FCC) investigated Jim and reported that he'd raised $350,000 that he claimed was going to foreign missions, when it was actually being used for the theme park. Additional donations were used to support their extravagant lifestyle. Bakker was forced to sell his TV station, but the Department of Justice did not press charges, and it wasn't until 1985 that the IRS reported that between 1980 and 1983, the Bakkers had diverted $1.3 million in donations (over $4 million in 2024 dollars) for their personal use.[24]

As if this weren't enough, the Bakkers were finished off by another scandal that broke in 1987. In 1980, Jim had had sex with former church secretary Jessica Hahn in a Florida hotel room, and Hahn had subsequently received over $350,000 ($1.1 million in 2024 dollars) in hush money. The story was leaked, however, bringing the wrath of other televangelists, especially Jimmy Swaggart, down on Jim, who was certainly giving them all a bad name. Bakker had kept a separate set of books to conceal the irregularities involved in keeping Hahn quiet; nevertheless, once the story broke, she claimed that she had been raped by both Bakker and Oklahoma City evangelist John Wesley.

24. Michael Isikoff and Art Harris, "PTL's Missing Millions," *Washington Post*, June 20, 1987, accessed September 19, 2024, https://www.washingtonpost.com/archive/opinions/1987/06/21/ptls-missing-millions/553aa246-42b9-49bd-954e-0c3b85349514/.

In the end, Bakker confessed to the sexual encounter but denied having raped Hahn. As further allegations of sex acts with both women and men came in, Bakker resigned his position at PTL and handed the reins to "Moral Majority" spokesman and Liberty University founder Jerry Falwell. The latter thanked him by calling him "a sexual deviant, an embezzler and a liar," and "the greatest scab and cancer on the face of Christianity in two thousand years of church history."[25] Jimmy Swaggart, one of Bakker's sharpest and most righteous critics, was later involved in his own scandal when he was caught visiting sex workers in New Orleans.

Eventually, Bakker was stripped of his position as an Assemblies of God minister and convicted on twenty-four counts of mail fraud, wire fraud, and conspiracy. Originally sentenced to a $500,000 fine and forty-five years in prison, the sentence was later reduced to eight years. He was released on parole in 1994, having been divorced while in prison by Tammy Faye, who remarried but died of colon cancer in 2007. Bakker emerged a free man but $6 million in debt to the IRS. (The doghouse, incidentally, went for $4,500 at auction.[26])

Ever the salesman, Bakker published a memoir in 1996 (*I Was Wrong*), and he has remarried and returned to televangelism. He's made a number of controversial statements, claiming that Hurricane Harvey was a judgment from God on America and that the mayor of Houston had ordered all area ministers to submit their sermons to her before preaching them. In the very same show, Bakker was selling "Tasty Pantry" food buckets for $175 apiece to hurricane victims, assuring them that the twenty-eight pounds of freeze-dried food in each bucket would stay fresh for twenty-five years.[27] Most recently, he was ordered by the attorney general of

25. "Bakker's Back," *Independent*, June 15, 2003, accessed February 26, 2025, https://www.independent.co.uk/news/world/americas/bakker-s-back-109104.html.

26. David Lauter, "The Faithful, Skeptics Flock to PTL Auction," *Los Angeles Times*, May 24, 1987, accessed February 26, 2025, https://www.latimes.com/archives/la-xpm-1987-05-24-mn-2561-story.html.

27. Brian Lisi, "Disgraced Pastor Jim Bakker Says Hurricane Harvey Was 'Judgment' from God While Selling Tasty Pantry Bucket for $175," *New York*

New York in 2020 to stop promoting colloidal silver supplements as a treatment for Covid-19.[28] Snake oil still sells.

The fall of the Bakkers brought attention from the public, the media, and government officials to the issue of televangelists and their finances. The Bakkers were not alone in their luxury. In 2015, Kenneth Copeland defended his fleet of private jets by claiming that he can't be expected to pray on a commercial flight in coach: "You can't manage that today, in this dope-filled world, [to] get in a long tube with a bunch of demons." Copeland seemed to miss the fact that those "demons" in coach are likely the same people he asks for donations.[29] Creflo Dollar (yes, *Dollar*) likewise defended his campaign to raise $65 million for a private jet: "Let me tell you something about believing God. I can dream as long as I want to. I can believe God as long as I want to. If I want to believe God for a $65 million plane, you cannot stop me. You cannot stop me from dreaming."[30]

A 2007 Senate investigation led by Iowa Republican Chuck Grassley certainly tried to slow him down, though. Dollar was one of a handful of televangelists whose personal fortunes raised the question of whether their ministries should maintain their tax-exempt status. The probe continued for three years, and while some preachers complied by providing financial records to the

---

Daily News, April 7, 2018, accessed September 19, 2024, https://www.nydailynews.com/2017/09/06/disgraced-pastor-jim-bakker-says-hurricane-harvey-was-judgment-from-god-while-selling-his-tasty-pantry-bucket-for-175/.

28. State of New York, Office of the Attorney General, March 3, 2020, accessed February 26, 2025, https://ag.ny.gov/sites/default/files/bakker_cease_and_desist_letter_notification.pdf.

29. Michael Brice-Saddler, "A Wealthy Televangelist Explains His Fleet of Private Jets: 'It's a Biblical Thing,'" *Washington Post*, June 3, 2019, accessed August 12, 2022, https://www.washingtonpost.com/religion/2019/06/04/wealthy-televangelist-explains-his-fleet-private-jets-its-biblical-thing/.

30. Carol Kuruvilla, "Televangelist Creflo Dollar Defends His Plans for $65 Million Private Jet," *Huffington Post*, April 23, 2015, accessed August 12, 2022, https://www.huffpost.com/entry/creflo-dollar-jet_n_7129548.

Senate Finance Committee, others did not. Yet none of those targeted for investigation received any penalties.

It should be noted that a televangelist may amass a personal fortune by selling books and other materials on the strength of their platform, without touching actual donations. Still, the limitless wealth of some of these preachers, while defended by them as proof that the prosperity message works, makes other conservative clergy outside the Prosperity Gospel movement nervous. Not only might the faithful tar them with the same brush, but there's concern that tax-exempt status could be reconsidered for religious nonprofits more broadly.

Among those investigated by Grassley's committee was Joel Osteen (b. 1963), pastor of Lakewood (formerly Baptist) Church, one of the largest churches in the United States. The church, which meets in a converted sporting arena, seats 17,000 people, and in multiple services sees an average of 45,000 attendees per week.[31] Millions more are reached weekly through its broadcast.[32] The church was founded and pastored by Joel's father John, a Southern Baptist minister, and its congregation originally met in the back of a feed store. Lakewood has come a long way since those early days.

Joel was one of six children born to John and Dolores Osteen. After graduating from Humble High School in Humble, Texas, he attended Oral Roberts University for a couple of years, where he studied communications. But he ultimately dropped out to return to Houston and put his father's sermons on television. He married Victoria Iloff in 1987. They have two children and live in

31. Amanda Cochran, "Lakewood Church: The Houston Megachurch by the Numbers," December 3, 2021, accessed August 13, 2022, https://www.click2houston.com/news/local/2021/12/03/lakewood-church-the-houston-megachurch-by-the-numbers/.

32. Dwight Adams, "Joel Osteen in Indianapolis: Why the Televangelist Is So Beloved and So Controversial, " *IndyStar*, August 9, 2018, accessed August 13, 2022, https://www.indystar.com/story/news/2018/08/09/joel-osteen-house-net-worth-lakewood-church-wife-why-televangelist-so-beloved-and-controversial/935789002/.

a house bought in 2010 for $10.5 million in an affluent suburb of Houston.[33]

John Osteen often encouraged his son to preach, but Joel consistently refused until January 17, 1999. It was the first and last sermon his father ever heard him preach, as John died of a heart attack only days later. Upon his father's death, Joel succeeded him as senior pastor, and has remained in that position ever since. He's built up the size of the congregation and its media outreach, and his best-selling books and well-paid speaking gigs have pushed his net worth up to over $50 million. He has not drawn a salary from Lakewood since 2005, however, and explains that "We make plenty of money from our books. But we just live normal lives. We try to be conservative and honor God with our life and with our example."

Kate Bowler describes Joel Osteen as a preacher of "soft prosperity."[34] Osteen's prescriptions for success reflect a more indirect notion of causality: instead of a simple "name it and claim it" approach in which the words themselves have supernatural power, Osteen's version is more infused with psychology and self-help: by affirming that "I am blessed. I am prosperous. I am healthy. I am talented. I am creative. I am wise,"[35] Osteen says a person can change their self-image, which doesn't directly lead to God's blessing. But that healthy self-image will cause believers to act in more positive ways, such as getting their spending under control, or working in a way that attracts the boss's attention and favor. And *that* is what is blessed.

Osteen's language is less filled with Christian jargon and more at home on an Oprah show, and indeed he has appeared on Oprah's "Super Soul Sunday." Listening to him, whether in conversation or at the "podium" (he doesn't call it a pulpit, and his church has no altar or cross, just a slowly spinning golden globe), he sounds

33. Adams, "Joel Osteen in Indianapolis."

34. Bowler, *Blessed*, 125.

35. Quoted in Bowler, 125.

like a pretty nice guy. He just wants people to live their "best life," to think positively about themselves and their prospects, to experience a divine transformation that will lead them to fulfill their potential.

The problems with Osteen's gospel are more sins of omission than commission. He is criticized by evangelicals for the noticeable lack of sin and hell in his preaching. Osteen responds that people generally know they're in trouble; what they need is help getting out. As one of his staff put it, "If you want to feel bad, Lakewood is not the place for you. Most people want to leave church feeling better than when they went in."[36] That feels like a soothing, compassionate message, one long overdue from a church that has berated and condemned people for too long. But there's no place for the cross in this plan of redemption, no place for the kind of brutally honest, searching self-examination and realism that the desert hermits embraced.

For those of a more mainline Christian bent, the main problem with Osteen's teaching is the absence of any attempt at theodicy, at accounting for the presence of evil in the world, especially evil that strikes the innocent. Where is God when a child has cancer? Where is God when innocent people become "collateral damage" when a great power commits an act of aggression?

Preaching a sort of "Christianity Lite," Osteen doesn't take on these problems. He also doesn't wrestle with political issues with his audiences, preferring to say that he might, for example, have disagreed with President Barack Obama on some things, but in general, he thought the president was a good person doing his best. This is actually pretty refreshing at a time when many conservative preachers explicitly take sides and tell their congregations how to vote. But the fact that Donald Trump is a "big fan" of Joel Osteen[37]

36. Edward Luce, "A Preacher for Trump's America: Joel Osteen and the Prosperity Gospel," *Financial Times*, April 17, 2019, accessed August 15, 2022, https://www.ft.com/content/3990ce66-60a6-11e9-b285-3acd5d43599e.

37. Luce, "Preacher for Trump's America."

suggests that this is not a prophet speaking truth to power. Pushed on how he manages to keep so much of the New Testament out of his preaching, "Osteen smiled awkwardly. 'I preach the gospel but we are non-denominational,' he replied. 'It is not my aim to dwell on technicalities. I want to help people sleep at night.' "

Osteen is a master at making himself likable. With his expensive suits, impressive head of hair, and a smile most often described as "megawatt" (and which can remain lit through an entire sermon), not to mention his pretty blonde wife, he models "success" in a way that invites you to come along. But he has, on occasion, found himself in embarrassing situations. One of the worst was in 2017 when, in the aftermath of Hurricane Harvey, Osteen did not open his church as a shelter for the people of his city displaced by the storm. While a member of his family claimed that the church couldn't open because of imminent flooding, Osteen himself claimed, to the contrary, that the church had been open from the beginning. Then he said it would open when other area shelters were filled. Finally, the church did open, but the damage to its image was done.[38]

There's one other prosperity preacher I'd like to include here, who in many ways is the most intriguing of all. Joyce Meyer was born in 1943 in St. Louis, Missouri. The names of her parents are typically not listed in online bios, presumably because Meyer has been outspoken about the sexual abuse and emotional neglect she endured as a girl, but also about her efforts to reconcile with them in their old age. By age nine, she summoned the courage to tell her mother what her father was doing, and her mother confronted him. When he denied it, Joyce's mother chose to believe him, despite the fact that she once walked in on them while it was happening. She later said that while she knew about the abuse, she

38. Stephanie Kuzydym and Kristine Phillips, "Joel Osteen Pushes Back Against Accusations He Closed His Megachurch to Harvey Victims," *Chicago Tribune*, August 30, 2017, accessed August 15, 2022, https://www.chicagotribune.com/nation-world/ct-joel-osteen-megachurch-harvey-victims-20170830-story.html.

couldn't bring herself to face it. She was also his victim, enduring beatings, which Joyce did not receive. She was, apparently, already sufficiently subdued.[39]

Always attracted to the spiritual, Joyce found Jesus at age nine, but also found astrology, fortune tellers, tarot readers and other occult practices, as well as a tendency to steal anything that wasn't nailed down. She was, nevertheless, a good and popular student, blessed with a sharp wit and an early flair for leadership. As soon as she turned eighteen and finished high school, Joyce moved out of her parents' house: one step forward toward independence. But it was quickly followed by two steps back into a disastrous marriage. He was a fifth-grade dropout, a philandering car salesman who worked sporadically and disappeared often, sometimes for months at a time. A miscarriage at twenty-one was followed by the birth of her son, and Joyce decided that even her parents' home was better than her own. She moved back home and sank into depression, trying to comfort herself with drinking, partying, and sleeping with random men.[40]

Soon after her divorce, Joyce met David Benjamin Meyer, who was a hard worker and just the kind of steady, godly influence she needed. They married after five dates, and he immediately adopted her son. Dave was good for Joyce, but she was carrying a lot of baggage and didn't instantly turn into the kind of wife she wanted to be. Short-tempered and demanding, she often tells stories now in her talks of how difficult she was, and how she tried the patience of the saintly Dave. They attended the nondenominational Life Christian Church together, but it took time and a mystical experience, in which she felt "full of liquid love,"[41] to bring about a real change

39. Bill Smith and Carolyn Tuft, "Meyer Traces Her Fervor to Early Abuse, Alcohol," STLtoday.com, November 15, 2003, accessed August 16, 2022, https://web.archive.org/web/20060127003333/http://www.stltoday.com/stltoday/news/special/joycemeyer.nsf/0/1D29266A7F855B2886256DDF00701F8A.

40. Smith and Tuft, "Meyer Traces Her Fervor."

41. Smith and Tuft.

of direction. Shortly after this, she began leading women's Bible studies in her home, though they soon had to change locations with the number of women in attendance swelling to five hundred.

Joyce has a genius for building, for growth: she eventually took to the pulpit at Life Christian and, between her preaching and Bible studies, was so popular that the struggling, thirty-member storefront church grew to over three thousand. She and Dave eventually took their show on the road; although Dave never appears on stage, he makes a lot of appearances in Joyce's talks as her wise, long-suffering, and ever-supportive spouse. Radio came first, and then conferences and television, plus a string of best-selling books. Except for a brief early period as associate pastor of Life Christian Church, Joyce has never served as a pastor, preferring a less conventional ministry in which she speaks to crowds in packed stadiums and on TV. Her show *Enjoying Everyday Life* reaches millions of people. She's written over a hundred books, which have been translated into a hundred languages, and she's landed on *The New York Times* bestseller list. Her audiences, mostly white, middle-aged women, want what she has to sell, and they're prepared to pay for it.

It's not hard to see why. Joyce is, above all else, proof that even the most screwed-up woman can become a spectacular success and remain open and honest about her failings once she's done so. She inspires people, not only through her messages, but also as an entrepreneur and the lone woman in this line of work who takes the stage while her husband stays in the wings. In this, she has shattered one of televangelism's most durable glass ceilings. And Joyce is fun to watch: she's folksy and funny, and she's candid about not only the darker passages of her story but also the many ways they made her a really annoying and immature person. She speaks often and with evident gratitude of how much Dave put up with before God turned her life around. And if Dave was a gambling man, it must be said that his faith in Joyce has paid off magnificently, at least in worldly terms. With a net worth estimated at $8 million, multiple houses, a private jet and more, until 2004 Joyce and her husband earned a combined $1.35 million per year from Joyce Meyer Ministries alone. In that year, she elected to reduce their salaries, but her stack of bestsellers alone makes for a pretty comfortable income.[42]

Joyce's luxurious lifestyle has, inevitably, brought criticism, as it has for other prosperity preachers. In one case, the criticism arose out of a laughable misunderstanding: in 2007, the word went out that Joyce had paid $23,000 for a toilet seat. It turns out that it wasn't a toilet seat at all, but an antique chest of drawers (a "commode") that had been donated to her for placement outside her office. This was one of the stories that brought the attention of the Grassley investigation, but Joyce Meyer Ministries cooperated with the committee, providing financial information, and was not stripped of its tax-exempt status. Yet it must be said that the Meyers live at a level her audiences can only dream of. Beyond the house, the car, and the private jet, there's Joyce's wardrobe ("If you want to know how many blazers I have, I'm not telling. It's a lot!"). In 2009, the organization was granted accreditation from the Evangelical Council for Financial Accountability, which indicated that its financial transparency and fundraising practices had met the standard for "responsible stewardship."[43] There's no knowing what Joyce's budget is for clothing, hair, and accessories, but it's obviously "a lot." And for these and other indulgences, she makes no apology. Defending her wardrobe and even plastic surgery, Joyce simply asserts that there's no reason a Christian shouldn't want to look her best for God. After all, what is attractive about a Christianity that requires people to look dowdy and dull?

Pushed in a *Nightline* interview about owning a private jet, she responded:

42. Naomi Karina, "Top 15 Richest Pastors in America and Their Impressive Net Worth," https://www.legit.ng/ask-legit/top/1627219-top-richest-pastors-america-impressive-net-worth/.

43. Bowler, *Blessed*, 196.

> "I really could not fly commercial at this stage of my life and do what I'm doing. I could not endure it physically if I had to do that. Do you know how hard it is to fly commercial now?"

In the same interview, Joyce was asked point-blank if she would consider herself a Prosperity Gospel preacher:

> [Joyce:] "Do I believe that God wants to bless us? Yes."
>
> [Reporter:] "Do you believe that if someone gives money to the ministry, that more will come back to them?"
>
> [Joyce:] "Yes."
>
> [Reporter:] "I think that's what they mean by prosperity gospel."
>
> [Joyce:] "Yes."[44]

Yet in 2019, Joyce joined several other televangelists who made statements pulling back a bit from a full-on prosperity message.[45] In a video posted on Instagram, she stated: "I'm glad for what I learned about prosperity, but it got out of balance." Joyce admitted that she'd overestimated the role of faith in keeping people out of trouble:

> "Well, that's not right! There is nowhere in the Bible where we're promised we will never have any trouble. I don't care how much faith you have, you're not going to avoid ever having trouble in your life. Jesus said, 'in the world, you

44. Cynthia McFadden, *Nightline* interview, April 13, 2010, https://archive.org/details/WJLA_20100414_033500_Nightline/start/480/end/540.

45. "Joyce Meyer Admits Her Prosperity and Faith Views 'Got Out of Balance,'" *Christian News*, January 12, 2019, accessed August 17, 2022, https://premierchristian.news/en/news/article/joyce-meyer-admits-her-prosperity-and-faith-views-got-out-of-balance.

> will have tribulation [but] cheer up, I have overcome the world.' "[46]

This seems like a promising withdrawal from the version of prosperity Joyce and others have preached over the last hundred years and more. If she holds to this position, she will be making some space for poverty in her message. It's encouraging that Joyce has embraced her own experiences of poverty, including the abuse she endured growing up:

> "I'm not telling you this to get you to feel sorry for me," she told followers in a crowded church in Tampa, Fla. . . . "I'm telling it to you to show you that people have awful things happen to them. . . . I know that my life is more powerful because of what happened to me than it ever would have been if it wouldn't have happened."[47]

Critics have found plenty of other reasons to consider Joyce's teaching heretical, but admirers will put up with a lot from this charismatic, eminently relatable woman who has suffered, who understands suffering, and assures them that God can give, in the words of the prophet Isaiah, "beauty for ashes" (see Isa 61:3).

Prosperity: Song of the Sirens

I have discussed the Prosperity Gospel and some of its main spokespersons at length because this movement is exactly what we might have predicted would eventually follow from what has been called the "curse of Constantine": a church that enjoys the favor and patronage of the powerful. Even as I imagine the relief of the ragged, persecuted bands of Jesus' followers throughout the Roman Empire following the Edict of Milan, I can hear the words of Dante Alighieri a millennium later:

46. Quoted in "Joyce Meyer Admits."
47. Quoted in Smith and Tuft, "Meyer Traces Her Fervor."

> Ah, Constantine, what wickedness was born— and not from your conversion—from the dower that you bestowed upon the first rich father! (*Inferno* 19.115-117)

By endowing the church (that "father") with temporal goods and advantages, Constantine had launched it down the path of corruption. There would be centuries of attempts to explain why the eye of a needle isn't after all that much smaller than a camel, and why Jesus didn't really mean any of the many things he said about poverty—of wallet or of spirit.

Kate Bowler shows that the Prosperity Gospel can be organized into four major themes. First, *faith* and words that speak faith have unseen spiritual power to overcome misfortunes of all kinds. Second, God desires to bless the faithful with *wealth*, and third, with *health*. Finally, the life of a believer should be characterized by *victory*: no obstacles should be able to impede the faithful from reaching their goals, including goals very much of this world.[48]

Is this message consistent with the Scriptures? In one sense, yes. The book of Deuteronomy contains a long passage in which God, having brought the children of Israel out of slavery in Egypt and to the edge of the Promised Land, assures them that if they'll keep their end of the covenant, they will prosper:

> Then you shall again obey the Lord, observing all his commandments that I am commanding you today, and the Lord your God will make you abundantly prosperous in all your undertakings, in the fruit of your body, in the fruit of your livestock, and in the fruit of your soil. (Deut 30:8-9)

So it's not that prosperity preachers are conjuring their message out of thin air; they do have this scriptural basis for their claims, as well as another one frequently drawn upon:

48. Bowler, *Blessed*, 7.

> Bring the full tithe into the storehouse, so that there may be food in my house, and thus put me to the test, says the LORD of hosts; see if I will not open the windows of heaven for you and pour down for you an overflowing blessing. (Mal 3:10)

Jesus himself, in Luke's Sermon on the Plain, said:

> [G]ive, and it will be given to you. A good measure, pressed down, shaken together, running over, will be put into your lap; for the measure you give will be the measure you get back. (Luke 6:38)

On the strength of texts like these, preachers of prosperity argue that God wishes to bless believers with abundant wealth, health, and victory. The problem, once again, lies in what is *omitted*: these preachers, unlike St. Paul, do avoid declaring "the whole counsel of God" (Acts 20:27 NKJV). Both the Hebrew and Christian Scriptures are full of examples and teachings that tell us that there will be suffering, even—perhaps especially—for the righteous among us: "Indeed, all who want to live a godly life in Christ Jesus will be persecuted" (2 Tim 3:12). In the parable of the rich man and Lazarus, Jesus makes it clear that those who enjoy material comforts in this world, without a thought for the suffering poor at their gates, will pay for it in the next. And in his Sermon on the Plain, Jesus warns the rich over and over:

> But woe to you who are rich,
> for you have received your consolation.
> Woe to you who are full now,
> for you will be hungry.
> Woe to you who are laughing now,
> for you will mourn and weep.
> Woe to you when all speak well of you, for that is what their ancestors did to the false prophets. (Luke 6:24-26)

So the Lord will reward the righteous with prosperity, but on the other hand, woe unto the rich. Is there a contradiction here?

I would say no: the faithful can hope for and even expect God's blessing. The mistake lies in thinking that the blessing will take worldly forms. Health, wealth, and victory may come, but they very well may not. Thomas Aquinas said that it may be the poor person who is actually blessed by God, because they have a chance to benefit spiritually from their poverty. The healthy and wealthy won't look to God for help, and as such are to be pitied for missing the spiritual blessings that would have come if they had.[49]

The church through the ages, seduced as she's been by the attractions of the world, has always come back to the centrality of poverty. The desert hermits, Saints Francis and Clare of Assisi, the medieval mystics of Helfta, the lovers of the Sacred Heart of Jesus—all have declared, along with the Scriptures, that poverty confers great spiritual blessing on those wise ones who pursue her. And from the 12-Step movement, we have learned that hitting bottom is often when healing begins. The journey to real wholeness and blessing can't get underway until we are convinced of the futility of our own efforts, the emptiness of our own resources. But when we reach that place, when we own our poverty and hold empty hands out to God, that is when the true riches come in.

In the chapters that follow, we'll look more closely at poverty in the Scriptures, and then investigate each of these poverty-centering traditions across history and in our own historical moment. By mining the wisdom of those through the ages who have held poverty as a precious, direct path to the heart of God and to our own healing, we will have an answer to the preachers of false prosperity. And we'll understand why Jesus wasn't crazy when he looked at the poor in spirit, and called them blessed.

49. Robert Barron, "Bishop Barron on the Prosperity Gospel," April 8, 2010, accessed August 17, 2022, https://www.youtube.com/watch?v=1ip4Jx92F94.

Chapter 2

Filled with Good Things

Poverty in the Scriptures

He has filled the hungry with good things,
and the rich He has sent away empty.

Luke 1:53 NKJV

The Prosperity Gospel movement is the logical extension of humanity's unwillingness throughout history to accept the fact that we are not God. The whole of Scripture, from the beginnings in the Garden of Eden through Israel's repeated rebellions, restorations, and renewed rebellions, can be read as the story of our very human reluctance to accept human limitations. Nor does this change in the New Testament, any more than it's changed in the centuries since. It was to imperfect humans that Christ came to offer reconciliation and restoration, and it's as imperfect humans that we struggle and rebel against the sublime gift of our poverty. Salvation history is the story of God mercifully punching holes in our illusions of self-sufficiency and the fantasies of our inflated egos so that, in true humility, we might hold out empty hands and receive all of God's abundance.

What is wrong with us? We're like little kids riding in a shopping cart. Our divine Mother has planned a sumptuous meal for us, a true holiday feast. But she can't get on with it as long as we're grabbing for the circus peanuts and spray-can cheese. This is just it: we were created to receive, but we don't receive because we're too busy grabbing. The opposite of poverty is not wealth but *entitlement*: we don't want to wait for what God greatly desires to give us, so we grab instead at what we think is our due. And in doing so, we miss the point of it all, which is *relationship*. Grabbing instead of receiving robs us of the joy, the fulfillment, of being in right relationship with God. It takes from us everything we were made for.

In this chapter, I'd like to show how this conflict between grabbing and receiving recurs again and again throughout the Scriptures, and how accepting and embracing our poverty is the way forward to healing. Because this theme turns up so often in the Scriptures, I'm going to have to be selective. But once you see the pattern a few times, you'll see it everywhere.

Eden, Babel, and Entitlement

So let's begin "in the beginning." In the creation story, God places the humans in a garden. What could more clearly communicate God's desire that we live in abundance, in lushness, not only with plenteous provision but surrounded by beauty as well? And the first couple were given free access to all the delights of Eden—with just one exception: the fruit of the tree of the knowledge of good and evil was off-limits, and if they ate of it, they would "surely die."

I spent thirty-some years as an academic, and I've always thought it odd that it was knowledge, of all things, that God forbade to Adam and Eve. Specifically, the knowledge of good and evil; I mean, of all the kinds of knowledge people could possess, moral understanding seems like it would be God's first priority. And yet, God forbids it to them, and the consequences of disobedience turn out to be catastrophic. Why?

It's been suggested[1] that what was forbidden here was not so much an *understanding* of the difference between right and wrong, but the right to *arbitrate* the difference. Humans were given by God the dignity of free will, the ability to choose to do good or evil. But to decide what is good and what's evil—that is for God alone. This is not a popular position to take in a time when moral absolutes are rejected by many.

To a degree, moral relativism is a healthy corrective to ethnocentrism and other forms of bigotry: moral meanings sometimes do depend on the context. For example, a cultural emphasis on the rights of individuals versus the needs of the collective is not good or evil in itself. How we judge a woman who puts her own career above the needs of her extended family will vary, depending on where the emphasis is placed in a given cultural context. In an individualistic culture like that of the United States, she may be applauded for her ambition,[2] but in a more collectivist culture like Japan's, she may be seen as selfish. Cultural relativism says that a society has the right to determine its values for itself. Compare this to the European global colonial adventure, which was supported by the idea of the "civilizing mission" and the "white man's burden," and it's clear how urgently that "corrective" has been needed.

And yet, even the most committed relativist cracks at some point. Western feminists who insist that a society's ways are not to be seen as right or wrong, just "different," will quickly change their tune when, for example, you bring up the issue of female genital mutilation—at which point we want to send in the Marines. We all have some values on which we believe you don't get to choose. Some things are just right or wrong in themselves.

1. Robert Barron, "Understanding Genesis: Adam, Eve, and the Fall," November 1, 2021, accessed November 26, 2024, https://www.youtube.com/watch?v=rAGyNe9hytc.

2. And of course, in a heterogeneous society like that found in the United States, there will be multiple variations between the dominant culture and those of minority communities.

From a biblical perspective, then, the right to choose *between* good and evil is given to humans, but the right to establish what *is* good and evil remains the prerogative of God. At least, it was supposed to. Being human, however, Adam and Eve needed only to be told that one tree in all the garden was off limits to make straight for that tree. They're tempted, and they eat. But it wasn't out of sheer orneriness, a desire to eat this fruit just because it was the only one God had forbidden to them. The tempter had planted the idea that God had withheld this fruit because it would bring them up to God's level, make them a competitive threat: "You will not die; for God knows that when you eat of it your eyes will be opened, and you will be like God, knowing good and evil."

But how likely was that? God does not compete with beings in creation, as if we're all engaged in some great cosmic game. So God didn't forbid the fruit because of a fear that humans would threaten God's fragile sense of divinity. It was because laying the boundary between right and wrong was always supposed to be God's job, and when humans grab at that prerogative, when we try to wrench it out of God's hands, we cannot be in right relationship with God or one another, cannot become what we were created to be.

We see it again just a few chapters later. The earth's population having rebounded a bit after human wickedness led to the great flood, the people still haven't learned. So they decide to build a tower, "with its top in the heavens" so they can get above themselves once again (see Gen 11:1-9). "Let us make a name for ourselves," they say, as if building giant towers in one's own name were a good idea. Seeing them tipping dangerously into narcissism, God confuses their language and scatters them abroad, because once again they were grabbing at a higher place, trying to wrest it from God, rather than receiving God's gifts in patience, humility, and gratitude.

Don't we recognize this impulse? Entitlement is a sin that is so basic, so pervasive. Thomas Merton called it the "Promethean problem"[3]: in Greek mythology, Prometheus stole fire from the

3. See Thomas Merton, *The New Man* (New York: Farrar, Straus and Giroux, 1961).

gods and was sentenced by Zeus to be chained to a rock and have an eagle peck out his liver every day. It's an extremely old story, and variations can be found in many cultures. Our tendency to grasp at things that aren't ours is the very impulse that is exploited in the marketplace, where we're constantly being offered things that we "must have" but can't afford. The market flashes a pretty leg at us, and we fall for the seduction. The result, among other things, is stratospherically high levels of debt. In the fourth quarter of 2024, Americans' collective consumer debt stood at $18 *trillion*; individually, that's an average of $105,056 per household.[4] This figure includes debt from credit cards, mortgages, student loans and other sources. Many Americans are so deeply in debt that they cannot realistically see a way out, ever.

Let's be clear, though, that a great deal of this debt comes, not from entitlement, but from living in a society that places basics such as education, housing, and health care out of the reach of many people unless they rely on credit. In my own state of Washington, for example, when I was in college in the 1980s, 80 percent of the cost of educating a student was paid by the state, and 20 percent by the student. That ratio is now reversed; moreover, free money in the form of scholarships has been disappearing for decades, replaced by loans that must be repaid. Further, housing costs here in Seattle, as in so many places, have driven even middle-class families out of the market, and many couples in their childbearing years are saying no to parenthood because they can't afford a pregnancy and childbirth, let alone child care after the baby is born. And many of us are just one diagnosis away from losing everything.

These are stark realities, and I don't in any way want to minimize them. But certainly a good-sized chunk of consumer debt comes from our simply wanting things and being unwilling to wait for them until we have the money to pay. Consumerism is at the heart of both our economy and our culture, and "consumerism" is just

4. Jack Caporal, "Average American Household Debt in 2025: Facts and Figures," *Motley Fool Money,* February 18, 2025, accessed February 26, 2025, https://www.fool.com/money/research/average-household-debt/.

another word for our tendency to grasp at what we want. As we've seen, the consumerist spirit has even worked its way into the Christian faith via the Prosperity Gospel: "I say you *ought* to be rich," Baptist preacher Russell H. Conwell roared at his congregation in 1915; "*you have no right to be poor!*"[5]

In each of Jesus' temptations in the wilderness, the devil struck right at this human tendency to grasp at things instead of waiting for them to be given. "Hungry, Jesus? You're supposed to be the Son of God. There's no reason for you to put up with discomfort. Command these stones to become loaves of bread." "Come on, Jesus, throw yourself off the roof of the Temple. You know your Father will protect you (*if* you are the Son of God, that is). Why wait for every knee to bow to you someday? You can have that today." "In fact, Jesus, there's no need to wait to take your place as Ruler of the world. Just one small bow in my direction, and it can all be yours right now" (see Matt 4:1-11).

But Jesus was having none of it. Secure in his identity as God's Beloved Son, he had nothing to prove to Satan and no need to grasp at the prerogatives of deity. He rejected all sense of entitlement and embraced the full humility of human poverty: although he "existed in the form of God, [he] did not consider equality with God something to be grasped, but emptied Himself . . . " (Phil 2:6-7, New American Standard Bible). That self-emptying, which in Greek is called *kenosis*, is the precise opposite of entitlement. It is, in fact, poverty of spirit at its healthiest. In his divinity, Jesus was entitled to everything. Yet in his humanity, he claimed nothing, but instead poured himself out, emptied himself of comforts, of honor, of power, even of life itself. And therefore, says the ancient hymn, God "highly exalted him" (Phil 2:9).

5. Tara Isabella Burton, "The Prosperity Gospel, Explained: Why Joel Osteen Believes That Prayer Can Make You Rich," *Vox*, September 1, 2017, accessed October 12, 2022, https://www.vox.com/identities/2017/9/1/15951874/prosperity-gospel-explained-why-joel-osteen-believes-prayer-can-make-you-rich-trump (emphasis added).

By refusing to grasp at what he had every right to regard as his, Jesus shows us a "more excellent way" to be human (see 1 Cor 12:31). Entitlement says, "I will have what I want, God's will or not," while kenosis says, "I will empty myself until the space within me is vast enough to hold God's gifts." Jesus knew, and we can trust, that what God seeks to give us is "abundantly far more than all we can ask or imagine" (Eph 3:20). This is because what God desires to give us is God's own self; as Jesus said, "If you then, who are evil, know how to give good gifts to your children, how much more will the heavenly Father give the Holy Spirit to those who ask him!" (Luke 11:13). If we're tempted to doubt this, it's worth remembering that right after his disciples had shamefully denied and deserted him in his hour of greatest need, the very next thing Jesus did when he saw them again was to breathe on them and say, "Receive the Holy Spirit" (John 20:22). Their emptiness was filled to overflowing, and they would never be the same.

Job and the Mystery of Suffering

But let's return to the Hebrew Scriptures, as we've barely begun to probe their wisdom on poverty of spirit. The ultimate meditation on poverty in the Hebrew Bible is the book of Job, so it will be worth looking at this book in a bit of depth. This is possibly the earliest attempt at *theodicy*, which is trying to understand the ways of God, particularly the thorny question of why an all-knowing, all-powerful, benevolent God allows bad things to happen to good people. Where is God's justice when the innocent suffer and the wicked flourish? Job, we learn in the first verse of the text, is "blameless and upright, one who feared God and turned away from evil." He had a wife, a family, great wealth, and position, and he was zealous in the service of the Lord. When God points this out to Satan, the tempter cynically responds that of course Job serves God, since God has given him everything a human could ask for. Who's to say his motives are pure? But take all this away, Satan says, and "he will curse you to your face."

So God allows Satan to take it all away: first his possessions and servants, then his children, and then his health. Job does the biblical version of a shrug and observes that everything he had came from God, who thus had every right to take it all back. Job blesses God's name instead of cursing it, even when he sits in such misery that his own wife invites him to "Curse God, and die" (Job 2:9). Instead of taking her advice, he simply tells her to stop being foolish and gets on with scraping at his sores.

At this point in the story, three of Job's friends show up (a fourth will appear later). For a whole week, they have the good sense to stay silent while Job gives voice to his suffering. He doesn't curse God, but he does curse the day he was born: "Why was I not buried like a stillborn child, like an infant that never sees the light?" (Job 3:16). Listening to his lament, his friends are finally moved to speak—a move they'd have been better off resisting, because their theodicy is neither wise nor helpful. Eliphaz goes first: "Can I give you some feedback? No offense, but . . . " and then essentially gives him platitudes along the lines of "God never gives us more than we can handle." Job responds by longing again for death, which is all the more bleak given that there is no suggestion in the whole book of belief in an afterlife.

Next comes Bildad, who accuses Job of blowing hot air and makes explicit what Eliphaz has only implied: Job and/or his children must have sinned. "Does God pervert justice?" Don't be one of those who forget God, Bildad says, and are like plants cut off from water. Instead, he urges Job to repent, and assures him that God will have him back. Job's reply shows increasing confusion and helplessness. He knows he is innocent, but he despairs in his weakness of defending himself before God.

Then Zophar takes a turn at Job and is even nastier than the other two: "Should a multitude of words go unanswered, and should one full of talk be vindicated?" (Job 11:2). "You've sinned, God knows it, stop denying it." But Job does deny it, and he calls on God to judge him rightly: "[L]et me be weighed in a just balance, and let God know my integrity!" (Job 31:6). There are more speeches, Job gives ever more spirited defenses of his innocence, and his friends continue to prove their uselessness.

Finally, God answers Job "out of the whirlwind: 'Who is this that darkens counsel by words without knowledge?' " (Job 38:1-2). God tells Job to pull himself together, that God is going to question *him* now, and he'd better get ready to answer. And so the grilling begins: *Where were you when I laid the foundation of the earth? Tell me, if you have understanding.* God goes through the cosmos and keeps questioning Job about its mysteries. Job is not given an answer to the mystery of his own suffering; instead, he is reminded of his own stature in the presence of God. "See," Job says, "I am of small account; what shall I answer you?" (Job 40:4). Finally, nearly speechless with awe, *Job assumes a posture of poverty*: "I despise myself, and repent in dust and ashes" (Job 42:6). With this, God rebukes Job's friends and requires them to humble themselves by offering sacrifices and asking for Job's prayers, that they might be spared the just recompense for their folly. Then God more than replaces Job's property, gives him new sons and daughters,[6] and restores Job's health so that he finally dies "old and full of days" (Job 42:17).

It's interesting that the theodicy question is never really answered. In fact, God seems to lay aside that question as of minimal importance. And indeed, for Job it's been of secondary importance all along. The main source of Job's suffering has lain in the apparent loss of his close relationship with God. In chapter 29, Job is nostalgic for the days when he and God seemed to be on the same side, when Job delivered justice to the people and God was his friend (see Job 29:4). When that friend seemed to turn against him, Job was thrown into a confusion rendered even darker by the

6. Some people find this restoration of Job's family troubling, as if lost humans can just be replaced. But we have to remember that the story takes place at a time when offspring are as close as one can get to eternal life. Furthermore, in a society based on honor, lacking them is a profound source of shame. Job doesn't get his children back, but this is a patriarchal culture, and he does get back his status as a patriarch. Besides which, it's a *story*.

misguided counsel of those who claimed to be friends but weren't. In reality, God has been his true friend all along, a fact that's seen less in the content of God's response to Job's questions than in the fact that God answered him at all.[7]

Job, unlike his companions, has skin in this game from the beginning. Yet for most of the book, the statements of all four mostly take place at an intellectual level. There's certainly no lack of emotion, especially on Job's part. But while Job is in deepening depression edging on despair, his exchanges with the others are still essentially a theological debate. I recognize the format from "Author Meets Critics" sessions at academic conferences. It's not until Job abandons all effort to justify himself, however rightly, and simply allows himself to come before God in his poverty, that his relationship to God is restored—or perhaps revealed—and he knows himself as God's beloved. As long as Job is full of the reasons why he doesn't deserve any of this misery, there isn't space within for God's loving presence to be known. The whole book is, for Job, a journey of kenosis that brings him at last into the place and stance for which he was created.

The Psalms: Hungering and Thirsting for God[8]

There is plenty of poverty in the book of Psalms, the songbook of Israel. The psalms are human life served up raw, full of every kind of emotion from grief, frustration, and hatred to overflowing joy, gratitude, and praise. The laments, thanksgivings, and hymns in the psalter are real life—specifically, Israel's life with their God.[9] In the psalms, God's chosen people pour out their heart, their suffering, their poverty, cry out to God for help, and give heartfelt thanks when they feel seen and heard. For Jesus, the psalms gave voice

7. Dianne Bergant, *The Collegeville Bible Commentary: Old Testament* (Collegeville, MN: Liturgical Press, 1992), 698.

8. Unless otherwise indicated, verses from the psalms in this chapter are from the New King James Version. The psalms are poetry, and poetry should be beautiful.

9. Bergant, *Collegeville Bible Commentary*, 754–55.

to his desolation on the cross: "My God, My God, why have You forsaken Me?" (Ps 22:1). For Jesus and other Jews of his time, the psalms would have been the soundtrack of their life, the music that expressed their full emotional repertoire, from agony to ecstasy.

It is in the psalms of lament that the theme of poverty is most obvious. A good example of a psalm of lament is Psalm 31. It begins with the psalmist addressing God:

> In You, O LORD, I put my trust;
> Let me never be ashamed . . . (v. 1)

Next comes the complaint:

> Have mercy on me, O LORD, for I am in trouble . . .
> I am a reproach among all my enemies . . .
> I am forgotten like a dead man, out of mind;
> I am like a broken vessel.
> For I hear the slander of many;
> Fear is on every side;
> While they take counsel together against me,
> They scheme to take away my life. (vv. 9, 11, 12-13)

This is followed by an expression of trust:

> But as for me, I trust in You, O LORD;
> I say, "You are my God." (v. 14)

The psalms of lament are cries from the heart that come from the depths of human poverty. Sometimes, as in Psalm 130, that poverty is a result of the psalmist's own sin, and these laments are called *penitential* psalms:

> Out of the depths I have cried to You, O LORD;
> Lord, hear my voice!
>
> Let Your ears be attentive
> To the voice of my supplications.

> If You, LORD, should mark iniquities,
> O Lord, who could stand? (vv. 1-3)

But even when the psalmist is in trouble of his own making, as in this psalm, the trust in God is there:

> O Israel, hope in the LORD;
> For with the LORD there is mercy,
> And with Him is abundant redemption. (v. 7)

Another well-known penitential psalm is Psalm 51, with its familiar opening lines:

> Have mercy upon me, O God, according to thy lovingkindness; according unto the multitude of thy tender mercies, blot out my transgressions.
> Wash me throughly from mine iniquity, and cleanse me from my sin.
> For I acknowledge my transgressions, and my sin is ever before me. (vv. 1-3 KJV)

For those moments when we are overcome with guilt and sorrow, feeling the full weight of our poverty, nothing says it quite like this. And yet, there is still hope. The psalmist trusts in God's mercy and even dares to hope that in God's eyes, *his very poverty is itself beautiful*:

> The sacrifices of God are a broken spirit: a broken and a contrite heart, O God, thou wilt not despise. (v. 17 KJV)

There are certain psalms, and I find these particularly affecting, in which the "lament" takes the form of a hunger or thirst for God which the psalmist despairs of satisfying. One beautiful example is Psalm 42, which begins:

> As the hart panteth after the water brooks, so panteth my soul after thee, O God.

> My soul thirsteth for God, for the living God: when shall I come and appear before God?
> My tears have been my meat day and night, while they continually say unto me, Where is thy God?[10] (vv. 1-3 KJV)

Psalm 63, which is another psalm that is partially a lament, begins with a similar expression of longing:

> O God, thou art my God; early will I seek thee: my soul thirsteth for thee, my flesh longeth for thee in a dry and thirsty land, where no water is;
> To see thy power and thy glory, so as I have seen thee in the sanctuary.
> Because thy lovingkindness is better than life, my lips shall praise thee. (vv. 1-3 KJV)

This theme of longing, of an overwhelming desire for God, appears powerfully in Psalm 27, in which the psalmist longs for the presence of God:

> One thing have I desired of the Lord, that will I seek after; that I may dwell in the house of the Lord all the days of my life, to behold the beauty of the Lord, and to enquire in his temple. (v. 4)

"One thing": this is the "one thing necessary," the *unum necessarium* that was the choice and focus of Mary of Bethany, for which Jesus praised her. The psalm continues:

> When thou saidst, Seek ye my face; my heart said unto thee, Thy face, Lord, will I seek.
> Hide not thy face far from me; put not thy servant away in anger: thou hast been my help; leave me not, neither forsake me, O God of my salvation.

10. A "hart" is a deer.

> When my father and my mother forsake me, then the Lord will take me up. (Ps 27:8-10)

I will do what I must to find You, and when even my own parents desert me, I will trust in You. This is poverty at its most beautiful, as the purity of heart, the "willing of the one thing" as Danish philosopher Søren Kierkegaard put it, that Jesus said would enable a person to see God (see Matt 5:8). In the end, we get what we most desire, whether that is God's own self or simply to be left alone.

Jesus and the Poverty of God

Jesus, whose incarnation was an act of self-emptying poverty, as we saw in the hymn from Philippians, announced in both his inaugural sermon and his sermon-manifesto that he had what Vatican II rather clumsily called a "preferential option for the poor." That seems to be church-speak for "a special place in his heart for the poor." Whatever we call it, it's clear throughout Jesus' ministry that he treats the poor with a special tenderness and reserves his anger and harsh words for those in power who oppress and exploit them.

It began with that early sermon in Nazareth, his first public statement in Luke's gospel, in which he announced the nature of his mission. Reading from the scroll of Isaiah, he declared to the assembly that:

> "The Spirit of the Lord is upon me,
> because he has anointed me
> to bring good news to the poor.
> He has sent me to proclaim release to the captives
> and recovery of sight to the blind,
> to let the oppressed go free,
> to proclaim the year of the Lord's favor." (Luke 4:18-19)

Sitting down, that is, taking the posture of a teacher, of authority, he then told his audience: "Today this scripture has been fulfilled in your hearing" (Luke 4:21). They took it surprisingly well at first, and turned against him only when he began to suggest that there were heroes of faith who did not belong to Israel. That was enough to rouse them into a murderous rage, in which they tried to deliver some vigilante "justice" by throwing him off a cliff. You can almost hear the devil: *You could have prevented this, Jesus. I did offer.*

Later, Jesus delivers his manifesto, the "Sermon on the Mount" in Matthew's gospel; in Luke's, the "Sermon on the Plain." He begins with a series of statements called the *Beatitudes*, in which he lists the types of people who are "blessed" (Latin: *beati*). The Greek word here, again, is *makarios*, which means "blessed," "happy," or even "lucky." And at the top of the list in both Luke and Matthew, signaling Jesus' reversal of worldly values, are the poor. There is a difference, however: in Luke's gospel, it's "the poor" who are blessed, full stop, while in Matthew's, it's the "poor in spirit."

Yet even in Luke, after blessing those who hunger, Jesus also blesses those who weep, and those who are hated because of him. So it's more than just economic poverty being blessed, even here. In Luke, too, Jesus calls down "woes" upon those who are the opposite of each: rich, full, laughing, well regarded. You can hear the song of Mary, the *Magnificat*, in Jesus' words: "He has filled the hungry with good things, and sent the rich away empty." There's an invitation here to meditate on the rich teaching Jesus must have had at his mother's knee. Meanwhile, Matthew omits the "woes," and adds to the blessed ones the meek, the merciful, the pure in heart, and the peacemakers. But you could say that Jesus' blessing on the poor is, in both gospels, the major premise of the Beatitudes. All of the others can be seen as forms of poverty, and they follow directly from it.

Matthew, then, begins with a broad definition of poverty—the "poor in spirit"—and his list, like Luke's, consists of variations on the theme. All of these "blessed" states are precisely the opposite of what the world considers "fortunate." Those who mourn are impoverished in that they've lost someone, or perhaps something, dear to them. We all dread grief; permanent separation from those we love is an intimation of hell. We shrink back from it in anticipation and mourn when it comes. The meek are certainly not considered fortunate by the world. No; instead, we say that "fortune favors the bold." It is the bold who are celebrated and rewarded in this world, even if they lie, cheat, and steal their way to the top.

Blessing those who hunger and thirst after righteousness takes us back to the psalms: we heard the psalmist hunger and thirst after the righteous One. This emptiness is the fruit of kenosis, and it creates the internal vacuum that draws God in: "they shall be filled." The merciful are those who don't act out of a sense of entitlement, as if the hard experiences of life could never happen to them. They know that they, too, are vulnerable. They are generous and free with the mercy that has been extended to them in their poverty, recognizing a fellow beggar, recognizing Christ himself.

Blessed are the pure in heart, those whose commitment to the *unum necessarium* is total, because every worldly ambition, all the glories of their personal empire, have been stripped away. Kenosis makes every one of us a fallen empire. Nothing is left for the pure in heart but the one thing necessary, and all their desire, their energy, and their passion are now focused on that one thing. There are no ruffles and frills; they are fiercely aerodynamic in their flight into God.

In pushing back against entitlement, peacemaking too displays a spirit of poverty. As the letter of James tells us:

> Those conflicts and disputes among you, where do they come from? Do they not come from your cravings that are at war within you? You want something and do not have it, so you commit murder. And you covet something and cannot obtain it, so you engage in disputes and conflicts. (Jas 4:1-2a)

When one country invades another, what is driving that but entitlement? When we start a fight with a sibling, a spouse, a colleague, doesn't that often come from our desire for something the other is unwilling to give us? Notice that I said when we *start* a fight; the entitlement I'm talking about is the motivation of the aggressor, not the one on the defensive. Some relationships are old enough and complex enough that it can be difficult to tell "who started it." But when we say "I'm ending it," that can come from a place of poverty, a place in which relationship is more important than rights, reconciliation a greater priority than what we believe—rightly or wrongly—we deserve.

Real life is complicated, and sometimes what looks like peacemaking comes, in reality, from codependency, a trauma bond, an impulse to people-please, or other unhealthy motivations. But the peacemaking that is born from God, that creates us as children of God, is that which says "I'm not taking what is yours, and you're not taking what is mine, or theirs. Let us each be content with what is our own gift from God." Entitlement has no place in that peacemaking.

Finally, Jesus calls blessed those who are persecuted, those who are insulted and falsely accused. Those who are bereft of honor, of reputation, of opportunities and even of life itself, are deeply poor, and Jesus calls them deeply blessed. "Rejoice," he says, "and be glad, for your reward is great in heaven." There is indeed a special place in God's heart for those who suffer any kind of poverty—those who lack money, for sure, but also those who lack hope, joy, or love. The Scriptures caution us not to grasp at things in a spirit of entitlement, but they also recognize that we sometimes lose those things God has greatly desired to give us. God's heart is tender toward us when we find ourselves in those places of poverty, and when kenosis opens up space within us, the Spirit of God is pleased to rush in and fill it.

Jesus and Our Belovedness: Cana

John's gospel gives us no Sermon on the Mount and no explicit teaching on poverty. What we do get is a series of seven miracles, or "signs," which reveal Jesus' true identity and purpose. These signs include the miraculous feeding of a crowd, Jesus' dominion over nature, healing the sick, and raising the dead. But one of these things is not like the others; one of these signs just doesn't belong. In the first of them, Jesus, along with his disciples and his mother, is attending a wedding. The hosts are in danger of running out of wine, which would be a humiliating end to the feast. In her compassion, the Blessed Mother brings the problem to Jesus, whose initial responses are that, first, it's not his business, and second, his time has not yet come.

Mary doesn't argue; she simply turns to the servants and offers the best advice ever given: "Do whatever he tells you" (John 2:5). Jesus has them fill the six stone jars of water for purification right to the brim. Each of these jars would have held twenty or thirty gallons, so this is a *lot* of water. He then has them draw some out and take it to the steward of the banquet. The steward observes that while most people serve the better wine while their guests still have their wits about them, and go to the inferior stuff when everyone's partied too long to care, in this case, the best wine is only now being brought out. So Jesus nails it on both quantity and quality. On both dimensions, his generosity goes well beyond what's needed to save the situation. Truly, it was a case of "My cup runneth over."

As I've said, this is the first of Jesus' signs in John's gospel. It's his debut, every bit as significant as the sermons in Matthew and Luke or his announcement of the kingdom in Mark. Yet in comparison to those introductions, providing more wine for a wedding feast seems to lack *gravitas*: it looks a bit frivolous next to identifying himself as the fulfillment of prophecy, or laying out a manifesto for his kingdom. But in John's gospel, everything is included for a reason; everything is significant. That Jesus shows up in John making wine for a wedding party has been the subject of much meditation over the centuries, and I could fill this book and more with the insights that have come from it. But let me narrow it down to those that draw the connection between Jesus' action in this story and our belovedness.

Appreciation for wine runs through the Hebrew Scriptures. The psalmist notes that God brings forth food from the earth, and "wine to gladden the human heart" (Ps 104:15). Wine is about joy. Wine is about life being good. Both the ideal wife (see Ps 128:3) and Israel itself (see Ps 80:8-11) are compared to fruitful vines, and in that great ode to lovers, the Song of Songs, the woman says of her love that "He brought me to the banqueting house [literally, a *house of wine*], and his intention toward me was love" (Song 2:4).

Occupied Israel, waiting in agony for the promised Messiah, was a lot like a party where the wine had run out a long time ago. But Isaiah had prophesied that the time would come when God would deliver Israel—and indeed, all people—from their oppressors:

> On this mountain the LORD of hosts will make for all peoples
> a feast of rich food, a feast of well-aged wines,
> of rich food filled with marrow, of well-aged wines
> strained clear.
> And he will destroy on this mountain
> the shroud that is cast over all peoples,
> the sheet that is spread over all nations;
> he will swallow up death forever. (Isa 25:6-8a)

Later in the book of Isaiah we see that God will vindicate his people; indeed, Israel will be able to say that "his intention toward me was love":

> You shall be a crown of beauty in the hand of the LORD,
> and a royal diadem in the hand of your God.
> You shall no more be termed Forsaken,
> and your land shall no more be termed Desolate;
> but you shall be called My Delight Is in Her,
> and your land Married;
> for the LORD delights in you,
> and your land shall be married.
> For as a young man marries a young woman,
> so shall your builder marry you,
> and as the bridegroom rejoices over the bride,
> so shall your God rejoice over you. (Isa 62:3-5)

Your builder—your creator, that is, the one who made you—wants to *marry* you. Unlike the pagan gods, who apparently just want to dominate and manipulate mortals, Israel's God seeks the closest and most intimate, loving relationship with his people. So when God-With-Us shows up as one of us, in his own person the marriage of God and humanity, the union of heaven and earth, is it any wonder that he would begin his work at a wedding? The belovedness of God's people has been the point all along. Moreover, when history comes to an end, and the whole work of redemption is completed, the Revelation to John tells us that the Lamb will call his bride, the church, to a great wedding feast. So it makes sense that Jesus would begin to reveal himself at a wedding, an occasion that's all about celebrating love.

And when the cups were filled with the water-become-wine, the prayer would have been offered: "Blessed are you, Lord our God, King of the universe, who creates the fruit of the vine." I wonder how Jesus felt when he heard those words that night. His disciples most likely missed their significance, missed the fact that the rabbi they were getting to know was indeed the One who'd just created and brought forth the fruit of the vine. But they didn't altogether miss the meaning of what had happened: John notes that in this first of his signs Jesus "revealed his glory; and his disciples believed in him" (John 2:11).

The Samaritan Woman

Soon after the wedding at Cana, Jesus continues the "marriage" theme. In chapter 4, we find him meeting a woman at a well. For first-century Jews, when a man met a woman at a well, it would evoke an expectation that a marriage might be in the works. It was at a well that Abraham's servant sought a wife for Isaac: when Rebekah turned up, the servant asked her for a drink and pretty soon she became Isaac's bride. Their son Jacob met his beloved Rachel at a well, and he got her in the end, though along the way he unwittingly acquired another wife and a rather shady father-in-law.

Moses met the daughters of the priest of Midian at a well, and after he defended them against some predatory shepherds, their father handed over his daughter Zipporah as a kind of thank-you note.

So in the stories of Israel, "man meets woman at well" brings with it nuptial expectations. In John's gospel, it's a hot day in Samaria, of all places—not friendly territory for Jews, for whom Samaritans are traditional enemies. The disciples have gone into the town to buy food, and we're told that Jesus is tired from the journey. Hot, tired, and hungry: most of us would be too absorbed in our own discomfort to be at our pastoral best, but Jesus is the Good Shepherd, and he loses his own concerns as he considers the woman arriving to draw water. At noon, and alone.

They're at a well, and not just any well, but Jacob's well. When Jesus sees the woman, whom Orthodox tradition has named Photini, like Abraham's servant he asks her for a drink of water. We hear from her that it's a deep well, and he has nothing to draw water out with, no container of his own. He is speaking out of his own poverty. His only option is to ask to use her container which, as Photini points out, is taboo for a Jew. Actually, the whole conversation, which is the longest Jesus has with anyone in the gospels, is a norm-busting exercise. But this, he assures her, does not concern him. He is more interested in giving her water that will satisfy her thirst forever.

She is skeptical. She knows exactly how much work is involved in coming to the well every day to draw water for a thirst that never ends. Saint Augustine saw the well as a symbol of Photini's concupiscent—that is, errant—desire:[11] her soul was parched with thirst, a deep thirst that no ordinary water could reach, a thirst she tried to satisfy again and again with all the wrong things. It's a picture of addiction, of turning again and again to something that promises satisfaction but never quite delivers. And we all have

11. Robert Barron, "4 Lessons on Divine Mercy from the Woman at the Well," *National Catholic Register*, June 9, 2016, accessed November 2, 2022, https://www.ncregister.com/blog/4-lessons-on-divine-mercy-from-the-woman-at-the-well.

our wells, the places where we go to soothe our restless, anxious souls. What well have you visited again and again? It might be wealth, status, or power; it might be alcohol, drugs, or food, or maybe retail therapy. Or it might be gambling, sex, or bad reality TV (though that last one may be redundant).

Over the years, Photini's predicament has been seen as the result of her own sexual sin. Jesus tells her to call her husband in for the rest of the conversation, and she tells him that she has no husband. "You are right in saying, 'I have no husband,'" he replies, "for you have had five husbands, and the one you have now is not your husband. What you have said is true!" It's at this point that we start imagining Photini jumping merrily from one bed to the next, a sex-crazed, fallen woman who is drawing water alone at noon because she has disgraced herself. How many sermons have you heard with this portrayal?

But let's think about this. It is, as I've said, a long conversation, and yet we never hear Jesus call her to repent. She is the first evangelist in John's gospel, the first to be told directly by Jesus that he is the Messiah, and yet he never tells her to "Go and sin no more." What if his comment about her five-plus husbands isn't said to shame or judge her, but to show compassion? She may have had those five because at least some of them died, leaving her vulnerable unless she remarried. She may have been forced to move on because of abuse, a situation Jesus would have understood, though her judgy neighbors and even the law might not have. And if her unusual conjugal career had been because she was sexually out of control, how do we explain those later marriages? What man would have taken a bride so thoroughly disgraced?[12]

Jesus treats her like a woman more sinned against than sinning. More: he treats her like an intelligent being, capable of having a sustained theological discussion. And he entrusts to her his mission to the Samaritans. But first there's that thirst to deal with. An

12. "Photini, Mother of Evangelists," *Know Your Mothers*, accessed January, 31, 2025, https://knowyourmothers.com/blog/photini-mother-of-evangelists.

interesting detail (and remember, in John's gospel, all the details matter) is that when she returns to the city to tell everyone that she's met the Messiah, she leaves her water jar behind. She's received the living water Jesus offered and has no further need for that old, addictive well. (Let's not be too literal about this; obviously she's going to need real water again.) And when the disciples come back offering Jesus food, he tells them that he's already been well fed: "I have food to eat that you do not know about." Jesus knows where true satisfaction is to be found ("to do the will of him who sent me and to complete his work"). Jesus is human, and poor, and has needs. He just doesn't try to meet those needs with things that don't satisfy. Instead, he uses his very poverty, his need, to build a bridge ("Give me a drink") to another person who, according to social norms, should be out of reach.

Throughout the gospels, we see Jesus reaching again and again across every kind of chasm to lift up the poor in spirit. Healing Gentiles, eating with tax collectors, those most hated collaborators with Rome—even calling one to be an apostle. He received lavish public displays of repentance and love from women, displays that made others around him very uncomfortable. He touched lepers, and in doing so, made them clean instead of becoming unclean himself. Jesus showed mercy and healed, even when he felt it drain power out of him. He could be fierce with the privileged and hard-hearted, but he was always tender with the poor, the outcast, the disgraced. To him, no matter the societal expectations, no one was out of reach. And he called, and calls, us to do the same.

Pauline Poverty

Jesus had to be pretty stern with Saul of Tarsus when Saul was "ravaging the church by entering house after house; dragging off both men and women . . . commit[ting] them to prison" (Acts 8:3). Throwing Saul to the ground and striking him blind was apparently the only way to get Saul's attention long enough for him to hear the question: "Saul, Saul, why do you persecute me?" (Acts

9:4). When Jesus sends a nervous Ananias to escort Saul through the process of conversion, he tells Ananias, "I myself will show him how much he must suffer for the sake of my name" (Acts 9:16).

And Saul, now Paul, would suffer. In his second letter to the Corinthians, he compares his dedication to that of his opponents by listing off the many ways he'd suffered more than they:

> . . . with far greater labors, far more imprisonments, with countless floggings, and often near death. Five times I have received from the Jews the forty lashes minus one. Three times I was beaten with rods. Once I received a stoning. Three times I was shipwrecked; for a night and a day I was adrift at sea; on frequent journeys, in danger from rivers, danger from bandits, danger from my own people, danger from Gentiles, danger in the city, danger in the wilderness, danger at sea, danger from false brothers and sisters; in toil and hardship, through many a sleepless night, hungry and thirsty, often without food, cold and naked. (2 Cor 11:23b-27)

"And, besides other things," he adds, "I am under daily pressure because of my anxiety for all the churches. Who is weak, and I am not weak?" (2 Cor 11:28-29a). The Corinthians need to emulate Paul in all of this: through slander and dishonor, through beatings and imprisonment, through hungry days and sleepless nights, "as sorrowful, yet always rejoicing; as poor, yet making many rich; as having nothing, and yet possessing all things" (2 Cor 6:10 NKJV).

We have seen in Paul's use of the famous Philippians hymn how the process of being poured out, of kenosis, is the path to the true riches. Paul poured himself out deeply, right down to the dregs, until his final moment, with his head on the block. But he knew the secret: "When I am weak, then I am strong," for as the Lord told him, "My grace is sufficient for you, for My strength is made perfect in weakness" (2 Cor 12:10, 9a NKJV). Paul learned to rejoice in his weakness, in his poverty, because he knew that poverty in all its many forms is blessed. He knew that to cease grasping, to open one's empty hands to God's gift, brings us "abundantly far more than all we can ask or imagine" (Eph 3:20).

This is the testimony of Scripture from start to finish. And as we'll see in the next chapter, it was the unshakeable belief of Saints Francis and Clare of Assisi. It has been the conviction of their followers in the eight hundred years since they began a movement that made poverty their first and central priority. This is because in poverty, they saw the poor Christ himself, and no one and nothing could turn their gaze from him.

PART TWO

The Personal Experience of Poverty

Chapter 3

Perfect Joy

Poverty in the Franciscan Tradition

Poverty is the language of love.

Ilia Delio, OSF[1]

Francis of Assisi has been dead for eight hundred years. This seems to have done nothing to diminish his popularity or his importance as a spiritual mentor and guide. Francis' appeal simply defies boundaries: from those who've made lifelong vows in one of the Franciscan orders; to the Baptist guy who called me to ask how he might incorporate Franciscan ideals into his own Christian practice; to the Jewish student in a group I took to Assisi who started wearing a Franciscan tau cross and said, "I don't know about Christianity, but I like this guy"—Francis seems to cut across the borders and charm most everyone who encounters

1. Ilia Delio, *Clare of Assisi: A Heart Full of Love* (Cincinnati, OH: St. Anthony Messenger Press, 2007), 3.

him. Hundreds of books have been written about him, and many movies have been made, including a few good ones. People who identify as "spiritual but not religious" and people who just want something pretty for their garden—all find something in this man whose charisma is as great after death as it was in life.

A Lasting Movement

Along with Clare, whom we'll get to shortly, Francis began a movement that is still going strong all these centuries later, when most new religious movements die out before anyone's really heard of them. One problem that besets all religious movements is what to do when the charismatic founder dies? This is what sociologists of religion call the "charismatic succession problem": a movement that forms around an inspiring leader will have trouble keeping the flame alive once that leader is dead. Purely from a sociological point of view (excluding, that is, any supernatural explanations such as the giving of the Holy Spirit), Jesus postponed the charismatic succession problem by appointing the apostles and investing them with authority before his death. After that, the doctrine of apostolic succession postponed the problem indefinitely, and by the time people began to question it, Christianity was well established. We'll come back to the issues of charisma, succession and authority in chapter 5.

Before diving into the theme of poverty in the Franciscan tradition, I'd like to deal briefly with this question of why there is a "Franciscan tradition" in the first place. How do we account for the posthumous charisma of this man? Why do so many in the twenty-first century still follow him? Even in his own time, it was a bit of a mystery why people followed Francis. Even his own followers weren't always sure why people followed him. Francis wasn't nobly born. Was he handsome? He was kind of short, which of course doesn't mean he wasn't handsome, but he didn't have a big, commanding presence. He wasn't very well educated, was nobody's idea of a scholar, and once he started writing important documents, his scribes often had to quietly correct his rather shaky

Latin. He wasn't even a great speaker; that is, he didn't have the easy, fluid eloquence of a serious orator.

But he did have an eloquence of the heart, which spoke to people where they were. So he was revered during his life, canonized within two years of his death, and the day after his canonization, construction began on a giant basilica in his honor—one of countless churches that would be dedicated to him, not only in Italy (where, with Catherine of Siena, he is the national patron) but around the world.

I have always thought that there are two main things that continue to draw people to Francis. The first was his *passion*: Francis was a man utterly in love with God. If you've ever been in love, you'll know that everything in your life falls into orbit around your beloved, who becomes the center of your universe. This is the cure for the problem of pride that I mentioned earlier, where *I* am the star around which everything revolves. When we're in love, we begin to understand Jesus' parables about selling everything to buy the pearl of great price or the field in which the treasure is hidden. No price is too high, no sacrifice too great, in the pursuit of the one you love—not if you love with real passion. And Francis was that kind of lover.

Francis was a real saint's saint, a man outstanding in a field of outstanding people. But I think the ability to zero in on the one thing that truly matters is a characteristic that is common to all the saints. That is, holiness is largely a matter of focus, the ability to "will one thing," as Kierkegaard famously defined purity of heart. And it's the pure in heart, Jesus said, who see God. As I mentioned in the last chapter, it was for this kind of focus that Jesus praised Mary of Bethany, explaining to her sister Martha that only one thing is necessary, the *unum necessarium*, and that Mary had chosen that good thing and it would not be taken from her. The thing that makes Francis' zeal so charming is that he didn't pursue the "one thing" with grim determination, but with joy—even in some of his darkest moments.

In the midst of hideous suffering from a painful eye disease, for example, Francis burst into a song of praise, the famous *Canticle of the Creatures*. It's interesting that he begins with praise for "Brother Sun, through whom you lighten the day for us," when that very light was virtually unbearable to Francis' weakened eyes. Those eyes would be treated with cauterization—with "Brother Fire," whom Francis called "beautiful and cheerful, full of power and strength."[2] Where most of us would recoil from such a horrifying "treatment," Francis simply entreated Brother Fire to be gentle with him, "for I have always loved you."

Born to wealth and comfort, Francis after his conversion lived a life so austere that he was dead at forty-five. In the *Canticle*, though, he even praised "our sister, the death of the body."[3] How was this little poor man able to be so at peace with terrible suffering and even death itself? The answer is both ludicrous and profound: he was in love. And when you love the One who created everything, you can love everything in creation. Francis shrank from none of it, not even death, because Jesus had been there before him, and Francis knew that Jesus would be there waiting when his own time came.

So Francis' passion is one thing that still draws people to him today. The other secret to Francis' lasting appeal lies in the way he wrestled with the big questions of his day, and sought ways to live an authentic and faithful Christian life in the face of formidable challenges. Every set of social arrangements poses certain questions to members of that society, and Christians will have to find responses to those questions in the teachings of Christ. The slave economy in the southern United States before the Civil War, for example, raised questions about humanity and who is included in the commitment to "all men are created equal." That African Americans were clearly not being treated as equals forced slavery apologists into some elaborate moral gymnastics. For Christians, though, slavery in the antebellum South, and in our own

2. *Devotional Companion* of the Third Order, Society of Saint Francis, Province of the Americas (2015), 58.

3. *Devotional Companion*, 58.

time, forces questions such as: What does it mean to be made in the image of God? Who is my neighbor? And if I willingly consume products made with slave labor, whether cotton clothing or iPhones, what have I done to Jesus in the least of his people?

In the same way, Francis struggled with the questions of his age. Francis lived at a time of macroeconomic change in Europe, when the land-based feudal order was giving way to merchant capitalism, the old nobility being displaced by an urban merchant class. The gap between rich and poor was growing, and the misery of the poor was growing with it. The urban poor have a harder lot than those who go begging on farms, where there's always an odd apple or bit of bread to be spared, and perhaps a barn where one might sleep. The economic changes also made some degree of class mobility possible. Francis' own family had experienced upward mobility as his father, a wealthy cloth merchant, was part of that rising middle class. In fact, Francis originally hoped to carry this even further by distinguishing himself in battle and becoming a knight.

This and every other worldly ambition would collapse when he fell in love with Christ. That love would reorder all his priorities, make everything that had once been bitter to him sweet, and the sweet things bitter. There's a famous story that took place during his conversion, in which Francis was out riding one day (so he had not yet "left the world") and came across a leper. Now, everyone was afraid of lepers in those days, but Francis' fear verged on the neurotic. He was always a generous guy, though, even in his worldly life. So he tossed the leper some coins and rode on.

After a few paces, however, he turned back. When Francis returned to where the man was standing, he dismounted, went up to him, and embraced him. In a kiss he never would have imagined possible, his revulsion turned to joy. After that experience, Francis spent a lot of time with lepers and other beggars, sometimes sharing food with them, sometimes exchanging clothing, often dressing their wounds. The urban dandy who'd always enjoyed being well dressed and well fed fell in love with the poor Christ, whom he met in the poorest and most despised of his own society. And when he discovered he could find Christ there, he became determined always to seek out the lowest places. He and his followers would be called the *Friars Minor*, the "Lesser Brothers": lower than all, subject to all, dependent on all. Francis took the economic values of his day—wealth, status, upward mobility, comfort, and exclusivity—and turned them upside down. Lady Poverty would be his companion for life, as she had been Christ's.

Francis' was also an era in which conflict and violence were a constant presence. On a local level, neighboring cities like Assisi and Perugia engaged in long-term sibling rivalries that periodically broke out in bloodshed. In one episode when Francis was about twenty, the Assisians were routed by the Perugians, and many of them were executed on the spot. Coming from a wealthy family, Francis was taken captive instead in the hope that a ransom would be paid for him. His father took a year to cough up the cash, during which time Francis contracted a serious illness. By the time he was released, Francis' eagerness for battle was considerably subdued.

On the larger European stage, there was the protracted pissing match between popes and emperors, and beyond that, the fiasco of the Crusades. One of the hallmarks of Franciscan spirituality is the reconciliation of enemies, and another episode in Francis' life highlights his role as a peacemaker. In 1219, during the Fifth Crusade, the Christians were laying siege to the Egyptian city of Damietta. The Muslim forces, under Sultan Malik al-Kamil, were holding them off, when Francis showed up with another brother. Francis asked Cardinal Pelagius, the papal legate, for permission to cross into the Muslim camp and received it only after Pelagius made it clear he would not be responsible for the friars' lives.

So they were received by the sultan, and unlike most Christians of that age (and many perhaps, of our own), Francis did not treat him like an infidel dog who needed to convert or burn in hell. He preached Jesus to the sultan, but gently and with respect.[4] And

4. See 1 Peter 3:15.

while neither converted the other, they came away with mutual regard. In short, Francis walked willingly into a situation that could easily have gotten him killed, and made peace. He didn't stop the military action, and some five thousand crusaders died (after ignoring Francis' warning that they were going to lose). Francis didn't make peace between Christendom and Islam, but he did make interpersonal peace, you might say, and showed us that the way forward is through respect and listening, even to one's enemy. *Islam* means "submission," and in a certain sense Francis made peace with the sultan by submitting to him in humility and love. Francis had eagerly armed himself to fight the earlier Fourth Crusade, but by this time, his response to violence was radically changed.

Why is there still a "Franciscan tradition" today? Why do people still follow Francis' lead in living according to gospel values? Because Francis found radically faithful responses to the questions of his time: changing economic structures that create a widening gap between rich and poor; the suffering of society's outcasts; the expectation of upward mobility and all the status striving that goes with it; our uneasy relationship to the created order; and the pervasiveness of violence, from the interpersonal to the international level. Does this set of issues look familiar? Because these are some of the greatest questions we face in our own era, Francis—even from a distance of eight hundred years—still has much to teach us. If he could come to a place of freedom and joy in such troubling times, maybe we, in our own troubling time, can too.

The Poverty of Francis

Francis is remembered as *il Poverello*, the "little poor man," and even at his death, he asked to be removed from the bishop's palace and placed on the ground outside the tiny church at the Porziuncula, the "Little Portion," called Our Lady of the Angels, which serves to this day as the spiritual home of the Franciscan family. He died as poor as he had lived, in the chill embrace of Sister Death. I suspect that when this dread Lady came for him, Francis recognized in her the Lady Poverty, to whom he'd pledged himself when he left the "world" spiritually. Now that he was leaving the world physically, I think Francis would have understood that all our poverty is the gift of Sister Death, because death is the ultimate poverty, the logical conclusion of all our limitations. Because Francis had always found Christ in poverty, he could release himself in peace from the final attachment—to life itself—and surrender to his unveiled bride in joy.

But let's not succumb to the hagiographic impulse here, the desire to romanticize our heroes in faith until they're larger than life—larger not only than our lives, but even their own. As Francis' health declined in his last few years, he faced challenges he hadn't known as the carefree youth who happily tossed his clothing back to his dad and walked away naked.[5] His body was showing signs of long-term neglect and abuse, and chronic insomnia meant the night offered no refuge from pain. He'd had to face up to his weakness as an administrator and allow others to take the reins, but the institutionalization that's inevitable to any religious movement that's going to survive was hard to take. Likewise, the order's increasing clericalism troubled Francis: more and more provincial superiors were priests, and even illiterate novices aspired to ordination, which meant an emphasis on training and scholarship that was never part of Francis' vision. Where all friars had originally been required to do physical labor, now some could fulfill this obligation with intellectual work. While he claimed in his letter to Anthony of Padua that he was "pleased" to make this allowance, it certainly signaled a turn away from the poverty Francis had cherished and a glimpse into the future of "his" order.

Even as Francis tried to step aside and go from superior to "ordinary brother," he faced a dilemma: always uncomfortable with leadership, Francis hated giving orders. Yet with others taking the community in directions that troubled him, he couldn't resist stick-

5. For the following, I am heavily indebted to Augustine Thompson, *Francis of Assisi: The Life* (Ithaca, NY: Cornell University Press, 2012), chap. 7.

ing his oar in, and as the founder, his orders were instantly obeyed. Then his lack of humility gnawed at his conscience. As his health declined, he became a difficult patient, berating his caregivers for making accommodations that singled him out as special, and demanding that his weaknesses be broadcast as exercises in humiliation. Of course, these in themselves singled him out as special, and at times his attendants had no idea which orders to obey and which to ignore. He was aware of how much trouble he gave them, which pained him even more. As he moved toward the end, Francis was "a deeply conflicted man,"[6] increasingly withdrawn from his brothers and frustrated and impatient in their presence, acutely conscious of his failures and of the changed direction of his movement.

It was a long crucifixion, but it would be wrong to say that Francis lost his joy in it. Perhaps it's more accurate to say that as death approached, Francis became more and more identified with the cross, both that of Christ and his own. Francis had long since learned to embrace suffering of all kinds as holy poverty; that is, he made the first transition I described early on. Francis possessed the romantic imagination: life was an adventure, and life in Christ was the greatest and most noble adventure of all. He'd never really abandoned his desire to become a great knight; he just transferred his fealty to a greater lord.

But it was toward the end that his identification with the Crucified One was fully consummated. A couple years before his death, his health broken, his celebrity a burden, and drained by inner conflicts, Francis rode off to the mountain hermitage of La Verna, where he pleaded for a sign that his life and actions were pleasing to God.[7] Francis could not find it within himself to share the public's confidence in his sainthood, and although the birds came and sang for him, he was also prey to agonizing thoughts and temptations. If there was a "sign" in the birdsong, it was a pretty ambiguous one, and his interior struggle dragged on.

6. Thompson, *Francis of Assisi*, 141.

7. Thompson, 146–52.

And then it came. After weeks spent on the mountain meditating on Christ's passion, and entering more deeply into Jesus' suffering and death, Francis had a vision in which a six-winged seraph appeared to him. The angel was fixed to a cross, but its face radiated a profound peace—more paradox, more questions. Francis was deeply affected by the vision, and soon afterward his body began to display wounds corresponding to Christ's crucifixion: nail prints in his hands and feet, and a bleeding gash in his side. Francis would bear these painful wounds for the rest of his life, but his immediate response to this intimate experience of the passion of the poor Christ was an outburst of praise, Francis' "Praises of God."[8] God is humility, wisdom and peace; joy and beauty, justice and gentleness, "all our riches," "our haven and our hope," "our great consolation . . . . God Almighty, Merciful Saviour." The words come cascading out of him; one senses that they can't come fast enough, and that Francis is, like mystics across the ages, trying to "eff" the ineffable.

It was here, I believe, that Francis fully made, in his own unique and spectacular fashion, what I've called the second transition. He entered into the heart of the poor, crucified Christ to such a complete extent that he knew it from the inside, and he would bear the marks of it on the outside of his own body until his death. Was his life pleasing to God? Francis had the sign he longed for, had in fact become a sign himself, an icon of the Crucified, so conformed to Christ that he would be remembered as *alter Christus*, "another Christ."[9] That Francis in his poverty could be given such a sublime gift tells us that the place of poverty—even the place of pain, regret, and agonizing self-doubt—is not necessarily a bad place to be. In

8. "St. Francis of Assisi's Prayer in Praise of God Given to Brother Leo," *Catholic Online*, accessed May 18, 2019, https://www.catholic.org/prayers/prayer.php?p=180.

9. We don't want to take the notion of *alter Christus* too far, as no one is suggesting that Francis is literally on a par with Christ, a Person of the Trinity. The idea simply emphasizes how closely Francis walked in the footsteps of Christ.

it, Francis knew himself to be united to God's "beloved Son," and knew himself beloved in his turn.

I wouldn't begin to offer this example as some sort of "standard" of the second transition. As C. S. Lewis once observed,[10] God does not do encores. Besides, our spiritual temperaments and "styles" are so diverse one from another, and our own mindsets and needs so different from one day to the next, why would we expect God to do the same exact thing again and again? As we'll see in the lives of St. Clare and others, sanctity looks different in different people. What all saints have in common, I believe, is that willingness to follow Christ, even when he takes the path of poverty. It's a path that brings them eventually to an intimate and powerful experience of Christ's own heart. And in that place of union, of "one-ing," these blessed ones learn an unforgettable sense of their own belovedness in God.

Poverty in Francis' Thought

Francis' understanding of poverty was complex and multivalent, going well beyond economics alone. Some scholars have pointed out that, in spite of the association of Francis with poverty, it may be more accurate to say that *humility* was his most fundamental value. The Dominican historian Augustine Thompson notes that Francis expressly rejected the name "Poor Brothers" for his fraternity, choosing instead the "Lesser Brothers" ("Friars Minor").[11] Francis' poverty, Thompson insists, was more about being the lowest and the least, subject to all, than it was about not "having stuff."[12] Explicit references to poverty come up infrequently in Francis' writing, given how closely he's associated with poverty.

10. C. S. Lewis, *Letters to Malcolm, Chiefly on Prayer* (New York: HarperOne, 2017), 27.

11. Augustine Thompson, OP, "Poverty in the Church and St. Francis of Assisi," accessed July 13, 2018, https://www.youtube.com/watch?v=3xaZnTR6xPQ.

12. Thompson, "Poverty in the Church."

Yet in his admonition to Clare and her sisters, which Clare was shrewd enough to incorporate into her own rule, Francis' love for poverty is obvious:

> I, little brother Francis, wish to follow the life and poverty of Jesus Christ our Most High Lord and of His Most Holy Mother and to persevere therein until the end. And I beseech you all, my ladies, and counsel you, to live always in this most holy life and poverty. And watch yourselves well that you in no wise depart from it through the teaching or advice of any one.[13]

Certainly Francis affirmed the value and practice of poverty in his followers, and it grieved him when some of the brothers began to water down the message while Francis was still with them. It wasn't long before some friars were searching for poverty loopholes: if members weren't allowed to own property, perhaps they could just "use" it, which, on a practical level, came out to the same thing. Most new religious movements at least wait until the founder is dead to lose sight of the original vision, but it was part of Francis' own poverty that he had to witness this weakening of conviction in his lifetime.

Yet there were those who remained faithful to the radical poverty Francis had taught them, and he cherished them for that. One of the stories in the charming collection of Franciscan legends called *The Little Flowers of St. Francis*[14] tells how Brother Leo, one of Francis' original band of followers, was praying at the bedside of St. Francis, who was quite ill. In the sickroom, Leo slipped into ecstasy and saw a vision in which a group of brothers were trying to ford a fast-flowing river. Some of them were carrying heavy burdens; these caused them to fall in and drown. Eventually an-

13. *The Writings of St. Francis of Assisi*, trans. Paschal Robinson (1905), accessed July 13, 2018, https://www.sacred-texts.com/chr/wosf/wosf08.htm.

14. Ugolino di Monte Santa Maria, *The Little Flowers of St. Francis of Assisi*, repr. ed. (New York: Vintage Books, 1998), chap. 36.

other group of friars approached the river carrying nothing but the radiance of poverty, and these made it across in safety. When Brother Leo told the vision to Francis,

> Saint Francis said: "That which thou hast seen is true. The great river is this world; the friars who were drowning in the river are those who follow not the Gospel profession and especially with regard to most high Poverty; but they who passed over without danger are those friars who neither seek nor possess in this world any earthly or carnal thing, but having food and raiment are therewith content, following Christ naked on the cross . . . "

Francis is referring here to material possessions, and he wasn't fond of people trying to spiritualize away his teachings on them. In his Testament, his final word to his order as he sensed the approach of death, he insisted that the strictures of his rule be taken at face value, that the brothers not come up with elaborate interpretations that allowed them to follow Christ well dressed to the cross.

Francis meant what he said about material possessions, yet another famous story shows that his understanding of poverty—how to live it, and why—went well beyond a simple lack of "stuff." Once when Francis and Brother Leo were traveling on foot in bitter cold from Perugia back to home base at the Porziuncula, Francis began to tell Leo that if the friars achieved a great reputation for holiness and good works, this would not give them perfect joy. The two walked on a bit, when Francis continued: the brothers might perform great miracles of healing, even raise the dead, but they would not find perfect joy in it. They might become exceedingly learned, mastering all the sciences; they might speak prophetically; they might preach with such power as to convert even the infidels to Christ, but they would not find in any of that "perfect joy."

This had gone on for a couple of miles, and Leo was tired and cold. I can imagine his impatience with his oblivious superior, and he finally begged Francis, for the love of God, to tell him where perfect joy could be found. Francis responded that if they got home and knocked at the convent gate and the porter didn't recognize them, and they had to spend the night suffering hunger and cold; and if they knocked again and again and the porter swore at them, called them imposters, accused them of trying to steal alms from the poor, and beat them with a stick; and if the two bore this abuse without complaint, thinking of the sufferings of Christ; then that, Francis insisted, would bring them perfect joy.

Francis was eccentric in some ways, but he wasn't stupid, and in this vignette he is showing remarkable insight. When we're enjoying success and attracting admiration, we may feel happiness at the surface. But the pleasure they bring tends to keep us at the surface. It's usually when suffering comes that we're motivated to go deeper, pushed to find something to hold on to that transcends our circumstances. The psalmist captures it well:

> Now in my prosperity I said,
> "I shall never be moved."
> Lord, by Your favor You have made my
> mountain stand strong;
> [Then] You hid Your face, *and* I was troubled. (Ps 30:6-7 NKJV)

Francis knew that it's from the depths that we most urgently cry out for God. Physical suffering, lack of love from those from whom we expect it, false accusations, and questions about our motives, rudeness, and violence—the list Francis gives Leo is partial but evocative. If we can hear in our woes some echo of the passion of Christ, can somehow connect our suffering to the One who connected his own suffering to each of us, then we'll have made that first turn: "I feel my poverty right now." If we resist the temptation to flee the discomfort of that place, then perhaps we'll receive the grace, as Francis did, to dive into the depths of Christ's own heart and find our refuge, and our belovedness, there.

Francis was deeply committed to material poverty, but even that poverty is broader than simply doing without money. After all, the body is "material" too. So illness, injury, and disability are all material forms of poverty, whatever one's bank balance may be.

But wounds of the mind, heart, or spirit are also forms of poverty because they all point to our self-*in*sufficiency. They all bring us to the end of ourselves so that we might, like the Prodigal Son, "come to ourself" and recognize the need to go home.

Clare: First Lady of the Poor Ladies

About twelve years after Francis' birth, a girl was born to a noble family of Assisi: Chiara Offreduccio di Favarone—Clare of Assisi—who founded a branch of Francis' movement for women. And in that sentence I have reproduced much of what is most annoying about Clare's story: it's most often told in relation to that of Francis. Some of that is inevitable. But Clare was an interesting and important person in her own right, and we do her a disservice when we reduce her to "Sister Moon," one who simply reflects the light of Francis, or "Brother Sun." Clare has her own light; *chiara* in fact means light, bright, or clear.

And the name was intentional: Clare's mother was nervous while carrying her, but she was reassured in a dream: "O Lady, do not be afraid, for you will joyfully bring forth a clear light that will illumine the world."[15] The story bears the hagiographer's touch, but it's true that Clare had a brightness that drew others to her and to the new religious life for women that she pioneered and fought for. As a medieval woman, her charisma was necessarily quieter than that of Francis, and she exercised it more in private than in public. But she was no less a charismatic founder than he.

There are many questions about Clare's relationship to Francis, and the relationship of their parallel movements, but one of the first concerns how they met. Did she seek out the man who was preaching a return to gospel simplicity and beginning to attract a following? Or did he seek out the young woman who was known for her piety and connected to one of the most powerful families of

15. Delio, *Clare of Assisi*, xi.

the town? Francis wasn't always entirely oblivious to the usefulness of well-placed allies, though at this point in his life he probably wouldn't have given the potential advantage of a "Clare connection" much thought. That he knew something of her is evident from testimony given at her canonization.[16] It strikes me as most likely that Clare, who had been raised in a household of devout women and rather more worldly men, and who was deeply pious herself, would have been interested in meeting this strange and intriguing troubadour of Christ.

It seems that they had several meetings before the Palm Sunday of 1212 when Clare, about eighteen years old, was received by Francis and entered religious life. We have no transcript of these meetings, but it's not hard to imagine that they spoke of their intense desire to follow Christ in all things, including a radical embrace of holy poverty—since this became the focal point of both their lives. We can also be pretty sure that they brought the bishop of Assisi into their plans, since he plays a role in Clare's flight from home.

It was the custom of the ladies of the town on Palm Sunday to go up during the liturgy and receive a palm branch, but Clare remained in her pew. Bishop Guido pointedly went to her where she was and handed the palm to her. Was it a signal? That evening, she and a female companion quietly exited the house through the "door of the dead" (Clare here seems to share in Francis' flair for the dramatic gesture) and made their way outside the city walls, through the forest, and down to the Porziuncula. Francis and the brothers, one of them her own cousin, were waiting for her. Francis cut her hair and gave her a habit in exchange for her fine clothing.[17]

On Clare's part, it was an act of defiance. The men of her family had been busy arranging an advantageous marriage for Clare—to

16. Delio, xi.

17. Joan Mueller, *The Privilege of Poverty: Clare of Assisi, Agnes of Prague, and the Struggle for a Franciscan Rule for Women* (University Park, PA: Pennsylvania State University Press, 2006), chap. 1. My account of Clare's flight from home and renunciation of the world owes much to this work.

their advantage, that is, not to hers. Having herself experienced violence and exile during earlier conflicts between parties within Assisi, Clare was likely fed up with the competition for wealth and power, and the means it took to get them. Uninterested in serving as a bargaining chip, Clare most likely saw the "little poor man" as representative of another way, one of freedom and peace.

Francis, however, had sense enough to know that conflict lay in their immediate future, and hustled Clare off to the Benedictine monastery of San Paolo near Bastia, perhaps an hour's walk from Assisi. Joan Mueller notes that the monastery had the protection of "canonical privilege," which meant that if a person claimed sanctuary there, anyone who tried to take them was automatically excommunicated.[18] It was a sound move on Francis' part, and suggests some serious advance planning. In fact, several of Clare's male relatives did follow her there, barging fully armed into the church and demanding that she return with them. But Clare grabbed the altar cloth and played her trump card: pulling the covering off her head, she revealed a haircut that utterly removed her from the marriage market—and would for years to come, after which she'd be too old to be much use. Her pursuers, faced with a fait accompli, left defeated. But by God, they would make her pay: Clare was disowned—poor and without a dowry, she wouldn't be sellable to anyone, husband or monastery.

As they spat out the curse, Clare must have rejoiced at the gift of her freedom. It wasn't as public a scene, perhaps, as Francis' stripping before the bishop, his father, and the entire town. But Clare's renunciation of family and, with it, the world, was every bit as defiant. She divested herself of the things that gave her status and worth, and, with them, her connection to the support, protection, and love of her family. Yet as Jesus predicted (see Matt 19:29), having given up family for the sake of Christ, Clare received plenty of family in return: her mother and two sisters would later become part of Clare's community, and they would be joined by

18. Mueller, *Privilege of Poverty*, 9.

many sisters in spirit. Moreover, in condemning her to a life of poverty, Clare's sneering relations unknowingly conferred on her the greatest blessing, as poverty was a "privilege" she would fight for throughout her life. Clare leaped off a cliff, blindfolded, in the dark and landed precisely where she most longed to be.

The Battle for Poverty

But it was only the beginning, and Clare would have to fight to the end for the "privilege" of being poor and vulnerable. Francis and his brothers managed to get unwritten permission for their way of life from Pope Innocent III as early as 1209, followed soon thereafter by approval of a written rule. It was an intriguing historical moment: the reign of Innocent III represented the high point of the papacy's earthly power. For Innocent, of all people, to see in this bedraggled band the work of the Spirit is astonishing. But the brothers were tonsured, commissioned to preach (something Francis was not necessarily that excited about), and sent on their way. By contrast, Clare got grudging, temporary, and limited permission to live in poverty early on, but she fought all her life for a rule that would guarantee that right across monasteries and in perpetuity, literally receiving approval of it on her deathbed.

I've mentioned that in Francis' mind, poverty and humility were closely intertwined, and that both were central to his spirituality. In her writings, Clare seems more focused on poverty *as* poverty. It's easy enough to imagine why: in a patriarchal society, by the time a woman is old enough to enter a religious community, she has already had long training in the virtues of humility and self-denial. So Clare would not need to beat the humility drum incessantly to her sisters in the way Francis did. But because Clare's first sisters (called "Poor Ladies," and, after Clare's death, "Poor Clares") came from wealthy families, poverty was what today would be called their "growth edge," the place where they might be vulnerable and uncertain but that invited them into the spiritual depths. Clare, understanding this, gathered her sisters and "set her face" toward poverty, refusing to be diverted by anyone, however powerful.

For Clare, poverty was not limited to material possessions, though it certainly began there. Most religious houses in Clare's time were Benedictine. For them, as well as for the other existing orders, a vow of poverty meant no personal possessions, but a monk or nun could live a relatively comfortable and secure life because of goods held by the community. Clare's idea of poverty went way beyond this. She stubbornly refused any kind of income-generating property: her community would have nothing beyond a very modest monastery and a small garden. But for Clare, poverty also meant vulnerability. In a time when conflict was rife, and both armies and brigands were known to turn up on one's doorstep, Clare declined the safety of the city walls. San Damiano, which was restored by Francis and the site where the first sisters settled, is down the hill from Assisi. It's in the middle of nowhere, utterly unprotected. A fine place, the authorities thought, for a group of upper-crust women to live. The sooner they got over this girlish fantasy, the less chance for something to go horribly wrong.

Clare was resolute, however; not only was she politically shrewd, but she also had some powerful allies and could counter even the pope's pressure with her own. She waged a lifelong battle with the church hierarchy, who kept trying to force her into the more moderate and sensible Benedictine way, urging buildings and lands and income on her. But Clare and her sisters were forging a new and radical way. Pope Gregory IX eventually granted Clare the Privilege of Poverty, "a papal exemption that guaranteed the right to refuse landed endowments."[19] But it was a partial victory and, after his death, his successors started furiously backpedaling: they required some of the monasteries of the growing order to accept property, made them live under the Benedictine Rule, and so on. It was one thing for Clare to cut a deal with a pope who liked and to some extent supported her. But a rule would make it law, and Clare fought for that rule until her dying breath.

19. Mueller, ix.

An example of Clare's resolve can be seen in the counsel she gave her correspondent, Blessed Agnes of Prague. Agnes was of royal birth, and had experienced all the family expectations of her life that the aristocratic Clare had, only more so. By age eight, Agnes' family started arranging marriages for her, each of which was meant to advance their political agenda. She declined them all, determined to pursue religious life. When Agnes turned down the emperor himself, her brother Wenceslaus, king of Bohemia, gave her some land on which she founded a Franciscan hospital. Choosing the Franciscan way, she began a correspondence with Clare and eventually established a community of nuns in Prague.

Like Clare, Agnes had to resist offers of property and money over and over, and to repeatedly insist on a life of poverty. Pope Gregory was turning up the heat on both women, and Agnes wrote to Clare for advice. What to do with a pope who had good intentions, but was undermining their vocation by trying to force them into the safer, more conventional Benedictine mold? Gregory applauded their piety, but he didn't want to see a bunch of high-born women starve to death on his watch. After all, the brothers went around preaching and begging their meals, but the nuns were *enclosed*. Food had to come to them, and if it didn't, they'd do without. Francis had pledged that the brothers would provide for the nuns, and for a while they did. After Francis' death, however, they got involved in other things and the relationship grew more distant. Gregory probably suspected from the beginning that it would. So to see the "Poor Ladies" as unsupported and unprotected as they demanded to be had to strike him as an unreasonable risk, and I can see his point.

But Clare was adamant. To Agnes she wrote, "What you hold, continue to hold. What you do, keep doing, and do not stop."[20] She told Agnes to walk with a quick and sure step, and not to raise any dust—in other words, stay true to your position, but try not to irritate powerful men if you can help it. And try to maintain

20. Clare's second letter to Agnes of Prague, quoted in Mueller, 68.

your own sense of peace. She advised Agnes to make an ally of Brother Elias, the friars' Minister General, which Agnes did. She was instructed to cherish his advice, and:

> If anyone [read "the pope himself"] would tell you something else or suggest something that would hinder your perfection or seem contrary to your divine vocation, even though you must respect him, do not follow his counsel. But as a poor virgin, embrace the poor Christ.[21]

Eventually, Agnes would fight Gregory not only with the spiritual authority of Clare, whom the pope highly regarded, plus the moral support of Elias, but also with the political clout of her brother. Gregory needed Wenceslaus on his side in the ongoing battle with Emperor Frederick II (one of Agnes' suitors—the *dramatis personae* get very involved here). Wenceslaus wrote the pope a very diplomatic letter, essentially saying that if His Holiness didn't hand over what Agnes wanted, he could expect no support from Bohemia. Gregory didn't appreciate being outmaneuvered, but Agnes was politically savvy and knew that the combined weight of Clare, Elias, and Wenceslaus would be irresistible. It wasn't the last round, but for now, Agnes had prevailed—and Clare with her.

Poverty in Clare's Thought

Why was it so important? It's no sin to own things, after all. If Jesus doesn't recognize me at the Last Judgment, it won't be because I'm writing this on a nice laptop with a full belly. Why was poverty the hill Clare was prepared to die on?

It wasn't just asceticism. Like most devout medievals, Clare was no stranger to the hair shirt, and the San Damiano community fasted every day of the year except for Sundays, Christmas Day, and Easter Week. Thursdays in Ordinary Time were at the

21. Quoted in Mueller, 48–49.

individual nun's discretion, but Clare herself often existed on bread and water—or nothing at all. At one point, Francis, fearing that Clare was getting a little carried away, actually forbade her to go a full day without eating. But when fasting practices became a point of contention between Agnes and Pope Gregory, Agnes wrote to Clare to ask what their observation was at San Damiano. Gregory had told her that Clare and the sisters there had eased up on following Francis' strict path. Agnes knew this wasn't true, but wondered how to negotiate with the pope on this issue. Clare's advice was both practical and revealed what she considered the "one thing necessary." She responded that poverty was their vocation, not fasting. It wasn't worth fighting this one out with Gregory, so Agnes should not fret over it. Agnes should, instead:

> Place your mind in the mirror of eternity.
> Place your soul in the splendor of glory.
> Place your heart in the figure of the divine substance;
> and through contemplation,
> transform your entire being into the very image of the
>   Divine One.
> In doing this, you will experience what his friends experience
> when they taste the hidden sweetness that God alone has kept
> from the beginning for those who love God.[22]

So Agnes should keep her eyes on the spiritual prize, which was poverty, and not worry about having to compromise on lesser matters. But why was poverty the fulcrum on which everything turned for Clare? If it wasn't primarily a matter of asceticism, of beating back the wants and needs of the flesh for spiritual gain, what was it? It was partly about seeing Christ in the poor, and living in solidarity with them. Some people, when they hear the call of Christ to "go, sell your possessions, and give the money to the poor . . . then come, follow me" (Matt 19:21), find that their

22. Clare's third letter to Agnes of Prague, quoted in Mueller, 82.

begging just places an extra burden on the poor around them and becomes a pointless act of spiritual self-indulgence. That was my experience in my extreme youth, when I had that kind of courage.

It wasn't the experience of the Poor Ladies, however. When they received alms, they shared with their poor neighbors. Unlike both Francis and Clare, Agnes was not estranged from her family when she embarked on religious life. So even after taking her vow of poverty, she continued to receive royal gifts. From the *Vita* written after her death, we learn that Agnes' practice was to divide the value of these gifts three ways: a third each to the church, to her sisters, and to the poor and needy around her. Caring for widows, orphans, lepers, and the rest of society's castoffs was a duty recognized to a greater or lesser degree by devout medievals in general, and certainly to a greater degree by Franciscans.[23] One reason to avoid owning property was to avoid taxing and exploiting the people who lived and worked on that property.[24] Yet the early Franciscans were not principally preoccupied with social justice. They cared for the poor, yes, but living that poverty was their vocation, not working for social change.

Why poverty, then? Recall Clare's directive to Agnes, quoted above. After telling her to disregard anyone who would divert her from the poverty central to her vocation, she goes right to the heart of that vocation: "[A]s a poor virgin, embrace the poor Christ." In short, it was about *love*. It was about finding a way deeper into God's heart, to experience her belovedness there, and to give her own heart in return. For Clare, this intimacy with her divine Spouse was everything, and she knew that poverty was how she would get there. In her first letter to Agnes, Clare praised her new ally and "unexpected soul mate"[25] for having had the wisdom and good taste to choose a greater spouse than Frederick II, one:

23. Mueller, 106.
24. Mueller, 92.
25. Mueller, 3.

> Whose power is stronger,
> Whose generosity more abundant,
> Whose appearance more beautiful,
> Whose love more tender,
> Whose courtesy more gracious.
>
> In Whose embrace You are already caught up;
> Who has adorned Your breast with precious stones
> and has placed priceless pearls on Your ears
> and has surrounded You with sparkling gems
> as though blossoms of springtime
> and placed on Your head a golden crown
> as a sign of Your holiness.[26]

This is the voice of a true romantic, which Clare and Francis both were, for all their fierce austerities. They both possessed the romantic imagination, which is not about erotic fantasies but rather the capacity to see a larger, nobler reality behind seemingly mundane tasks and events. Francis cast aside his ambition to be a knight and propel his family higher on the status ladder. His family's status no longer mattered to him, any more than his own did. But he was still drawn to the nobility of the dream of knighthood, and all the courtly culture of courtesy and honor that went with it; he just chose the service of a greater lord.

Likewise, Clare and Agnes both rejected the path that was normative for women of their time and place: a marriage that would bring honor and power to their families. Like Francis, they rejected those earthly goals but sought instead the ultimate Spouse, the one who contained and embodied all that was fine and noble and true. Franciscan men and women alike had the imagination to see in a creative reworking of the roles society defined for them the possibility of a greater, if paradoxical, way: to rise to the heights by seeking the depths, to renounce what they had in order to receive

26. Claire Marie Ledoux, *Clare of Assisi: Her Spirituality Revealed in Her Letters*, trans. Colette Joly Dees (Cincinnati, OH: St. Anthony Messenger Press, 2003), 45.

the whole kingdom in return, to give themselves body and soul to the One, as the *Book of Common Prayer* puts it, "[in] whose service is perfect freedom."

So Francis married Lady Poverty, and Clare took her divine Spouse. For medieval mystics, marriage was often the metaphor of choice for the spiritual life because it represented total, lifelong commitment, a comprehensive act of self-giving and intimacy. This is why they so often fell back on it as a picture of the life devoted to God. Since many of them were vowed celibates who hadn't much experience of the day-to-day realities, they perhaps had a somewhat idealized notion of marriage. But it doesn't matter; marriage was the closest relationship they could imagine, and they were going for what it's like when it's working. They longed for that intimacy with the Divine, and they longed to embrace that total commitment, the kind of pledge lovers want to shout from the rooftops when love is new.

Like Francis, Clare longed with all her being for this relationship, the pearl of great price, the treasure buried in a field. Both were prepared to sell everything to get it, because they understood that *poverty is the way in.* As Ilia Delio puts it, "Poverty is not only the starting point of relationship with God but it is the *deepening* of poverty that enables the seeker to enter more *deeply* into the mystery of God."[27] What Jesus was getting at with images like the pearl of great price, and what Clare and Francis wanted, was a relationship of depth, a commitment that gives all and receives all in return. No superficial, conventional religion that punctuates the year with fun festivals and the week with tedious obligations was going to satisfy that hunger for depth. The founders of the Franciscan movement saw discipleship as a grand adventure. It was a quest, one that would demand everything of them. And like the quests romanticized by the troubadours of their day, it was all about love—a love that might never be fully satisfied in this life, but would bring the sweetest rewards to those who believed in and fought for it.

27. Delio, *Clare of Assisi*, 8; emphasis added.

And it wasn't just that they saw the beauty of the poor Crucified—though it began there. They would also come, in him, to see their own beauty, their own belovedness. The answer to Francis' question on the mountain, *Who am I?* came in the stigmata: he was so conformed to Christ that he would bear Christ's wounds in his own body. It was a sign that said, "This is my beloved son," with words written on Francis' flesh in letters of fire.

As for Clare, she communicates her own deep sense of belovedness in her fourth and final extant letter to Agnes. She begins with the poor Christ, "Whose beauty all the blessed hosts of heaven unceasingly admire . . . *the brilliance of eternal light and the mirror without blemish*." She then advises Agnes to

> [g]aze upon that mirror each day, O Queen and Spouse of Jesus Christ, and continually study your face within it, that you may adorn yourself within and without with beautiful robes, covered, as is becoming the daughter and most chaste bride of the Most High King . . . [28]

Here we see the romantic imagination vividly expressed. Clare delights in recognizing her King in disguise. After all, Isaiah had tipped us off:

> [H]e had no form or majesty that we should look at him,
> nothing in his appearance that we should desire him.
> He was despised and rejected by others;
> a man of suffering and acquainted with infirmity;
> and as one from whom others hide their faces
> he was despised, and we held him of no account. (Isa 53:2b-3)

Clare understands that all royal expectations were upset by Christ in the glorious paradox of his incarnation, from the very beginning right through to the end:

28. Clare's fourth letter to Agnes of Prague, quoted in Ledoux, *Clare of Assisi*, 91; original emphasis.

> O marvelous humility, O astonishing poverty! The King of the angels, the Lord of heaven and earth, is laid in a manger! Then . . . consider the holy humility, the blessed poverty, the untold labors and burdens which He endured for the redemption of all [hu]mankind. Then . . . contemplate the ineffable charity which led Him to suffer on the wood of the cross and die thereon the most shameful kind of death.[29]

The romantic imagination enabled Clare to look past the humble birth and the humiliating death and not only see her King, but also see the great adventure in sharing his poverty. After all, when a medieval woman married, she assumed the rank and status of her spouse. Clare, seeing with eyes of the spirit, recognized that to take upon herself Christ's poverty would be to share ultimately in his riches and reign. This is why for Clare, a life lived hungry and in poor health, within the walls of a small complex in the forest outside Assisi, could be the greatest and most romantic adventure. And it's why she could assure Agnes that in turning her back on the most exalted position a European woman of the time could occupy, and embracing instead poverty and obscurity, she had made a *sacrum commercium*—a "good deal."[30]

When Clare invited Agnes to "embrace the poor Christ," she was calling her to take on a life of vulnerability and dependence. But that went well beyond material needs. As Delio puts it:

> To identify poverty in relationship to God is to quickly dispel the notion of poverty as merely material want or need. . . . The poor person is not the one in need of material things but the one in need of God and the one who needs God possesses God and to possess God is to possess all.[31]

For the earliest Franciscan women, poverty meant taking on a radical dependence on God to feed hungers of both body and

29. Clare's fourth letter to Agnes of Prague, quoted in Ledoux, 92.

30. Mueller, *Privilege of Poverty*, 61.

31. Delio, *Clare of Assisi*, 1–12.

soul. In the text of the "Privilege of Poverty," Pope Gregory IX assures them that when they are enfolded in the embrace of Christ, his left hand will supply their every material need, while they will ultimately find that "his right arm will more *blissfully* embrace you in the greatness of his vision."[32] This kind of confident reliance is not for the casual acquaintance or distant relative; it's for spouses, for those who are all in, who have given everything, and have burned every bridge back to safety. To be poor is to have no plan B, to know that if there is no God after all, nothing in your life makes sense and you've thrown it all away for naught.

Poverty is, ultimately, the price of ecstasy. Intimacy with God is no less risky than intimacy with a human partner. Both require us to be vulnerable, to be authentic, to strip away (returning to the marriage metaphor) every covering until all is known, and shared. For Clare, for Agnes, for Francis and all their companions, economic poverty was the first step. Is it a necessary one? For some people, that is indeed God's call. And I believe that every Christian (and indeed every decent human being) must consider their own spending habits in light of the needs of others. But I don't think having no money is necessarily the first step into poverty for all. The alcoholic who "hits bottom" is poor whether they're penniless or not. The parent who loses a child will never be the same, no matter what resources they have. The kid who's bullied all day at school knows poverty, even if she returns to a big house when school is over.

There's no point in multiplying examples. Poverty begins when I come face to face with my own insufficiency, my own lack of control over my circumstances, my life, my very self. And *holy* poverty begins when I welcome my helpless vulnerability as the one thing that will enable me to draw close to the crucified Christ, to share in both his anguish and the promise of paradise. As Delio points out, Clare knew this:

> Clare profoundly connected the prayer of the passion with the ecstasy of glory. Only the lover stays with the rejected

32. Quoted in Delio, 121; original emphasis.

> and despised Christ at the foot of the cross. . . . Agnes was to stay beneath the cross and to love the Love who loved her until she was brought into the wine cellar—the place of intimacy with her Beloved Christ.[33]

It was in that place of intimacy that she would know, not just her Beloved, but herself as beloved too. When we're willing to shed all pretense of self-sufficiency and illusions of control, we can begin to get a sense of our deep belovedness in Christ. Clare was willing to embrace that radical dependence, including the illness of some fifty-seven years that confined her often to her bed. And yet her last words bore no sense of regret but were a burst of joy from within the circle of God's embrace: "Blessed are you, O Lord, for having created me!"

Beyond the Founders: Franciscan Poverty Evolves

I've noted that even within Francis' lifetime, there were those in his order who took a more flexible view of poverty—not so much broadening it to focus on non-economic forms, as I have done here, but relaxing the practice of economic poverty itself. This grieved Francis while he lived, but the cracks would grow wider after his death.[34]

Francis died in October 1226 and the following year, Cardinal Ugolino, long an admirer of Francis and protector of his order, was elected pope. As Gregory IX, he moved forward quickly with Francis' canonization and the construction of a basilica in Assisi in his honor. We have already met Gregory through his negotiations with Clare and Agnes; he was a supporter of the Franciscan movement, but he was also a practical man. Gregory felt that extreme

33. Delio, 120.

34. For the following account of developments in the first generations after the death of Francis, I am indebted to "History of the Franciscan Movement (1)," The Franciscan Experience, FIOR (Franciscan Institute Outreach—Malta), accessed July 20, 2020, https://web.archive.org/web/20110805051354/http://www.christusrex.org/www1/ofm/fra/FRAht01.html.

poverty was all very well for saints and founders, but expecting it of thousands of rank-and-file members of a growing movement was a bit much. Many Franciscan women in fact accepted an "Ugolinian" Rule, in which expectations concerning poverty, asceticism, and property ownership were considerably relaxed. Clare and the other stubborn holdouts at San Damiano, plus a few other "Damianite" monasteries, continued to follow poverty as envisioned by Clare and Francis.

It was Gregory whose bull allowed the brothers to "use" property and other resources through agents who would see to their material needs, so that they technically would not have to "own" them. Gregory also deputized Brother Elias to oversee the building of the basilica, the giant shrine that would contain the remains of Francis and serve as a lavish tribute to *il Poverello*. The irony was apparently lost on Elias, but not on Francis' earliest followers, such as Brother Leo, who smashed a marble collection box set up for donations toward construction (for which Elias had him beaten). The public, revering Francis as they did, were generous. But those brothers who held to a strict interpretation of Franciscan poverty saw all of this as going in the wrong direction.

Indeed, two parties developed within the order around this issue of how strictly the rule had to be observed when it came to poverty, and they did go in different directions. In 1230, Pope Gregory relaxed the rule and in 1232, Brother Elias fulfilled his ambition of becoming Minister General (head) of the Franciscans. In that capacity he promoted the construction of large friaries or "convents" next to urban churches (such as the basilica in Assisi) where the friars, who came to be known as "Conventuals," could study and carry out other work. Despite Francis' own suspicion of academic study, Franciscans didn't take long to become influential in the academic world. Around 1236—just ten years after Francis' death—an English scholar at the University of Paris, Alexander of Hales, entered the Franciscan Order and became the first Franciscan to hold a university chair. And so began what would become the "Franciscan School," whose notables included Giovanni di Fidanza, known to us as St. Bonaventure. He was most likely one of Alexander's students and certainly brilliant, but his own academic career would be cut short when he was elected Minister General in 1257. We'll return to Bonaventure shortly.

Franciscans also quickly came to assume positions of authority in the church: the first Franciscan pope, Nicholas IV, reigned from 1288 to 1292. And the church found other uses for them. Probably the most regrettable was as inquisitors, a job that required education and orthodoxy. One might have thought that the numerous Benedictines around Europe would have been the obvious choice. But there was a snag: the Benedictine vow of stability meant they couldn't travel like the mobile mendicants. Along with the Dominicans, the Franciscans were road warriors and thus were able to investigate cases of alleged heresy in the places where the accusations were made. So Pope Gregory IX began appointing men from both mendicant orders as inquisitors early as 1231.

Meanwhile, some friars stuck closely to the original way of life followed by Francis: they held strictly to the principle of *sine proprio*, or "without anything of one's own." These friars tended to live in spartan, isolated hermitages, the kinds of places Francis himself had loved, and they shunned the large and increasingly privileged convents in the cities. Known first as *Zelanti*, they eventually came to be known as "Spirituals" or "Observantists." They strove to remain faithful to Francis' original vision, while the "Conventuals" were willing to see the order evolve in directions Francis likely would not have approved.

It's easy to valorize the Spirituals and condemn the Conventuals as sellouts. Certainly, the Spirituals tended to see the Conventuals as compromisers. The Franciscan mystic and poet Jacopone of Todi (1230–1306) lamented the increasing involvement of friars in the academy. Like Francis, he suspected that the scholarly life was not the best soil in which to cultivate the virtue of humility. Here's a fed-up Jacopone:

That's the way it is—not a shred left of the spirit of the Rule!
In sorrow and grief I see Paris demolish Assisi, stone
by stone.
With all their theology they've led the Order down a
crooked path. . . .

See how these theologians love one another!
One, like a young mule, watches and waits
For the right moment to kick the other in the chest.[35]

Having spent thirty years on a university faculty myself, I can't say I blame either Jacopone or Francis for their judgment, though I doubt it's a worse environment than most. Jacopone wrote some truly lyrical mystic texts, and I love him for them. But I admit that it's the cranky Jacopone that most often came to mind in the middle of a lecture:

You who enjoy talking, consider—
Does all that talk serve any purpose?[36]

The Spirituals certainly viewed the worldliness of the Conventuals with a jaundiced eye, but they too came in for criticism. Many of them embraced the apocalyptic writings of Joachim of Fiore (ca. 1135–1202), who often teetered on the brink of heresy. Further, a group within the Spirituals considered the emperor Frederick II (d. 1250) to be the Antichrist, and that is living rather dangerously. It should be noted that when the arch-Conventual Brother Elias was excommunicated, it was the emperor Frederick who gave him shelter. No wonder the Spirituals took a dim view of him.

A lot of poverty politics went on over the next few centuries, and I'm not going into the details of it all here. At times the Spirituals would prevail, but in general the church hierarchy tended to support the Conventuals and edge the Spirituals out toward the

35. Jacopone of Todi, *The Lauds* (Mahwah, NJ: Paulist Press, 1982), 123.
36. Jacopone, *Lauds*, 218.

margins. Some of the more stubborn among them were handed over to the Inquisition and burned. Bonaventure, as Minister General, as well as some of his successors, tried to steer a moderate course between the two parties. But by 1322, a papal bull ended even the appearance of *sine proprio*, forcing the friars into property ownership. At the same time, the order was becoming more centralized and clericalized. In 1525, an Observant named Matteo Serafini da Bascio launched a reform movement within the Franciscan Order that embraced greater austerity. It grew quickly, and in 1619 became a fully separate order, the Order of Friars Minor Capuchin. (Incidentally, *cappuccio* is Italian for "hood," and the brown hooded habits with white cinctures or roped belts of the Capuchins gave us the word *cappuccino,* a "little Capuchin.")

This pattern of growing laxity, the call for a stricter observance, and the subsequent splitting off of a more rigorous section of an order has been repeated many times in monastic history (not to mention the history of the church in general). We can see it in the Benedictines, with the Cistercian (1098) and Trappist (1664) reforms, as well as with the Discalced Carmelite reform, which was founded by St. Teresa of Jesus (Avila) and St. John of the Cross in 1562. But among the early Franciscans, it was Bonaventure who tried to hold things together. He was a gifted scholar and a good administrator, but, unusually perhaps, those gifts were accompanied in him by a rich spiritual life. So it's worth taking a quick look at Bonaventure's own understanding of Franciscan poverty.

The Seraphic Doctor

Born Giovanni di Fidanza in the town of Bagnoregio, Bonaventure (1217/21–1274) was one of the second-generation Franciscans. He was just a boy when Francis died, but by the time Bonaventure went off to the University of Paris, the Franciscan Order was growing rapidly. He himself entered the order in Paris in 1243, having studied under some of the great scholars of the newly established Franciscan School there. Unlike Jacopone of Todi, Bonaventure saw no conflict between the intellectual focus of Paris and the simplicity of Assisi:

> Do not be upset that in the beginning the Friars were simple and unlettered. This ought rather to strengthen your faith in the Order. For I acknowledge before God that what made me love the life of blessed Francis so much was the fact that it resembled the beginning and growth of the Church. As the Church began with simple fishermen and afterwards developed to include renowned and skilled doctors [i.e., scholars], so you will see it to be the case in the Order of Blessed Francis. In this way God shows that it was not founded by the prudence of men but by Christ.[37]

Bonaventure completed the equivalent of a doctoral degree in 1255, but there was to be no refuge for him in the ivory tower. He became Minister General shortly after finishing his studies, and he served in that capacity for seventeen years, a moderate in a time of extremes.

For Bonaventure, the vision and values of Francis mattered, but so did the need for institution-building in a rapidly expanding movement. What kept him from being a bland, fence-straddling bean-counter was the winning combination of his sharp intellect and deep personal holiness. So greatly was he respected for these, plus a much-needed gift for reconciliation, that he has been called the second founder of the Franciscan Order.[38]

Among Bonaventure's works are three books of particular importance. One is an official and politically motivated biography of Francis that Bonaventure was tasked by his superiors with writing. It replaced the two previous biographies by Thomas of Celano, which were subsequently suppressed, and put forward a vision of Francis and Franciscan life that served some parties better than oth-

37. Quoted in *Bonaventure*, translated and introduced by Ewert Cousins (Mahwah, NJ: Paulist Press, 1978), 6.

38. *Bonaventure*, 7.

ers. Bonaventure's *Tree of Life* reflects and builds on the Franciscan devotion to the human Christ: the drama of his birth, the labors of his life, and the pathos of his passion and death. Franciscan spirituality is incarnational: it's interested in the sensate experience of God *touching* and *participating* in the world with all its creatures, including humankind. It meditates on the smell of the manger and the heaviness of blood dripping from a body tortured and dying. Franciscans tend not to be abstract in their devotion, and although Bonaventure was a sophisticated theologian, he was also a man in love, as Francis himself had been, with the poor Christ.

Bonaventure's inspiration for *The Soul's Journey Into God* came from time he spent meditating on Mount La Verna, where Francis had received the stigmata in his vision of the six-winged seraph fixed to a cross. Bonaventure, a couple years into his demanding job as Minister General, was longing for a bit of peace and withdrew to this sacred place to reflect and re-center. As he meditated on Francis' vision and sought a way to connect a changing order to Francis' original ideals, Bonaventure conceived of a six-stage journey, reflecting the six wings of the seraph, by which the soul finds union with God. Note that Bonaventure speaks not of the soul's journey *to* God, but its journey *into* God,[39] and this journey to intimate union has only one route: "There is no other path but through the burning love of the Crucified."[40]

To contemplate Christ crucified is to see him at the extreme of his poverty; for Bonaventure, as a Franciscan, it always comes back to that. And as a Franciscan, the response must always involve the heart: no dry analysis, no safe scholarly distance, but a personal and emotional involvement in the poverty of the poor Christ. And yet, Bonaventure was indeed a scholar, so he also avoided dissolving into sentimentality and schmaltz. In fact, he delighted in the "coincidence of opposites," those paradoxes on which the spiritual life is built (How is Christ both human and divine? How

39. *Bonaventure*, 21.
40. Quoted in *Bonaventure*, 21–22.

can strength be perfected in weakness? And how are the poor in spirit blessed?). In Bonaventure himself, we find just such a reconciling of opposites: an exceptional theologian, he could articulate a theory of the spiritual journey drawing from Francis, Augustine, Pseudo-Dionysius, and others, taking the intuitions of Francis and honing them into a rational, intelligible framework.

And yet, he knew that all frameworks, like all metaphors, eventually find their limits. The intellectual who's been made steward of a great mind must push reason this far, because it is given to humans to "know in part" (1 Cor 13:9-10 NKJV). But when the journey brings us face to face with "that which is perfect," then reason surrenders in poverty, and we open empty hands to receive it. Our journey ends in mystical ecstasy, in union with God, but we cannot study our way there. If we confine ourselves to study, we'll be like a pilgrim whose desk is stacked with maps but who never leaves the house. Bonaventure, in closing *The Soul's Journey*, impresses this on the reader:

> But if you wish to know how these things come about,
> ask grace not instruction,
> desire not understanding,
> the groaning of prayer not diligent reading,
> the Spouse not the teacher,
> God not man,
> darkness not clarity,
> not light but the fire
> that totally inflames and carries us into God
> by ecstatic unctions and burning affections.
> This fire is God,
> and his furnace is in Jerusalem;
> and Christ enkindles it
> in the heat of his burning passion,
> which only he truly perceives who says:
> My soul chooses hanging and my bones death.[41]

41. *Bonaventure*, 115, emphases removed.

Lady Poverty had made another conquest, brought another bride to the divine Spouse. As a philosopher and theologian, Bonaventure helped launch the Franciscan intellectual tradition. Canonized in 1482, he was known as the "Seraphic Doctor" and was formally made a Doctor of the Church in 1587. He was a capable leader, a moderate, and a reconciler. But not even a saintly genius could settle for good the question of how Franciscans should live out the poverty beloved of their founder. Every generation of Franciscans, in their different contexts, has had to confront that challenge for themselves, and that's only considering the economic side of poverty. The side of poverty that's virtually indistinguishable from humility—that is, poverty of spirit—is a mystery that must be worked out between God and every Franciscan soul.

Franciscan Poverty Today

What about Franciscans today? What is the twenty-first-century Franciscan take on poverty? Naturally, different Franciscans would answer this question in different ways, but an interesting opinion has been offered by Casey Cole, OFM, a young friar, priest, and blogger, on his YouTube channel called "Breaking In the Habit." In one episode he takes on the question: How does the life lived by friars today, which is far from the austerities of Francis, constitute an authentic model of Franciscan poverty?[42]

Brother Casey begins by acknowledging that the question of what true Franciscan poverty should look like has been contested from the beginning, as we have seen. There were partisans on both ends of the continuum, but most brothers were then, as now, somewhere in between those advocating bread-and-water poverty and those for whom a relatively comfortable life was acceptable. Cole tells of visiting a Franciscan house from the sixteenth century, in which the rooms the friars slept in were small enough to touch all

42. Casey Cole, "Let's Talk about the Elephant in the Room," accessed August 3, 2020, https://www.youtube.com/watch?v=XcU4o3VgvXw.

four walls with your hands, and also mentions a tiny courtyard in the center. It looks so austere that it's tempting for us in our time to look back with nostalgia on those brothers of centuries past and how true they were to their vocation. And yet, Cole points out that those friars didn't live in that house in the twenty-first century; they lived there in the sixteenth century, when it would have been a luxury to have a courtyard at all, never mind a room of your own. Most people had none of that. Friars have never lived like the poorest of the poor; being destitute and dying of starvation in the street has never been the goal. If you're trying to "win" at poverty, so that no one is poorer than you, you'll quickly find yourself without the strength to carry out any sort of ministry at all.

In fact, as we have already seen, economic poverty itself is not the goal. It's never been about what "stuff" you own; Francis was more concerned with humility, with the renunciation of status and privilege and entitlement. And it's about how we relate to the stuff: if I claim no "right" to the things I have, then I'm getting close to the goal. (A helpful exercise is to imagine that your house burns to the ground with everything you possess in it. How do you feel? That can give you some sense of where you are with this.) I think that the reason humility was emphasized so much more by Francis is that, while he realized that the "stuff" could so easily come between us and the love of God and neighbor, getting on top of that is entry-level poverty. It's not that it isn't important, but it's rudimentary. The deeper level of poverty, in which we claim no rights, expect no deference, and accept our personal insufficiency and the ego-shrinkage that comes with it, is poverty of spirit and closer to what Francis and his "Lesser Brothers" sought.

Like Francis and Clare in their time, Franciscans today focus on poverty because it's the key to freedom. As the Franciscan priest and writer Richard Rohr puts it:

> Poverty for Francis is not just a life of simplicity, humility, restraint, or even lack. Poverty is the freedom to recognize that *myself—by itself—is powerless and ineffective.* This is

> not a low self-image but a very liberating and utterly honest self-image.[43]

Poverty is freedom because once we've relinquished our hold on things, they relinquish their hold on us. This is true of material objects: the Quaker writer Richard Foster suggests that if you suspect you're too attached to a possession, you can break the attachment by giving it away. I tried this once with a costly china platter that someone had given me years before. I decided to take it to a party as a "hostess gift," and it turned out it completed a set my friend had in the same pattern. She was delighted, and I felt just a tiny bit more free.

A contemporary Franciscan writer who powerfully connects poverty to belovedness, as well as to beauty and transformation, is one I've already cited several times: Ilia Delio, OSF. With PhDs in both science and theology, Delio is certainly a woman who sees connections. For her, poverty is "the language of love," "that which allows me to become fully human," the "love that unveils the beauty of the divine image within me."[44] It's worth pausing to recognize how dramatically these statements depart from the dominant values of Western culture; Delio's going to have some explaining to do. She also clarifies what is, and what is not, the role of material poverty in the Franciscan way: "material poverty is only sacramental of the deeper poverty of being human."[45] That is, material poverty can be an outward and visible sign of an inner poverty of spirit. Following Bonaventure, she hones poverty down to its essence: "The poor person is one who realizes his or her need for God."[46] Whether we need God to supply our next meal, to keep us from drinking, to

43. Richard Rohr, "The Franciscan Genius: Integration of the Negative," *Franciscan Poverty*, June 18, 2015, accessed August 5, 2020, https://cac.org/franciscan-poverty-2015-06-18/ (original emphasis).

44. Ilia Delio, *Franciscan Prayer* (Cincinnati, OH: St. Anthony Messenger Press, 2004), 87.

45. Delio, *Franciscan Prayer*, 83.

46. Delio, 79.

give us the compassion to forgive our spouse one more time, or to stick out a loathed but inescapable job, it's about the *fact* of our need more than the particulars of *what* we need.

We all share an existential poverty: the vulnerability of being human, of being created, of our dependence on God and our interdependence with each other. With Bonaventure, Delio sees sin as the rejection of our poverty, the tendency to grab at things instead. As we saw in chapter 2, this is the voice of entitlement: "I want this. I deserve this. My will be done." But Delio points out that in Jesus, God takes on the poverty of the human condition. Jesus, as the Philippians hymn has it, did not regard equality with God as something to be grasped at. Instead, he emptied himself, humbled himself, became like a slave, and finished up by enduring an agonizing and humiliating death. Recall that the Greek word for "emptied" is *ekenōsen,* and we speak of "kenosis" as the self-emptying in which the Son of God gave up every right and entitlement and embraced our poverty.

He "emptied" himself, poured himself out. What does that mean? If God is love, then what is being poured out here but love? In the extravagant outpouring of God's own self on humankind and all of creation, while divesting himself of every prerogative of his own, Jesus shows us the deep connection between poverty—holy poverty, that is, chosen poverty—and love. This is why Jesus said that there is no greater love than to lay down your life for another—to give, that is, the very last thing you have (see John 15:13). And just as Jesus embarks on his public ministry, in which he will do just that, we are told that the Voice from heaven affirms to all: "You are my Son, *the Beloved*; with you I am well pleased" (Mark 1:11; emphasis added).

So well pleased, indeed, that "Therefore," that is, because he emptied himself, "God also highly exalted him and gave him the name that is above every name . . . " (Phil 2:9). Poverty is the self-emptying that receives everything in return. This is Bonaventure's "coincidence of opposites," the paradox of embracing poverty, of giving all away, and receiving everything in return. "As having nothing," Paul says, "and yet possessing all things" (2 Cor 6:10 NKJV). Once poverty clears out some space within us by pouring out the nasty byproducts of an ego that refuses to be dependent, there is more and more room to take in an infinite love. And that love teaches us to know ourselves as beloved, as Jesus was. Not because we're innocent like Jesus, but because *we were created for this.*

Franciscan spirituality, as I have said, is deeply incarnational. It is grounded in the meeting of earth and heaven in the person of Jesus Christ, the "God-man." Saint Athanasius claimed in the fourth century that "God became man that man might become God," that is, deified or divinized, "participants of the divine nature" (2 Pet 1:4). Francis and Clare understood, as have their spiritual heirs since, that while the divinization process will take us to our most exquisite joy, that process is going to be painful at times. It has to strip us down, empty us out, tear away our illusions of self-sufficiency; in short, it requires poverty. We cannot return to Eden as our entitled selves; there's an angel with a flaming sword in the way. As long as we're full of ourselves and grasping at things, we remain broken, and our deep wound, the "original wound," needs healing. While we desperately want to know ourselves to be "beloved," it just seems too good to be true.

But that's because the wound has clouded our vision, robbed us of the ability to see ourselves as we truly are in God's eyes. We were created by God to be loved and to give our love in return. That is our mission and purpose; it's what we're *for.* It's simply in God's nature to love, and while needing nothing from us, God chooses to desire our love. So the salvation accomplished by Jesus is meant to sweep us into the embrace, the "group hug," of the Trinity itself. And every experience we have of poverty—of diminishment, of struggle, of longing—brings us closer to that place where we see ourselves truly, as God does: utterly dependent, but utterly loveable. We are a work in progress, but God sees the end product and, by divine choice, is helpless to resist us.

It took Francis most of his life to grasp this. But when he questioned his identity and worth, God's answer was the stigmata: a powerful affirmation of how closely Francis resembled "My beloved Son." The message of the stigmata brought it all together: "You are poor and wounded. But in those very wounds, like those of Christ, you know that you, too, are my beloved son." Clare also found in poverty the truth about herself. After spending decades of illness and suffering secreted away with her divine Spouse, Clare was so grounded in her own belovedness that on her deathbed she erupted in gratitude for her own existence. The Franciscan tradition teaches us that "Sister Death," in the words of Francis' famous canticle, is to be welcomed, not feared. She is the clearest vision of Lady Poverty, who has accompanied us all along and will carry us in her embrace to our final home, to the place where we know our value in God's sight. Here, in the wholeness and abundance for which we were created, poverty is no longer needed because ours is the kingdom of heaven.

Chapter 4

Into the Heart of God

O divine fire . . . consume me and I will not resist. . . .
Your lively flames make those live who die in them.

St. Margaret Mary Alacoque[1]

The Sacred Heart has the potential to alienate and annoy most everyone: Protestants because it's too Catholic, older Catholics who remember pre–Vatican II family devotions awash in sentimentality and bordering on superstition, and post–Vatican II Catholics because, well . . . it's so pre–Vatican II. Finally, those who retain a devotion to the Sacred Heart can be annoyed because this powerful symbol is so much misunderstood and so widely dismissed.

The heart of the unchanging Son of God has been through a lot of changes in the popular imagination. In this chapter, I want to trace those developments from the beginnings up to the present, being particularly attentive to how the Sacred Heart tradition, which includes devotion to the sacred wounds of Christ, weds our poverty to our belovedness in God. When Jesus promised

1. Quoted in David Richo, *The Sacred Heart of the World: Restoring Mystical Devotion to Our Spiritual Life* (Mahwah, NJ: Paulist Press, 2007), 86.

that the poor in spirit would be blessed, it wasn't because they'd find out that, after all, poverty turns out to be a lot of fun. No, it was because "theirs is the kingdom of heaven." They would find that it is precisely when we come to the end of ourselves and our resources—whether that takes a lifetime of denial and resistance or whether our insufficiency is so obvious that we're forced to give up early—it is when we accept our emptiness that grace rushes in. When that happens, we can see ourselves truthfully "as having nothing and yet possessing all things" (2 Cor 6:10 NKJV).

I once put up an image of the Sacred Heart on a screen in a roomful of Roman Catholics, and the entire room groaned and rolled their eyes. I had an idea what was going on, but figured I should hear it from them. They told story after story of Thursday night family prayers and First Friday communions; sentimental, over-the-top devotional language; and being threatened as children with piercing the tender heart of Jesus if they took an extra cookie or pulled the cat's tail. The heart of Jesus was represented as a frightening, disembodied organ tightly bound with thorns and shooting flames out the top: admittedly, kind of hard for a kid to relate to. Or it appeared as a kind of radioactive glow on the chest of a simpering Aryan Jesus who looks like he's just back from brunch.

Not having been raised Roman Catholic (or really, much of anything), I don't have any of that baggage. I come to this through my own experience of being brought repeatedly to the wounds of Christ in prayer, and then finding that instinctive devotion validated in Wendy M. Wright's beautiful book *Sacred Heart: Gateway to God*. Sometimes you stumble around on your own for a long time and then come across something that makes sense of it all. This was my experience of Wright's book, which informs much of what I'll have to say in this chapter.[2]

2. Wendy M. Wright, *Sacred Heart: Gateway to God* (Maryknoll, NY: Orbis, 2001), 1–4.

The Early Church: Making Sense of Christ's Body

Although the Feast of the Sacred Heart only made it onto the Roman Catholic calendar in 1856, the history of devotion to the body of the incarnate One can be traced right back to the beginning. There was the reverence with which Jesus' body was deposed from the cross and laid in the tomb: in haste, but with as much dignity as wealthy friends could give it (see John 19:38-42). Who doesn't feel the Virgin's anguish captured in Michelangelo's famous *Pietà*, her soul pierced with the arrow that had been prophesied long before? When I was eleven years old and my family spent a summer in Rome, I fell in love with that sculpture, which was not yet surrounded by bulletproof glass. To my family's amusement, I insisted on having a cheap plastic replica in my room, which became the focus of all my childish piety during that long summer spent at once inside and excluded from the heart of the Catholic Church.

The women who had loved and served Jesus went, before dawn on the first day of the week, to finish up the last things they could do for the One they had lost. If nothing else, they could at least anoint his body (see Luke 24:1-3). In John's gospel, Mary Magdalene goes alone to the tomb. I smile when she mistakes the risen Christ for the gardener and says, "[T]ell me where you have laid him, and I will take him away" (John 20:15). "You and what pair of burly men you brought with you," I always think. But then, the name: "Mary." Or rather, in Aramaic, *Mariam*. Regardless, it is heart reaching out to heart, calling her "Beloved." She cries out: *Rabbouni*! "Teacher," "Master," regardless, it's "Beloved." Hearts rejoice in a moment of recognition, mingle, and are exchanged.

Jesus pushes gently against Mary's impulse to grab hold of his body and never let go; with no way of understanding what it will mean to have his Spirit instead, I'd have done the same thing. After Jesus' appearances to the other disciples, in which he approaches them wounds-forward, his broken body and shed blood become the ritual center of their worship. In time, St. Paul will work out the idea that they *are*, in a mystical sense, his body, continuing his presence in the world. Even the hideous instrument of torture on which his body was broken would become the primary symbol of their faith, but that would take time. For the earliest Christians, crucifixion was still a little too real to turn it into jewelry, though it certainly appeared in St. Paul's letters as a summary of everything the church stood for: he speaks, for example, of being "persecuted for the cross of Christ" (Gal 6:12).

Even before Jesus was taken down from the cross, John's gospel tells us that when his side was pierced by the soldier to make sure he was dead, "at once blood and water came out." This is followed by the assertion that "He who saw this has testified so that you also may believe. His testimony is true, and he knows that he tells the truth" (John 19:34b-35). I used to wonder why the evangelist made such a big deal out of the flow of blood and water following the stabbing of a victim who'd died like this. Surely you'd expect to see something come out when a spear is withdrawn from someone's chest—especially if death had already occurred, and the "water" that escaped was the collection of fluid around the heart and lungs known as pericardial effusion.

But there are so many layers of meaning here. Nearly fifteen hundred years before, Moses had led the Israelites out of Egypt. In the fourth gospel, Jesus has already explicitly compared himself to the healing serpent that Moses "raised up" on a pole in the desert: when he is similarly "raised up," it will be to give eternal life to those who believe (see John 3:14-15). Nearing the Promised Land, when the people complain for the *nth* time that they have no water and surely they'd been better off in Egypt, Moses is told to place the trusty rock before the people and command it once again to yield its water. But Moses, whether in a fit of pique or for some other reason, strikes the rock twice instead (see Num 20:1-13). He'll be punished for his disobedience, and yet the people are saved as the water pours forth. At the crucifixion, the Rock is struck in disobedience, yet the water pours forth and the people are saved.

Jesus as a source of saving water is a theme in John's gospel. Not stagnant water but life-giving, gushing, abundant, "living water." On the last day of the Festival of Booths (*Sukkot*), he stood in the Temple and declared, "Let anyone who is thirsty come to me, and let the one who believes in me drink. As the scripture has said, 'Out of the believer's heart shall flow rivers of living water'" (John 7:37-38). Earlier, in his encounter with the Samaritan woman Photini, Jesus had assured her:

> If you knew the gift of God, and who it is that is saying to you, "Give me a drink," you would have asked him, and he would have given you living water . . . those who drink of the water that I will give them will never be thirsty. The water that I will give will become in them a spring of water gushing up to eternal life. (John 4:10, 14)

A spring, gushing up. Notice the lavishness of the language here: the water Jesus gives does not trickle; it gushes, it flows, it's *alive.* Here's another interesting detail—and it's good to keep in mind that, as I said earlier, in John's gospel the details are always significant. There are only two instances in this gospel when Jesus asks someone for a drink: in the encounter with the Samaritan woman Photini, and in his last moments on the cross: "I am thirsty" (John 19:28). He sips sour wine from a sponge and says, "It is finished" (John 19:30). And he dies.

The puzzle here is why, after everything he's suffered, when he knows the end has come—why at that moment ask for a drink? He's about to bow his head and give up his spirit, and the text strongly suggests that these things happen in quick succession. It's not as though he needs to hydrate for the long stretch ahead; he's reached the end. Why a drink now? This takes us back to his encounter with Photini, the only other time he'd expressed his thirst, which was followed by the promise of "living water." On the cross, we see a mirror image of that conversation: Jesus, thirsty in his humanity, becomes in his divinity the source of "living water."[3] Lavish, abundant water, gushing forth from his side to sustain life.

3. JP Nunez, "The Blood and Water That Flowed from Jesus' Side," *Catholic Stand*, October 10, 2018, accessed April 24, 2020, https://catholicstand.com/the-blood-and-water-that-flowed-from-jesus-side/.

For desert people, water equals life. At the beginning of creation, we hear that "a river flows out of Eden to water the garden" (Gen 2:10). And at the end of all things, the seer of Revelation tells us of a "river of the water of life, bright as crystal, flowing from the throne of God and of the Lamb through the middle of the street of the [New Jerusalem]" (Rev 22:1-2a). These two scenes are like bookends, and in between, God comes in person to provide that "living water," the water of life, out of his own wounded side.

But there's more. The blood and water pouring from Jesus' pierced side have been seen from the earliest days of the church as sacramental images. Saint John Chrysostom (349–407) preached a famous sermon, still read today, that makes this connection.[4] The waters of baptism initiate us into life: as Jesus said to Nicodemus, "no one can enter the kingdom of God without being born of water and the Spirit" (John 3:5). Just as Eve is born from the side of Adam in the second account of creation in Genesis (see Gen 2:21-22), so the church corporately, and each member individually, is the bride born from the water that flows from Jesus' pierced side. In the Eucharist, the blood sustains that life throughout our lives: "Those who eat my flesh and drink my blood have eternal life, and I will raise them up on the last day" (John 6:54).

So when the evangelist draws our attention to the blood and water flowing from Jesus' side wound, he is drawing us deep into the mystery of how God creates and sustains life, even out of death—even out of his own death. The layers of meaning in John's brief observation can keep us meditating for years, but in the first centuries of its history, the church was chiefly concerned with a more pressing issue: how to make sense of a three-Personed God in the context of a fiercely monotheistic religion? What to do with a divine, resurrected human who spoke of himself as distinct from, yet one with, God the Father? And what about the Holy Spirit?

4. "Good Friday with St. John Chrysostom," The Catholic Defender, *Deeper Truth* (blog), accessed April 24, 2020, https://www.deepertruthcatholics.com/single-post/2017/04/14/The-Catholic-Defender-Good-Friday-With-St-John-Chrysostom.

How do you avoid becoming a polytheistic religion, when Jesus came not to abolish the Law but to fulfill it?

Medievals and the Heart of the Human Christ

That question would take time, plus a lot of arguing and creed-crafting, to work out. But by the Middle Ages, the orthodox position was firmly identified, if still really hard on the rational mind. But now, a church that had a reasonably firm grasp of the implications of Christ's divinity could turn with new energy to contemplate his humanity. With St. Francis, they would gather around the infant King in the first Christmas crèche. But they also gathered around his crucified body. As we've seen, Francis longed to know the suffering Christ experienced in his passion and longed to know the love that enabled him to endure it. The stigmata were God's answer to that longing: the *wounds*, in his *flesh*.

The Franciscans, along with the Helfta mystics we'll meet in the next chapter and others of their time were increasingly being drawn to the details of Jesus' earthly life, especially the parts that were the most painful and most obviously connected to our redemption. They were drawn to his wounds: two in his hands, two in his feet, and the one in his side. Saint Clare composed a beautiful litany that begins:

> Praise and honor be given Thee, O my Lord Jesus Christ, by reason of the Sacred Wound in Thy Right Hand. *By this adorable wound, I beseech Thee to pardon me all the sins I have committed by thoughts, words and deeds, by neglect in Thy service, and by self-indulgence, both waking and sleeping* . . .[5]

She continues through the wounds in his left hand, each of his feet, and finally to the wound in his side: five in all. Others noted that

5. Quoted in "Catholic Prayer: St. Clare's Litany of the Sacred Wounds," *Catholic Culture*, accessed April 24, 2020, https://www.catholicculture.org/culture/liturgicalyear/prayers/view.cfm?id=1120 (original emphasis).

there would have been plenty more wounds than those made by the nails and lance: St. Gertrude of Helfta reported a vision which revealed to her that, together, Christ's wounds numbered 5,466. Gertrude would say a prayer each *day* for every one of them, while others were happy to spread them out over three years.

Another very famous prayer, the *Anima Christi* (Latin for "Soul of Christ"), dates probably from the fourteenth century, and exemplifies the kind of extravagant devotion to the body and wounds of Christ characteristic of the time:

> Soul of Christ, sanctify me.
> Body of Christ, save me.
> Blood of Christ, inebriate me.
> Water from the side of Christ, wash me.
> Passion of Christ, strengthen me.
> O Good Jesus, hear me.
> Within your wounds hide me.
> Permit me not to be separated from you.
> From the wicked foe, defend me.
> At the hour of my death, call me
> and bid me come to you
> That with your saints I may praise you
> For ever and ever. Amen.[6]

For a time, this prayer was popularly attributed to St. Ignatius Loyola (1491–1556), though much earlier versions of it have been found. Medieval in tone, perhaps, the notion of union with Christ through his wounds was loved by Pope Francis, himself a Jesuit. In a 2018 homily, Francis acknowledged that it "may sound a bit medieval," but he urged the congregation: "When we pray that Our Father, let's try to enter through Jesus' wounds and arrive deeper

6. From *Finding God in All Things: A Marquette Prayer Book* © 2009 Marquette University, quoted in "Anima Christi," *IgnatianSpirituality.com*, accessed April 24, 2020, https://www.ignatianspirituality.com/ignatian-prayer/prayers-by-st-ignatius-and-others/anima-christi/.

and deeper, to his heart. Enter into his wounds and contemplate the love in his heart for you . . . "[7]

What Pope Francis is expressing here is indeed a "medieval" idea: that one might enter the very heart of God through the wounds of the Crucified. The person of Christ is the place where heaven and earth meet; this is what incarnation is about. Jesus' body is Jacob's ladder (see Gen 28:10-22): as he promised an astonished Nathanael, "[Y]ou will see heaven opened and the angels of God ascending and descending upon the Son of Man" (John 1:51). By entering mystically into that body, our humanity is swept into the current of his divinity, and becomes one with it. In himself, in his own person, Jesus is the marriage of divinity and humanity, and in him, our humanity is married to the God who had said through the prophet Isaiah:

> [A]s a young man marries a young woman, so shall your
> builder marry you,
> And as the bridegroom rejoices over the bride, so shall your
> God rejoice over you. (Isa 62:5)

The theme underlying the whole story of God's dealings with humankind in the Scriptures is that it's a *courtship*. A long and rocky one, with a lot of drama and breakups and tearful reconciliations, for sure. But it's meant to end in marriage. That's why the language of covenant rather than contract: it's a relationship, not a deal, and God will remain faithful even when his people go "whoring" all over the place.[8] To Moses, God speaks of Israel as "my treasured possession out of all the peoples" (Exod 19:5). Through

7. Cindy Wooden, "Five Wounds of Christ: Pope Urges Recovery of Traditional Devotion," *National Catholic Reporter*, March 22, 2018, accessed April 24, 2020, https://www.ncronline.org/news/vatican/francis-chronicles/five-wounds-christ-pope-urges-recovery-traditional-devotion.

8. For a lengthy treatise on the sluttiness of God's people, see Ezek 16. Special thanks to the Rev. Doyt Conn of Epiphany Parish, Seattle, for a particularly memorable Bible study on the subject.

Isaiah, he tenderly claims them: "Do not fear, for I have redeemed you; I have called you by name, you are mine" (Isa 43:1). That God's heart becomes vulnerable in this process is abundantly clear in the book of Hosea. After recounting a long list of Israel's infidelities, which were vividly acted out by making poor Hosea take "a wife of whoredom" (Hos 1:2), God speaks of a day of reconciliation:

> On that day, says the LORD, you will call me, "My husband," and no longer will you call me "My Baal" [*master*]. . . . And I will take you for my wife forever; I will take you for my wife in righteousness and in justice, in steadfast love, and in mercy. I will take you for my wife in faithfulness; and you shall know the LORD. (Hos 2:16, 19-20)

When God takes human flesh, a marriage is taking place. So it makes sense, as we've seen, that the first of Jesus' "signs" in John's gospel is at a wedding, where he turns water into wine. Later, Jesus tells a story about unworthy guests who don't accept a wedding invitation, and another wedding guest who doesn't even respect the occasion enough to dress up (see Matt 22:1-14). And in the book of Revelation, the rejoicing in heaven is represented as a wedding feast: an angel says to the one who receives the vision, "Blessed are those who are invited to the marriage supper of the Lamb" (Rev 19:9). The bride is dressed in fine linen, multitudes burst out in praise, and the whole scene is so wildly exciting that the seer falls down to worship the angel, who quickly redirects his worship.

We seem to have wandered far from devotion to the wounds and heart of Christ here. But in fact it's because many medieval mystics understood their relationship to God and the whole of salvation history in terms of courtship, with marriage as the goal ("I will take you for my wife forever"), that they so earnestly desired to experience union with the heart of their divine Spouse. Their language can get a little gushy at times, and it's easy for readers of our day to over-literalize these texts and go all Freudian, wondering about suppressed sexuality among a bunch of celibates retreating into fantasies of "Jesus is my boyfriend." But this is a mistake, and it does a real disservice to the profound mystery these writers are trying, within the limits of human language, to convey.

Their desire is to be one with God—specifically, one with a *suffering* God. That being the goal, it's not surprising that they found a "way in" through the portal of God's wounds. Especially the side wound, from which the new life had first poured, and which became, as Wright observes,

> the entryway to God's most secret life. It was, devotionally speaking, only a short step inward from the side wound to the heart [which would] become the supreme symbol of the loving intimacy between creator and creatures. Medieval Christians moved deeper and deeper into the body through the side wound into the divine-human heart where the mystery of a love that poured itself out in death could be explored.[9]

Medievals layered image upon image: the heart beat beneath the breast of Jesus, where the beloved disciple had reclined in confident intimacy at the Last Supper. The heart was the "cleft in the rock," spoken of in the Song of Songs, where the dove takes refuge:

> O my dove, in the clefts of the rock,
>   in the covert of the cliff,
> let me see your face,
>   let me hear your voice;
> for your voice is sweet,
>   and your face is lovely. (Song 2:14)

Once when Gertrude of Helfta was praying for another nun, she was told to advise her to make a nest in the side of Christ and receive honey and instruction there.[10] The heart is a banqueting

9. Wright, *Sacred Heart*, 20.

10. Carolyn Walker Bynum, *Jesus as Mother: Studies in the Spirituality of the High Middle Ages*, vol. 16 (Berkeley: University of California Press, 1984), 197.

table, an overflowing fountain, a fiery furnace, which one can enter and not be consumed. In the book of Ezekiel, God promises to replace the stony heart with a heart of flesh (see Ezek 36:26), and medieval mystics such as Catherine of Siena reported experiencing an "exchange of hearts" in which Christ took their hearts and replaced them with his own. In a time of intense spiritual revival, the mystics of the Middle Ages seemed to frolic in their imagery, and the Sacred Heart became a multivalent and powerful symbol of the lavish love of God.

The Heart in the Early Modern Age: The Salesian Tradition

The sixteenth century was of course a time of tragic religious conflict in Europe, but also a time of reform and revival, on both the Protestant and Catholic sides. Laypeople as well as clerics and religious had a tremendous interest in both accessible Christian writings and practical Christian living.[11] But they were also interested in exploring the depths of prayer, and the long tradition of the Sacred Heart came to be a central focus of early modern piety. This was largely the result of the spirituality of St. Francis de Sales and St. Jane de Chantal plus, nearly a century later, St. Margaret Mary Alacoque. By the time they were done with it, the Sacred Heart had become one of the most universal and important symbols of Catholicism. It sounds like a triumphalist story, and it had its political moments, but in the spirituality of its proponents, the Sacred Heart is really a story of the tenderness and sacrificial love of God.

Saint François (Francis) de Sales (1567–1622) was born into an aristocratic Catholic family in the French province of Savoy. Educated by the Jesuits, he was, like Martin Luther, intended by

11. Wendy M. Wright, *Heart Speaks to Heart: The Salesian Tradition* (Maryknoll, NY: Orbis, 2004), 24. I am indebted to this book for much of what follows in this section.

his father for study of the law, an impressive legal career, marriage, and worldly success. Like Luther, however, Francis took his studies and vocation in a religious direction, and he subsequently had a crisis of faith in which he despaired of his own salvation. Francis' image of God was strongly shaped by the Song of Songs: God as lover in fervent pursuit of the beloved. And yet the notion of predestination in Augustine and Aquinas painted a very different picture, leaving him in grave doubt, not only about the state of his own soul, but also about how to reconcile such dramatically different understandings of God.

The crisis was resolved when Francis settled on a theology that placed the love and mercy of God, and God's desire that all might be saved, at the center. He envisioned a "world of hearts," based on the premise that God is love. The heart of God seeks union with human hearts; once this is accomplished, the human soul "in imitation of the beloved disciple, will repose with complete confidence on the lovable breast, actually *in the loving heart*, of the Loving Savior."[12] This union with the very source of love transforms disciples so that they become, as intended, channels through which that divine love flows. Far from an individualistic "Jesus-and-me" piety, Francis insisted that "whoever has Jesus Christ in his heart will soon have him in all his outward ways."[13]

Francis de Sales became a priest and, in his thirties, bishop of Geneva—by then, a Protestant stronghold. One of the distinctive features of his ministry was that he was an exceptionally generous spiritual advisor. He carried out an extensive correspondence, offering guidance to rich and poor alike. In a characteristic letter to one Madame de Veyssilieu, written in 1619, he gave the following counsel:

> Do not think about what will happen tomorrow, for the same Eternal Father who takes care of you today will look out for

12. Quoted in Wright, *Heart Speaks to Heart*, 27; emphasis added.
13. Quoted in Wright, 34.

> you tomorrow and always. Either He will keep you from evil or He will give you invincible courage to endure it. Remain in peace. Rid your imagination of whatever troubles you.[14]

It's still excellent advice, and the kind of thing that attracted the attention of Jeanne-Françoise (Jane) Frémiot, Baroness de Chantal (1572–1641). Born in Dijon in the French province of Burgundy, Jane's father was in the Parliament of Burgundy; her mother died when Jane was just eighteen months old. At twenty-one, she entered into a warm and loving marriage, but at twenty-eight, her husband was killed in a hunting accident.

The distraught young widow was invited by her father to return to Dijon for a series of sermons to be delivered by Francis de Sales. Like Francis and Clare of Assisi, the two quickly became soul friends and remained close until Francis' death in 1622. Jane survived him by nineteen years, and was eventually buried beside him. Francis served as Jane's spiritual director, but their relationship was essentially collegial, and they collaborated on a great project that was close to both their hearts: the founding of a new religious community based on the spirituality of the Sacred Heart.

When she was widowed, Jane longed to throw herself into the service of God with the same passion with which she'd loved her husband. But she had four children to consider, and a religious vocation would have to wait until she was nearly forty. Her living situation, in her father-in-law's irregular household (which included a mistress and "illegitimate" children), was not her first choice, but she would have to see her own children settled before she could move on. During this time, her formation in the way of the Heart continued, and ultimately she and Francis would realize their shared vision of a community that would become, in Jane's words, "a tiny kingdom of charity":[15] the Order of the Visitation of Holy Mary.

14. Quoted in Wright, 25.
15. Quoted in Wright, 52.

The Visitation was a creative and flexible alternative to existing monastic options. It filled a need for women not suited either to the enclosure or the mission field, but who sensed a call to a deep love of God and neighbor. Indeed, it was such a good solution to the existing demand that by Jane's death, the number of Visitation communities had grown to eighty-six.

There was no enclosure, no solemn vows (only simple vows to be renewed annually), no getting up in the small hours, and minimal fasting. There was enough solitude for prayer, but members were also expected to practice the little virtues of charity, both within the Visitation community and with their immediate neighbors. There was even provision for married women to join temporarily for a bit of spiritual respite.[16]

It was a gentle way; in fact, gentleness (*douceur*) was a virtue particularly claimed by the Visitandines. As Jane, the first superior, put it to another leader in the community:

> In the name of God, my dear daughter, wait for the improvement of these good sisters with great patience, and bear with them gently. Treat their hearts affectionately, making them see their own faults without undue emotion or strong feelings or harshness, but so that through your help they will be encouraged . . .[17]

The Visitation was a place for women who had great love, but not necessarily great stamina or spiritual ambition, those who might not be physically or otherwise up to life in a highly rigorous and ascetic order. In fact, the Visitation was not meant to be an order at all, but once they expanded outside Bishop de Sales' diocese, they were forced to become an order: there would be enclosure, and there would be solemn vows. Yet they still managed to retain their charism, and they continued to accept women who were

16. Wright, 49–50.
17. Quoted in Wright, 56.

disabled or elderly and thus unqualified for more traditional monastic communities.

Salesian spirituality is above all the way of the heart. It comes from, and brings us back to, the Trinitarian God who is inherently relational. The God who is utterly One in the love that unites three divine Persons created us specifically to participate, to be caught up, in that loving union. How do we get there? The heart that is both human and divine becomes the way of entry into the current of love flowing between the Persons. The heart of Jesus is the place where we can "jump in"; from there, love will carry us forward.

It's important to recognize that the Salesian notions of "heart" and "love" are not romantic fancies. However sentimental Sacred Heart imagery would eventually become, when Francis and Jane spoke of the heart, they did not primarily have emotions in mind. Their idea of love is more consistent with that of Thomas Aquinas: "[F]or Aquinas to love means to consistently will and choose the good of the other. To love neighbor as self means seeing their sharing in the good as constitutive of your own sharing in the good."[18] That means that all the "mystical" sighs and raptures in the world are pointless if they just end in personal emotional thrills.

They have to lead us to action, a point we'll return to in chapter 7. The love of God may begin in intimate contemplation, but if it's genuine, it will not end there. A union of hearts, an exchange of hearts with Christ, means that the Jesus whose heart ignites our own is the same one who gave his life for the world. The heart of Christ is not divided. You can't choose union with the part that builds up your true self without the part that pares away your false self. Any notion of a union with Christ that doesn't produce the fruit of self-emptying care for one's neighbor is delusional. God's heart is the soul's refuge, but from there the soul reaches out. After all, the visitation was Mary's *meeting* with Elizabeth: she left home to be with her kinswoman, to share the experience of unexpected

18. Tom Neal, "To Will the Good of the Other," *Word on Fire* (blog), February 24, 2016, accessed May 12, 2020, https://www.wordonfire.org/resources/blog/to-will-the-good-of-the-other/18268/.

life within. Mary didn't stay home and hoard the experience of the divine touch to herself. And the fruit of it was that the "prophet of the Most High" leapt for joy in Elizabeth's womb when he *met* the Most High himself (see Luke 1:76, 44).

The story is all about *relationship*. It's about love:

> The mystery of the Visitation for Jane and Francis summed up all the Christian mysteries, and as such it was first and foremost a mystery that expressed the dynamics of love. As divine love is ecstatic and communicative, pouring itself out into creation and drawing creation back to itself, the divine action in the world might be seen as a lover's visitation. Since love wants to be shared, it likes to visit.[19]

For Visitandines, to follow Jesus is to love, with gentleness and humility: "Take my yoke upon you, and learn from me; for I am gentle and humble in heart . . . " (Matt 11:29-30a). It's a simple way, one that seeks to practice small virtues with great love. Yet it is also a way of depth and power. How could it not be, when it begins within the heart of God?

The founders of the Order of the Visitation did a lot to develop the tradition of devotion to the heart of Jesus but, as we've seen, they didn't invent that tradition. Nor were they primarily responsible for spreading it—beyond giving it an institutional home in the growing Visitation community. The Society of Jesus (founded 1534), too, had made the wounds and heart of Christ a focus of devotion, which was also spreading among other religious orders and to the laity. But it was a particular Visitandine and her Jesuit spiritual director who campaigned for universal devotion to the Sacred Heart and who would do much to make it the ubiquitous and powerful Catholic symbol it would become.

Saint Marguerite Marie (Margaret Mary) Alacoque (1647–1690) was a fairly new member of the Visitation community in Paray-le-Monial, in eastern France, when she began having visions of

19. Wright, *Heart Speaks to Heart*, 53.

Jesus and the Sacred Heart. She'd been a deeply pious child and had already experienced visions before entering the monastery in 1671 at age twenty-three. But she was a bit of a misfit, and her profession didn't happen on schedule. Mystical raptures can be inconvenient for others when they occur on the job and lead to neglect of one's duties. Margaret Mary wasn't particularly good, either, at her assigned work in the infirmary. As an ex-nurse, I can sympathize with this: nursing is a tough job. But it seems her sisters didn't hold her in especially high regard.

When she began to have a series of visions involving the Sacred Heart, which were spread over eighteen months, Margaret Mary took them to her superior. Mother de Saumaise was skeptical of the notion that God would choose such an unimpressive nun to promote a new devotion to the Sacred Heart, and she reprimanded Margaret Mary for her presumption. When Margaret Mary collapsed and became seriously ill, however, the Mother Superior began to question her original response and vowed to give the nun's story another chance. Although Margaret Mary survived, she was put through a painful examination by a group of theologians, who concluded that she was delusional.[20]

It wasn't until a new confessor was assigned to the Visitation convent at Paray in 1675, Jesuit Fr. Claude la Colombière, that Margaret Mary found a more sympathetic ear. She told him about three revelations she'd received: in the first, which occurred on the Feast of John the Evangelist, she was invited by Jesus to recline on his breast, as John had done at the Last Supper. There was an exchange of hearts, and a declaration by Christ of his passionate love for humanity in general and Margaret Mary in particular. She would participate in his suffering and be an agent through which his love would be communicated to the world.

20. "St. Margaret Mary Alacoque," *My Catholic Life!*, accessed February 2, 2025, https://mycatholic.life/saints/saints-of-the-liturgical-year/october-17-st-margaret-mary-alacoque/.

In the second revelation, she was told to promote a Mass honoring the Sacred Heart on the first Friday of each month. The third proposed an hour of Eucharistic adoration on Thursday nights, remembering Christ's agony in Gethsemane. A fourth and final revelation was given after the arrival of Fr. Claude, which prompted the annual Feast of the Sacred Heart.

Convinced of the genuineness of these visions, Fr. Claude made a vow with Margaret Mary to take on this mission. In spite of various obstacles, he did write and preach on the Sacred Heart and did much to advance its devotion before dying at age forty-one. Meanwhile, a new and more sympathetic superior was elected, and Margaret Mary's position in the convent improved dramatically. She was made novice mistress, Fr. Claude's writings about the Sacred Heart were read aloud during meals, and chapels dedicated to the Sacred Heart were built within and outside the cloister.

Before long, communal devotion to the Sacred Heart spread to other Visitation houses, and laypeople too were taking it up. Margaret Mary wrote a short book of devotions to the Sacred Heart, which was published posthumously and gained widespread popularity. In time, there would be art, from inspiring to full-on kitsch, there would be churches, and hospitals, and schools named for the Sacred Heart. During the French Revolution, the Sacred Heart became a symbol of conservative Catholicism against the revolutionary forces; later it would be "the standard flown over the late-nineteenth-century church in its reactionary battle against the modern world."[21] While in prison, King Louis XVI of France made a secret vow promising that, if he survived (he didn't), he would consecrate himself, his family, and all of France to the Sacred Heart. In 1899, Pope Leo XIII did Louis one better and consecrated to it all of humankind.

There's a kind of drift going on here, and I wonder if perhaps the mistake lay in taking the Sacred Heart from an expression of intensely felt private love and dedication to a collective act that

21. Wright, *Sacred Heart*, 4.

would not necessarily be heartfelt by all concerned. That kind of variation could occur even within a Visitation monastery. But what does it mean to consecrate a country, or all of humanity, to the heart of Christ? Is it not actually a bit presumptuous to consecrate non-Christians to a symbol of Catholic devotion? What possible significance could it have?

There was, too, a budding transactional quality to the devotion that bordered on superstition: "You do this for God, and God will do that for you." Margaret Mary recorded twelve promises Jesus made to those who were devoted to his Sacred Heart. Some of these ("I will comfort them in all their afflictions") seem reasonable enough, but others get dangerously close to magic (". . . My all powerful love will grant to all those who receive Holy Communion on the First Fridays in nine consecutive months the grace of final perseverance; they shall not die in My disgrace, nor without receiving their sacraments"[22]). Magic is when we imagine we can control God because if we do something, God is bound to a certain action in return. I don't wish in any way to demean the sincere piety of generations of faithful Catholics. But this doesn't sound to me like a Spirit who blows in directions we can't predict or control.

Margaret Mary was canonized by Pope Benedict XV in 1920, while Fr. Claude was canonized in 1992 by Pope St. John Paul II. In the years prior to the Second Vatican Council, Sacred Heart devotions were a regular part of Catholic piety. After Vatican II, however, the whole idea of "devotions" fell out of favor: quaint and old-fashioned, they were part of the dust that the open windows of the council would allow to blow away. The emphasis shifted from popular devotions to a liturgy that was now accessible to the person in the pew. In *Sacrosanctum Concilium*, the very first document to issue forth from the council, the liturgy was identified as "the summit toward which the activity of the Church is

22. "The 12 Promises of the Sacred Heart of Jesus to St. Margaret Mary Alacoque," *Welcome His Heart*, accessed February 2, 2025, https://welcomehisheart.com/12-promises.

directed." Further, "Popular devotions of the Christian people are to be highly commended. . . . But these devotions should be so drawn up that they harmonize with the liturgical seasons, accord with the sacred liturgy, are in some fashion derived from it, and lead the people to it, since, in fact, the liturgy by its very nature far surpasses any of them."[23]

That seemed to put the Sacred Heart in its place. There are always, of course, those who are content to be old-fashioned, and it's not as though Sacred Heart devotion disappeared, especially among older Catholics. But for many in the post-conciliar generations, it doesn't really resonate. In recent years, however, there have been calls for another look at the Sacred Heart. Wendy M. Wright, whose work I've made extensive use of here, is one. Another is James Martin, SJ, known among other things for his advocacy of LGBTQ+ Catholics and hardly a backward-looking figure. Father Martin acknowledges some of the reasons why Sacred Heart devotion has waned: the "kitschy and off-putting" art featuring a "doe-eyed Jesus"; the "yuck factor" of the images of the heart cinched by a crown of thorns and dripping blood; and the "disbelief factor": is the notion of such a frail, delicate-looking carpenter remotely credible?

Yet Martin notes that "It's a tragedy that art has distanced many Catholics from a powerful way of looking at Jesus."[24] I would add that a second tragedy is that, in Wright's words, "The Sacred Heart is such a Catholic thing."[25] It's a great pity that Christians outside the Roman church are mostly not introduced to this powerful symbol that *links our poverty to our belovedness in Christ*. The Sacred Heart is an old and multivalent symbol: it's rich and complex, with many layers of meaning. Now that we've traced its history,

23. *Sacrosanctum Concilium* 10, 13, December 4, 1963, accessed May 20, 2020, https://www.vatican.va/archive/hist_councils/ii_vatican_council/documents/vat-ii_const_19631204_sacrosanctum-concilium_en.html.

24. James Martin, SJ, "Reviving the Sacred Heart," *America: The Jesuit Review*, June 15, 2012, accessed May 20, 2020, https://www.americamagazine.org/faith/2012/06/15/reviving-sacred-heart.

25. Wright, *Sacred Heart*, 42.

let's turn our focus to the heart itself, examine its contours, and see how it might help us make sense of Jesus' statement that it's the poor in spirit who are "blessed."

Thorns and Wounds and Blood and Fire

If you do a Google image search on "Sacred Heart," you'll find a lot of variation in how the heart has been represented. Often, it's the blond, sappy-looking Jesus pulling aside his cloak to reveal an anatomically incorrect heart outside his tunic. The heart emits rays of light, is surrounded by a crown of thorns, and has flames coming out the top, surmounted by a cross. It looks a bit like a red, upside-down artichoke. Alternatively, the heart is completely disembodied. Early versions, from the High Middle Ages, tended to show the heart with the instruments of the crucifixion: the nails, the crown of thorns, but also the lance and the soldiers' dice. The pierced hands, feet, and side were often included as well.[26] It might be surrounded by saints and angels. Most later versions are somewhat simplified, but the basic components seem to be the heart itself; the crown of thorns, often with drops of blood; and flames. Even the most streamlined versions nearly always have some version of thorns and flames.

Let's go through these components and see what they have to say to us about the heart of the God who is love. Perhaps the most immediately noticeable feature of the Sacred Heart is that it's surrounded, and pierced, by the crown of thorns. It's bleeding. This obviously calls to mind the passion, the uniquely Christian idea of a God who assumed human flesh, walked among us, and submitted to the worst things humans could find to do to him. We know that crucifixion was physically agonizing: the piercing of hands (or wrists) and feet, the struggle for air, hauling one's body up on the nails in order to draw breath, the final asphyxiation when the body was too weak to continue. All of this under a hot sun, and

26. Wright, 18.

sometimes the birds didn't wait until death to peck at the eyes. The total vulnerability of arms pinned down. The human spectators during the day; the circling dogs at night.

We know all of that, but I think we often focus on the physical misery to the exclusion of the emotional. In Jesus' case, of course, we know he felt abandoned by his Father. That most intimate of relationships seemed to fall away at the very moment when he felt the greatest need of it. But I wonder if we consider the utter humiliation that crucifixion imposed? We realize that passersby mocked Jesus as he hung there, because the gospels record it. But consider the shame of hanging there naked. Public nakedness was abhorrent to the ancient Jew. To strip Jesus of his clothing was to strip him of his dignity. Christian art tends to cover up this fact, along with Jesus' genitals, by giving him a loincloth. We don't have conclusive evidence about this, so opinions differ. But the Romans used crucifixion not just to execute, but intentionally to humiliate. Regardless, consider that crucifixion went on for hours or days, and there were no bathroom breaks. Blood and sweat, urine and feces—it wasn't a pretty sight. Add to that the betrayal and abandonment of his friends, the miscarriage of justice by the authorities, and the mocking and torture of the soldiers that preceded the crucifixion itself, plus the sense of utter spiritual desolation, and we begin to get the picture. The part we can't begin to get is whatever was involved in the battle to defeat sin and death. Maybe we'll get that story later.

So the first thing the Sacred Heart tells us is that the God who endured all of this, the God who is love, was willing to go to the last extremes of human suffering to bring us back into relationship, back to our place in that swirling current of love that flows within the Godhead. There are plenty of theories of how exactly that worked: Paying a ransom? Substituting himself for us and taking the suffering in our place? Descending all the way down to us at our lowest so he could draw us back up with him? My own sense is that the atonement is such an immense and complicated mystery that no one "theory" can capture it. They're all reasonable views from different angles, and all find some basis in the Scriptures. But all views are limited.

As an aside, the idea that "substitutionary" theories make God the Father into an abusive parent who's in such an unholy snit that he has to take it out on someone, so he sends his innocent son in for us and beats the crap out of him—that idea fails to take the doctrine of the Trinity seriously. God is one, with one will, and when Jesus hung on the cross, God hung on the cross. Yes, Jesus speaks of himself as "sent" by the Father. But he also says, "The Father and I are one." The divine Persons are not divided, and they don't beat the crap out of each other; God is love. And there is substitutionary language in the New Testament; for example, "He himself bore our sins in his body on the cross" (1 Pet 2:24). But any faithful story of substitutionary atonement is a story of love, not abuse. If any of our attempts to understand what God is up to are not consistent with love, then we've got them wrong, and we need to start again.

But back to the Sacred Heart. It's a wounded heart; in fact, it's a broken heart. A heart torn open: Jesus is torn open at his very core (*cor* is Latin for "heart"). In this image, we are shown a heart that is accessible, vulnerable. When artists depict Jesus drawing his cloak aside to reveal it, it's a heart that is *offered*, an invitation. In Jesus, God willingly becomes vulnerable: extending an invitation and giving us the freedom to refuse it.

This choice just seems bizarre; what could motivate it? God needs nothing from us; we weren't created because God was lonely. The Trinity is complete in itself. This is good news, though, because it means that God's pursuit of us is never motivated by self-interest. We've been given the power to wound God's heart—because to love is to give away that power—not because God needs us, but because God has *chosen* to long for us, and to be wounded when we refuse the invitation. It's a choice God made in absolute freedom out of a pure, self-giving love.

It's a costly love: we're reminded of that by the drops of blood. But they also remind us that it's a life-giving love. The idea that the life force dwells in the blood was established in the Hebrew Scriptures long before Jesus was born: "For the life of the flesh is in the blood" (Lev 17:11a). This is a love that's willing to give everything to deal with the wreckage we've made of ourselves, of each other, and our world—because we are the beloved.

The association of blood in Leviticus with life and atonement suggests that blood carries both physical and spiritual life. The latter, of course, points us toward the Eucharist: as Jesus said in the synagogue at Capernaum, "Those who eat my flesh and drink my blood have eternal life, and I will raise them up on the last day" (John 6:54). It was a "difficult teaching" then, and it's still pretty mysterious today. But besides the Jewish tradition of locating life in the blood and associating blood with sacrifice, it's basic to Christian sacramental theology that God uses material things to do spiritual work.

Yet the theology of all this is not what matters most here. The point is that when we contemplate the Sacred Heart, the blood reminds us of the incalculable price paid to give us life. And it was paid because in Jesus, the God who needs nothing nevertheless longed for us so deeply that he considered us worth that price. Not just all of us, but *each* of us. As St. Augustine said to God, "You are good and all-powerful, caring for each one of us as though the only one in your care," or in Marilynne Robinson's paraphrase, "God loves each of us as an only child."[27] It's a deep love, a costly and particular love.

One aspect of the heart is less affective and more cerebral: in addition to the blood and flames, portrayals of the Sacred Heart usually show it emitting rays of light. "I am the light of the world," Jesus said. "Whoever follows me will never walk in darkness but will have the light of life" (John 8:12). Jesus is the light that illumines everything else. That light makes clear what is obscure; it

27. Both quotations in Lisa Deam, "What I Wish St. Augustine Had Said," February 19, 2015, accessed May 22, 2020, https://lisadeam.com/what-i-wish-st-augustine-had-said/.

also reveals things we might prefer to keep hidden. We are commanded to love God with our minds as well as our hearts, and intellectual sloth is as bad as any other kind.

By the early modern period, however, priority was more firmly on the affective side: on the emotions and the will.[28] This emphasis was not limited to the Roman Catholic Church but found its way into Reformed churches' thinking as well. Devotion to the heart of Christ, and emphasis on "a personal, *heart-felt* relationship with God through Jesus Christ,"[29] remains prominent among, for example, members of the Moravian Church (founded 1457), the first of whom were followers of the early Czech reformer Jan Hus (1369–1415). In the eighteenth century, the Wesley brothers, who'd begun as Anglican priests and later founded the Methodist movement, both spoke the language of heart devotion. John Wesley famously described a conversion experience as feeling his "heart strangely warmed," and Charles Wesley wrote exquisite, highly affective hymns like "Jesus, Lover of My Soul." Another hymn, by Bianco da Siena, speaks directly to the passionate desire of God's heart for ours, and ours for God's:

> Come down O Love divine
> Seek Thou this soul of mine
> And visit it with thine own ardour glowing.
> O Comforter, draw near;
> Within my heart appear,
> And kindle it, thy holy flame bestowing.[30]

The Sacred Heart is a heart *on fire*. The flames tell us that this is a God who is "all in," who holds back nothing, who loves us

28. Wright, *Sacred Heart*, 63.

29. "Who Are Moravians?," *The Moravian Church*, accessed May 27, 2020, https://www.moravian.org/2018/07/who-are-moravians/ (emphasis added).

30. "Come Down, O Love Divine," *Hymnary.org*, accessed November 26, 2024, https://hymnary.org/hymn/HPEC1940/376.

unreservedly, fervently, unconditionally. Think of what it means to be loved infinitely by a God who *is* love. This God is omniscient, so cannot be disappointed by us. Omnipotent and unchanging, God cannot be worn out, isn't subject to moods, doesn't get bored, or like us one day and not the next. I've spent over twenty years meditating almost exclusively on what it means to be loved like that, and I can tell you that it changes everything. It has the power to transform us at our very *cor*, a transformation so deep and so powerful that mystics through the ages have described it, as St. Catherine of Siena did, as having Christ exchange his own heart for theirs. "The Sacred Heart," as David Richo has said, "is the ring of flames God places on our finger after the courtship of the ages."[31]

But we are made in the image of God, so to gaze into the heart of Christ is to see something of our own heart, our best and most authentic self. We too are capable of passionate, joyful self-abandonment and painful self-sacrifice. Although rational, we are capable of loving absurdly, beyond all reason. Recall the story from the desert fathers, in which Abba Lot asked Abba Joseph, "Tell me, what else should I be doing?" And as Abba Joseph stood up, he raised up his hands toward heaven, and his fingers turned into ten jets of flame. His response: "Why not become fire?"

This is what we were made for: to be ignited by the "consuming fire" that created us, like an ember falling off the bonfire and setting the grass around it alight. A friend of mine was recalling that story in her meditation and asked Jesus: "Why can't I become fire?" The answer: "What makes you think you're not fire?" Sometimes the Spirit has already done more of the work of transformation within us than we realize. Of course, there are plenty of times when we show others our brokenness instead. But when we are true to our call, then, in many small, unconscious ways that we may learn about only in the life to come, we shed light and warmth on the dark and chilly corners of the world. When this happens, it's the

31. Richo, *Sacred Heart of the World*, 9.

work of the Holy Spirit, who came with a rushing wind at Pentecost and set the disciples' hair on fire.

Like Jesus, we blaze, but we also suffer: we open ourselves to others, making ourselves vulnerable by issuing invitations they can refuse. We can know enlightenment and offer it to those around us, and they can refuse that too. The exquisite peace in the heart of Christ is indeed a place where our troubled souls can go for respite and renewal. As I suggested earlier, it usually takes some whittling down of our egos to be able to get into that space. But oh, when we do. It is a place where peace is palpable, where you cannot doubt that, as Julian of Norwich said, "All will be well." But if our hearts are mirrors of Christ's, is there a place within us that holds that kind of peace for others too?

Yes, and like union with God and inner transformation, this place of peace is God's work; our job is to find it and settle in. Thomas Merton called it the *point vierge*, the virgin point:

> At the center of our being is a point of nothingness which is untouched by sin and by illusion, a point of pure truth, a point or spark which belongs entirely to God, which is never at our disposal, from which God disposes of our lives, which is inaccessible to the fantasies of our mind or the brutalities of our own will. This little point of nothingness and of *absolute poverty* is the pure glory of God in us. It is so to speak His name written in us, as our poverty, as our indigence, as our dependence, as our sonship. It is like a pure diamond, blazing with the invisible light of heaven. It is in everybody, and if we could see it we would see these billion points of light coming together in the face and blaze of a sun that would make all the darkness and cruelty of life vanish completely. . . . I have no program for this seeing. It is only given. But the gate of heaven is everywhere.[32]

32. Thomas Merton, *Conjectures of a Guilty Bystander* (New York: Bantam Doubleday Dell, 1994), 158; emphasis added.

Merton speaks of a "virgin" point within each of us, but since the church's history of fetishizing virginity is a little disturbing, we might think of it as the "Eden" point. It's the place where all that we were made for remains untouched, innocent, whole. It's never been corrupted, never broken, never touched by evil. It's never been driven by self-interest, never lost sight of its divine Source. In spite of all the rest of what we are, God never looks at us without seeing this primal "virginity," and this is why God doesn't just tolerate us; God loves us, longs for us, longs to be one with us. It's this place at our very core that bears the name *Beloved*, and God's work of restoration aims to bring all the rest of us into line with this still point. When that work is complete, we will be utterly authentic and fully alive. And we will be perfectly aware of our own belovedness.

But notice that Merton calls this glorious place within us a "little point of nothingness and of absolute poverty." Here we see the link between poverty of spirit and our belovedness. The *point vierge* doesn't have layers to peel back. It is perfectly pure and simple, perfectly itself: no adornments, no accessories. "Blessed are the pure in heart," Jesus said, "for they will see God" (Matt 5:8). Poverty is a kind of spiritual, Edenic nakedness. It helps our vision, makes it possible to "see God," because we're not trying to look through layers of veils and masks and other coverings with which we've tried to protect ourselves. As God told Moses, "[Y]ou cannot see my face; for no one shall see me and live" (Exod 33:20). Once stripped down, however, we are at last ready to see God's face and live. One of Elizabeth Barrett Browning's *Sonnets from the Portuguese*[33] contains a beautiful description of this intimate seeing:

> When our two souls stand up erect and strong,
> Face to face, silent, drawing nigh and nigher,
> Until the lengthening wings break into fire . . .

33. Elizabeth Barrett Browning, *Sonnets from the Portuguese* (New York: Doubleday, 1990), 32.

To see God face to face is to *blaze*, to break into fire. It is to answer God's fire with our own, divinely ignited. Why not indeed become fire, when that is what we're made for?

Why is poverty so essential to reaching this point? It's because our poverty is a purifying fire that burns away our accumulated junk. We are like hoarders who live in a splendid house: we can't appreciate or even see the beauty of the place because of the rubbish piled everywhere. If you've ever watched reality shows about hoarding (which typically feature the most dramatic cases), you know it's not a question of simply organizing what's there. At some point, you have to just shovel it out and burn it. Most of us are not particularly eager to submit to the spiritual equivalent of that process. We're attached to our stuff because of fear and a need to be in control, even if that control is purely illusory.

So God allows life to burn away our possessions, often beginning with that very sense of control. Our expectations of life will turn to smoke and ashes. Ambition? Up the chimney. Our children being perfect little replicas of us? Into the bin. And on and on it goes, this process of shedding our attachments, until at last we can stand naked before the God who has called us "Beloved," and *be loved*.

The Sacred Heart at Work

That purifying process will look different in different people, just as what it means to "become fire" will look different. Humans are not mass-produced, and while some people are big bonfires, others become the soothing log on the hearth. They aren't less "fiery"; it's all the same stuff, just built for different purposes. For each of us, it's our job to become the fire that God lights in us, not to despise or envy the fire of another. Fires also have to be kept under control; we've all seen the destruction that wildfires unleash.

Let's get practical for a moment. Controlling our own fire will involve, among other things, life in community and accountability, because people who don't have that end up starting their own cults. Also critical are discernment and commitment regarding the spiritual disciplines and forms of active service to which we are called. Again, the specifics will differ from one individual to the next: some people find the liturgies of Morning and Evening Prayer deeply fulfilling, while others prefer to make it up as they go, or pray the beads, or sit in silence. But some form of prayer is a basic requirement. Some form of accountability, whether sacramental confession or spiritual direction or just regular tea with someone who will tell you the truth, is vital as well. And how can we claim to be pursuing deeper intimacy with the heart of Christ if there's no evidence in our lives of compassion? Love always results in action (more on this shortly), whether that's marching in the streets, donating a kidney, or being confined to bed and praying for the healing of the world.

Going deeper into the heart of Christ will always make us more like Christ:

> Beloved, we are God's children now; what we will be has not yet been revealed. What we do know is this: when he is revealed, we will be like him, for we will see him as he is. And all who have this hope in him purify themselves, just as he is pure. (1 John 3:2-3)

These few words bring it all together: our journey of purification, which is always going to involve some painful letting go and embracing our poverty. The transformative process of seeing: "we will be like him, *for* we will see him as he is." Our belonging and our belovedness as children of God.

Growing into this is a lifelong process. Eventually, we may hope to become spiritual grownups, ready to pull our share of the weight in this family. Maybe at this moment we're spiritual toddlers, just learning to stand and falling over a lot. What parent ever got mad at a toddler for falling? Their goofiness is part of their charm. It's only when they're older and still falling that we start to get concerned. In the same way, God loves us exactly as we are, where we are at this stage in the process. God isn't upset with us for not being further along than expected. Though if we're eighteen now and falling down because we're stoned, that's something that's going to need to change, and God needs our consent to take us through those changes.

This is no ordinary journey we're on; it's a pilgrimage, sometimes dull, sometimes scary, occasionally thrilling, paradoxically exhausting yet energizing. To ponder the Sacred Heart is to look toward the destination and be strengthened for the steps ahead. It's a pity that the Sacred Heart devotion became such a "Catholic thing," and then fell out of favor even among Catholics. Perhaps the time has come to reclaim this image, to pull away the superstition and sentimentality that got draped on it over the centuries and spend some serious time contemplating its depths. For as the Jesuit James Martin has said, "the Sacred Heart is nothing less than an image of the way that Jesus loves us: fully, lavishly, radically, completely, sacrificially."[34] To fix our attention on that love is to fall into the embrace of the God who loves us with infinite tenderness and infinite power.

34. Martin, "Reviving the Sacred Heart."

PART THREE

Collective Forms of Poverty

Chapter 5

Gender, Poverty, and the Question of Authority

Charisma is the gift from above where a leader knows from inside [herself] what to do.

Max Weber

Thirteenth-century Europe experienced a profound spiritual revival in which poverty assumed different forms and took on multiple meanings. Francis of Assisi, *il Poverello* himself, fell hard for Lady Poverty, that personification of his longing for the lowest place. In that low place, his identification with the poor Christ became so complete that the wounds of Jesus' passion were inscribed in Francis' own flesh. Clare shared Francis' uncompromising commitment to radical material poverty, in which this nobly born lady found her highest "privilege."

Elsewhere, pious medievals experimented with different kinds of poverty. The Beguines, a movement of laywomen based mainly in the Low Countries, Germany, and France, lived lives that were simple rather than precarious: economically self-sustaining, their number included businesswomen, tradeswomen, teachers, care givers, poets, and others. They weren't enclosed, took no formal vows, and had only local rules, so they were more independent than either wives or nuns. Beguines were subject to competition from tradesmen, persecution from officials within and outside the church, and suspicion from the public. But the writers among them (most famously Beatrijs of Nazareth, Hadewych, Mechtild of Magdeburg, and Marguerite Porete) left exquisite mystical texts that not only convey something of their own interior experiences, but suggest some of the spiritual priorities of their communities as well. In these texts, poverty is seen in the welcome given to suffering because of its association with the suffering Christ.

Most vividly, perhaps, the Beguines' poverty lay in their longing for God: the thirst that can never, in this life, be slaked. Poverty is, finally, the realization of limitation, of finiteness—ultimately, of mortality. It is the knowledge that the satisfaction of my greatest longing can only come from relinquishing life itself. The Beguines were courageous women, not only in their willingness to face opposition, but because they allowed themselves to need things they had no way to get. In this they identified with the poverty of God, who invites us into relationship and longs for us to accept, while giving us the freedom to refuse.

In this chapter, I want to explore a different type of poverty—namely, one that's group-based rather than strictly individual. Individual-level poverty of spirit can come, as we've seen, from disappointment, failure, loneliness, grief, addiction, and more. But some forms of poverty are collective: they come from membership in a *group* that is socially marginalized. People who are the "wrong" race or religion, the "wrong" gender or sexuality, whose bodies are "different"—all experience a type of poverty that's based on group membership. This means that, whatever their personal achievements may be, they will always carry with them the stigma attached to their group. The Black lawyer who comes to work on the weekend in jeans and a T-shirt, and isn't allowed into the building because he "doesn't look like a lawyer," is an example.

The challenges faced by both Clare of Assisi in seeking the "privilege of poverty," and the Beguines in their unconventional (and un-conventual) mode of living, arose specifically because they were women. The Franciscan brothers instantly got the church's permission to live the very deepest poverty, and men who wished to live in mutually supportive groups while they worked at trades and moved about town as needed would have had no problem doing so. But as women, Clare and her sisters, like the Beguines, had to fight for the right to live out the deepest devotion to Christ in ways that were new and therefore suspect.

Being female in a patriarchal church and society is a group-based form of poverty, in that the most talented and accomplished woman can, purely on the basis of gender, be shut out of various roles. I'm going to examine this from a particular angle: that is, by looking at the interface of competing sources of authority. This may seem like a strange digression, but stay with me. All of the figures we have met so far experienced to some degree the friction that occurs when one whose authority is based in their connection to God confronts those whose authority is institutionally derived. Jesus himself is the ultimate example of this tension, and we know how it played out for him.

But I'd like to introduce a set of fascinating women to illustrate a poverty that is perhaps more subtle than those we've seen so far, but that remains powerful and pervasive to this day. These women, the sisters Gertrude and Mechtild of Hackeborn, plus Gertrude the Great, as well as the Beguine Mechtild of Magdeburg, show us what happens when institutional self-preservation confronts divine gift. Before we get to them, however, let's look at authority itself: different types with their different sources, and the interests and conflicts they create. I hope this will give us some perspective on issues of group-based poverty that are still alive today. The "group basis" in this case is gender, and while we can't make simplistic equivalences between different forms of inequality (race, class, sexuality, and so on), I do think we can learn something from this case about *collective* poverty—that is, the ways group membership can be used to exclude people and voices that God very much wants to include. And I hope to highlight some of the interesting ways God finds to amplify voices we might prefer not to hear.

Power and Authority

"Thy will be done," Christians around the world pray daily, but let's face it: most people, including most Christians, are more interested in "my will be done," however infrequently it actually is. Which individuals and groups in a society are able to get their own way? And where does that ability come from? These questions have preoccupied sociologists from the very beginning, and one of the earliest and still the most influential social theorists to comment on them is Max Weber. Weber (1864–1920) was, along with his fellow German Karl Marx and the Frenchman Emile Durkheim, one of the founding thinkers of the discipline of sociology. Weber's ideas about power and authority formed the basis of much later work, and they are still foundational and will be useful in bringing a certain form of poverty into view.

Weber defined *power* as "the probability that one actor in a social relationship will be in a position to carry out his own will despite resistance, regardless of the basis on which this probability rests."[1] It's being able to get what you want when others don't want it, and Weber identified several ways this can happen. One form of power is *decision-making*: this is simply the ability to control the behavior of others and is a direct and obvious form of power. A police officer who pulls over a driver, a public health official who orders a quarantine, a dictator who suppresses voting: all are wielding power.

A form that's less obvious is what Weber called *agenda control*. This is the ability to determine which issues will even come up for discussion. When the US auto industry prevented the consideration of developing an extensive, nationwide public transportation network, it exercised control over the national political agenda so that this issue never came up for a vote. This kind of power may be more subtle than decision-making power, but it's perhaps even

1. Max Weber, *Economy and Society* (Berkeley: University of California Press, 1978), 53.

more important. If you can keep an issue from ever coming up for discussion, then you're never in danger of losing a vote on it.

Even more potent is what Weber called *systemic* power. This is what you have when the world is essentially set up to serve your interests. If you are a white person, an affluent person, a citizen of a superpower, or otherwise privileged, the world makes it easier (a little or a lot easier) for you to get what you need and want. In short, you have systemic power. More accurately, your *group* has systemic power. For example, consider the ways we punish white-collar vs. street crimes. Corporate decisions that degrade the environment, or business practices with disastrous consequences for the economy, can affect thousands, even millions, of people. These corporations may be punished with fines, which likely won't cause the decision-makers any real suffering. But one addict who holds up a 711 to support his habit can be put away for years.

This isn't the decision of one prosecutor or one judge, or even of a twelve-member jury. It's the *system*, it's how it's set up, which means that members of groups whose crimes are more likely to be of the "street" variety are routinely subjected to harsher penalties than those who commit crimes from their corner offices. So just obey the law, you're thinking, and you won't have to worry about it. Sure, but the point is that the guy in the 711 and the one in the boardroom are *both criminals.* Our criminal justice system is set up to serve the interests of wealthy people, who are also more likely to be white, and whose crimes may harm far more people. And that's before we even consider things like differential access to legal representation and bail, racial differences in the imposition of the death penalty, and the rest. We'll look at these dynamics more deeply in the next chapter.

So power is being able to get your needs met and your wishes fulfilled even over opposition. Naturally, the exercise of power often leads to resentment and instability, especially when that power is seen as illegitimate. Non-whites in apartheid South Africa, like the Jews of Jesus' day, lived in subjection to groups who not only had power, but whose power they also defined as illegitimate. What they lacked was authority. According to Weber, authority also concerns the probability that commands will be obeyed by specific groups, but unlike power, the exercise of authority is seen on both sides as legitimate. The leaders we get through free and fair elections might make decisions we don't like, but we do accept their right to make those decisions because they arrived at their position through a process we see as legitimate. Most of the time.

Weber also identified three forms of authority, and this brings us to the kind of poverty I will focus on in this chapter. First, *traditional* authority is based on long-standing cultural practices whose origins may be lost in the mists of time. Monarchies, patriarchy, the authority of parents over children: these are all forms of traditional authority, and, like most forms, they are tied to what sociologists call "ascribed statuses": being the firstborn son in a royal house, being male, being the parents or guardians. Traditional authority is vulnerable to criticism and delegitimation as social norms change; both monarchy and patriarchy are examples of that. But it has its advantages: a tradition of primogeniture means that the line of succession is unambiguous, and succession can take place without a lot of violence and drama. But there's always the risk that the firstborn may be incompetent: Elizabeth II was admirable, but remember George III?

When the United States decided against monarchy, it centered the government on what Weber called *rational-legal* authority. It's based, as the name implies, on rules and regulations, and is usually accorded on the basis of statuses that are "achieved" rather than ascribed; that is, they are allocated according to demonstrated competence. Degrees, civil service exams, moving up the ranks through a recognized path of advancement, all increase the likelihood that leaders will be competent. And if they aren't, procedures for removing and replacing them are well established. The problem with this kind of rule-based, institutionally centered authority is that it can be rigid, and it leaves little room for genuine talent that takes unexpected forms or comes from unexpected places. "Is not this the carpenter's son?" (Matt 13:55).

When someone like Jesus comes along, with no authority but that generated by his own personal qualities—that is, *charismatic authority*—institutions shudder. Saul of Tarsus had the kind of authority that religious leaders of the day understood: he'd studied, after all, "at the feet of Gamaliel . . . according to our ancestral law" (Acts 22:3). But when Jesus taught in the Temple, the institutional authorities "were astonished at it, saying, 'How does this man have such learning, when he has never been taught?' " (John 7:15)—never, that is, been taught through any process or by any expert they recognized. Jesus' response gets right to the heart of the question: "My teaching is not mine but his who sent me. Anyone who resolves to do the will of God will know whether the teaching is from God or whether I am speaking on my own" (John 7:16-17).

This is the kind of thing that makes institutions, and the humans within them, crazy. It's a spiritual "you'll know it when you see it—if, that is, you're close to God." How can such things be measured? More to the point, how can they be controlled? What made Jesus such a threat was that his authority came from within himself: "You have heard it said . . . but *I* say unto you . . ." Jesus' teaching scandalized religious leaders because "he taught them as one having authority"—that is, his own authority—"and not as their scribes" (Matt 7:29), who taught by citing earlier authorities right back to Moses.

Charismatic figures have no one's imprimatur; they attract a following because their ideas are compelling, or they make a convincing claim to personal connection with the Divine ("The Father and I are one" [John 10:30]). Their followers sense something in them that is the "real deal," and because of that, they may be prepared to do most anything their leader asks. This is why charismatic leaders, who may start out with a small band of family and friends, can quickly find themselves at the center of a movement. And that movement can promote any kind of agenda: Hitler and Mussolini were both highly charismatic figures, as was Martin Luther King Jr. In US presidential politics, both Barack Obama and Donald Trump could be considered charismatic leaders. And most new religious movements are founded by people whose personal gifts (*charismata* in Greek) attract eager disciples.

Charismatic leaders are good at motivating people to get things done, and they can also provide solace to their followers during hard times—whether by assuring them of God's goodness or by blaming their troubles on a convenient scapegoat which they intend to eliminate. Their movements are vulnerable, however, because as Jesus predicted, once the shepherd is gone, the sheep may scatter (see Matt 26:31). This is the "charismatic succession problem": when a charismatic leader dies, the movement that gathered around their personal gifts may disintegrate or drift far from the original vision. There may be no obvious successor, but even if there is, that person probably lacks the ability to generate the kind of excitement stirred by the founder—whose gifts, after all, are rare by definition. An example of this is Thabo Mbeki, groomed to follow Nelson Mandela after the latter's single term as president of a newly democratic South Africa. Mbeki turned out to be a disappointing leader, and his tenure was disastrous to his party and the country.

Institutionalizing Excitement

With new religious movements, the problem is often that there is not only no inspiring successor, but there also may not be enough institutional structure in place to give people a sense of direction when the founder is gone. Jesus held off this problem for a generation by passing his authority to the apostles: "As the Father has sent me, so I send you" (John 20:21). That gave the church time to build a bit of structure, including a mechanism for transferring apostolic authority to future generations. Of course, Christians will also factor the gift of the Holy Spirit into the equation, but I'm sticking to the sociology for now.

In that first generation, we see the earliest versions of what would eventually become the threefold office of leadership: bishops, priests, and deacons. We learn a lot from the New Testament and other early sources about what Christian communities of that era looked like: their worship, evangelizing techniques, dispute resolution, forms of discipline, and so on. In the centuries since, Christians have often looked back on the first-century church as a kind of Golden Age of simplicity, unity, and uniformly Christlike behavior. I'm not sure how that image survives a reading of the New Testament, but there's often a suspicion that if only the church hadn't turned into an "institution," we would have prolonged that Golden Age until Jesus returned.

This is naïve. Once their founder is no longer physically present, a new religious movement must either institutionalize or die. They must establish structures and procedures, not only for the identification of new leaders and the transfer of authority, but also for how all kinds of decisions will be made, how to attract and incorporate new members, and how to disseminate the message. Will there be full-time, paid positions that will free up some members to focus entirely on the movement, and if so, how will they be funded? What kind of influence will go with those positions? All of these questions and more must be decided if the movement is not to fragment and disappear; institutionalization is essential to the survival of a religious movement. And yet, with every step in that direction, something at the heart of the movement dies a little. This is why the twin challenges of charismatic succession and institutionalization are so crucial. The religious movement that doesn't get these right will die, and most of them do.

The tension between what we might call the structure and the fire also creates different constituencies within a movement and tension among them. On the one hand, you have the personnel whose authority is based on their position within the institution: that is, they possess Weber's "rational-legal authority." They have achieved their place in the hierarchy by a recognized process established by the institution itself; consequently, they have a stake in the status quo within that institution. On the other hand, as these people take the movement in the direction of increasingly rigid bureaucracy, the original vision gets lost as the institution itself becomes the priority. When this happens, parties dedicated to recovering that original vision may form. If they don't succeed in pulling the entire movement back, they may form breakaway movements of their own; in time, those splinter movements will likely be tempted to commit to the institution over the mission as well.

We don't have to look far to see examples of this temptation in our own day. Consider the sex abuse scandals plaguing the Roman Catholic Church, in which covering up the most horrific crimes for the sake of institutional self-preservation came to outweigh the church's commitment to protecting the vulnerable. The "least of these" just weren't important enough to risk the careers and reputations of men of consequence. The victims were of no consequence; they didn't register, they didn't matter. In short, they were *poor*.[2] This is just one example; there are plenty to choose from. But it shows that while institutionalization is necessary to the church's survival, when carried to this extreme it becomes idolatry, and it is deeply destructive. The poor Christ, and those who share in his poverty, are pushed aside as the great seek to shore up their positions and the benefits that come with them.

'Twas ever thus. Right from the beginning, in the letter of James, we hear churches being admonished to stop giving special treatment to the rich and stiff-arming the poor (see Jas 2:1-7). In our own day, our discomfort with those who differ from us can cause us to behave in very un-Christlike ways. A friend of mine has an autistic son, and her family was once asked to stop bringing him to church because he was a "distraction." He was sitting quietly with his family, super-focused on whatever he was doing. But the

2. The Roman Catholic Church is by no means the only institution, or even the only church, that has had a problem with the abuse and exploitation of children and vulnerable adults. Indeed, on November 12, 2024, Justin Welby, then archbishop of Canterbury and head of the global Anglican Communion, resigned over just such a failure to pursue complaints against an abuser of young people. But the size and complexity of the Catholic hierarchy have made it uniquely capable of developing structures and cultures that have protected perpetrators and made reform agonizingly slow and difficult.

claim was that others found his appearance "creepy"; as a result, neither he nor his family set foot in that church again.

There are churches that are thoughtful in their hospitality to people with disabilities, and others that build a ramp and call it good. There are churches that are used to being joined for their services by people who live on the surrounding streets, and others whose members would find Jesus' presence in that particular disguise quite unsettling. There are churches that are racially integrated—but let's face it, precious few. And the experiences of people of color in primarily white churches honestly make me wonder how they keep coming back. I could say the same for people whose sexuality or gender identity is considered either downright sinful or at least in really bad taste.

All of these are forms of poverty. Group identities are subject to a kind of centrifugal force that throws anything "different" out to the margins, and marginality of any kind is poverty. A narrow economic definition allows us to forget that, with at least two important consequences. First, while Christians often enough fail to respond with sacrificial love to those in economic need, at least we know we're supposed to. When we don't recognize other forms of poverty *as* poverty, we may take people's needs even less seriously. We dismiss their experiences of prejudice and stigma. We don't notice that an elder's friends have died and they struggle with loneliness and depression. We dismiss a young parent's struggles with childcare because we think we had it harder. We break the second great commandment: not loving our neighbors as ourselves.

Secondly, when we don't understand the multidimensional nature of poverty, we can also fail to name it—and respond to it—in ourselves. When that happens, we miss the opportunity to unite it to the poverty of Christ and find our peace there. Instead, we may live with self-loathing and shame. But often enough, we live with illusions of self-sufficiency, of security and control, failing to see ourselves as God sees us. After Jesus has told the Laodiceans that their lukewarmness makes him want to vomit (see Rev 3:15-16), he continues: "[Y]ou say, 'I am rich, I have prospered, and I need nothing.' You do not realize that you are wretched, pitiable, poor, blind, and naked" (Rev 3:17). The good news is that, even as he delivers this painful reality check, God assures the Laodiceans of his love and of his desire to be close to them: "Behold, I stand at the door, and knock . . . " (Rev 3:20 KJV).

In drawing this distinction between institution-based authority and charismatic authority, my point is that *charismatic authority usually stands in a position of poverty vis-à-vis authority located in institutions*. Those whose only claim to the attention and allegiance of others is their gift and their gut-level appeal tend to be at a disadvantage when up against structures, offices, policies, and procedures, not to mention organizational cultures with their own ways of doing things and their own reasons for doing them. The poet Kathleen Norris once recalled the painful experience of participating as a "resident scholar" in an academic program where she was the lone nonacademic. A poet surrounded by highly credentialed professors, she felt her marginal status acutely. Poets, she noted, have no authority but that which is given them by their readers. Likewise, charismatic religious leaders usually have no authority but whatever their followers find appealing in them.

"You have heard it said . . . *but I say unto you* . . ." To be without credentials in a world where credentials are everything is like speaking in an auditorium where you're the only one without a mic. It's poverty, and for some people, their group membership can make microphones hard to come by. Such was the position of Jesus ("No prophet is to arise from *Galilee*" [John 7:52; emphasis added]—you can almost see the eye roll), and such was the experience of the women to whom he first entrusted the good news of his resurrection: "But these words seemed to [the men] an idle tale, and they did not believe them" (Luke 24:11). The apostles in that moment set a precedent nearly as continuous as the apostolic succession itself. Excluded from preaching and positions of leadership by a church that had little interest in breaking with the patriarchy of the outside world, women have often found themselves not taken seriously.

And yet, the God who created and cherishes them has at times provided the means to amplify their voices, and one of these is through the charismatic authority that is based in mystical experience. Without lofty institutional positions or credentials, women have at times been so convincingly touched by the Spirit that men—at least some men, and sometimes important men—were compelled to pay attention to them. Let's take a look at what mysticism is and how, as a version of charismatic authority, it can present a challenge to the institutional church. Then I'd like to introduce some women from an era in which female mysticism flourished and see how the poverty they began with as women was overcome by their charismatic gifts.

The Mystic Vocation

"Mystic" is one of those words that gets used in different ways, which is not necessarily a bad thing, but it does mean I need to be very clear about how I'm going to use it. Skeptics have been known to say that mysticism "starts in mist and ends in schism" meaning, as far as I can tell, that mystics tend to make it up as they go and consequently create a lot of confusion and trouble. Certainly that's a pattern the religious world has seen time and again, but I'd like us to put cult leaders to one side for now and focus on genuine mystical experience.

I'd like us to, but that's easier said than done since mystical experience is not subject to empirical verification. What makes the visions of St. Catherine of Siena more credible than those of the founders of movements like the Unification Church, Heaven's Gate, and the People's Temple, to name just a few of the more notorious examples? Spiritual authenticity is a judgment call, and it's easy to slip into a kind of facile relativism here, in which what I think is absurd might be "true for you."

Sociology is not in the business of distinguishing between genuine and false religious phenomena; it has to stick to aspects of religious behavior that can be empirically verified. But the church has always taught that private revelations (beyond simple reassurances of things we already know, such as "I created you, and I love you more than you can imagine") must be subjected to a rigorous process of discernment involving consistency with Scripture and those teachings the church has traditionally affirmed, the guidance of recognized leaders and the collective wisdom gained in community, as well as the criterion Jesus offered: "You will know them by their fruits" (Matt 7:20). Admittedly, this kind of discernment is more art than science, but it does take us well beyond making it up as you go.

So what is a mystic? First, let me say a couple of things a mystic is not. A mystic is not necessarily someone who experiences dramatic supernatural phenomena: stigmata, levitation and bilocation, the ability to read thoughts or diagnose souls. These things make for great hagiographies, but they're not common and not central to the mystic vocation. A mystic is not even necessarily one who sees visions, hears locutions, or is swept into ecstasy—though they might be. A mystic could as easily be someone who goes into prayer and experiences nothing at all, but in that "nothing" finds God. The more vivid spiritual experiences are associated with the *kataphatic* form of spirituality, which was the style of Francis of Assisi: everything from receiving the stigmata to playing air violin and dancing before God marks Francis as a kataphatic mystic. The great sixteenth-century Spanish mystic John of the Cross is associated more with the *apophatic* way, the way of silence and "unknowing." God cannot be known; God is ultimate mystery, so the apophatic approach is not to pile up images and analogies to say what God *is* (powerful, infinite, compassionate, merciful); rather, apophatic souls are more interested in shearing away all of that as inadequate, leaving only what God is *not*. Both of these are well-trodden spiritual paths, and they both ultimately arrive at union with God. Neither is better than the other; the important thing is to find the path with your name on it, and follow it.

Mystics come in a wonderful but possibly bewildering variety of styles. So what do they share that makes them all "mystics"?

I'm going to go with a common and fairly straightforward definition: a mystic is one who has an *unmediated* experience of God. Unmediated, that is, by liturgies, sacraments, or clergy—in short, the mystic's experience of God is *direct*. Stuck on a desert island, or perhaps in quarantine, the mystic's spiritual life does not disintegrate, because she or he is watered by the hidden spring, nurtured by God's own hand. And if that's true, then all of us are mystics to some degree. If we're taking our faith at all seriously, we bring it out of church and into our lives outside, where the Spirit continues to guide and strengthen us.

On such grounds, there are those who claim that we're all mystics, full stop. I prefer to add "to some degree" because, while all of us get glimpses, if we're paying attention, of the reality that is unseen, there have always been those for whom that reality is more consistently visible than anything they can see. I've helped lead groups exploring the works of famous mystics, and I've been wonderfully surprised at how many people can immediately describe intense spiritual experiences of their own, which I would certainly call mystical. Of course, people gathered to read and discuss the works of mystics are more likely to report these experiences than a random sampling of church members would be. But these visits to the world behind the veil are not so rare as I might have supposed. Still, I would define mystics as people who don't so much visit that country; rather, they live in it year-round as locals.

Well, what's the point? It's common in contemporary spiritual writing to downplay mystical experience—particularly experience of the kataphatic variety—to brush it aside as unimportant or even a distraction. Some of this is driven by the current popularity of apophatic spirituality over kataphatic: better than anything we might know about God is *unknowing*. But some of it is just good sense. We are cautioned, and rightly so, not to seek *experiences* of God but to seek *God*. I don't need to go through a list of ways we chase positive feelings and avoid negative ones; you will have your own list, and I have mine. In the spiritual life, no doubt there are people who go to God in prayer for the consolations they can find there—that is, for the same reason they might watch a "feel-good" movie or listen to up-tempo music. C. S. Lewis spoke pointedly to this tendency: "I didn't go to religion to make me happy. I always knew a bottle of Port would do that. If you want a religion to make you feel really comfortable, I certainly don't recommend Christianity."[3]

He was right: authentic faith is often a struggle, and the feelings that arise as we face hard truths about ourselves, die to ourselves so as to live sacrificially for others, and confront the fact of our own mortality rather than living in denial? Those feelings can be brutal. And that's before we even get to the brutal feelings that come when God chooses to withdraw any sense of his presence from us. It happens to the best of us—literally to the best of us, as John of the Cross explained. The "dark night of the soul" described by John can feel like an experience of Godforsakenness, but it is actually a sign that God is drawing us closer into a more intimate embrace. Saint Teresa of Calcutta spent years in this desert, and she was hardly on God's B-list. When we cry with Jesus, "Why have You forsaken me?" we need to remember that *we are with Jesus*. Knowing that can console us even when the feelings are at their worst.[4]

John of the Cross is one of those mystics who's seen as kind of a specialist in the darker feelings, while Francis of Assisi, as I've suggested, is one who's associated mostly with joy. Yet Francis knew periods of intense suffering, as we have seen, and John's words are at times exultant:

> What more do you want, O soul! And what else do you search for outside, when within yourself you possess your riches, delights, satisfactions, fullness, and kingdom—your

3. C. S. Lewis, *God in the Dock* (Grand Rapids, MI: Eerdmans, 1970), 58.

4. For a fuller treatment of where the sense of desertion fits into the spiritual journey, and the connection of those desolate feelings to God's invitation to a more intimate relationship, see Susan R. Pitchford, *God in the Dark: Suffering and Desire in the Spiritual Life* (Collegeville, MN: Liturgical Press, 2011).

> Beloved whom you desire and seek? Be joyful and gladdened . . . for you have Him so close to you.[5]

A serious spiritual journey is going to take us to dark places at times. And we need not shrink from those challenges: Jesus cautioned us that if we want to find our life, we must be willing to lose it (see Matt 10:39). But it's possible to overdo this and forget that both desert and oasis are part of God's creation; eventually, most of us will spend time in both, and both will lead us to God. We get plenty of reminders in writings on spirituality that we must be very brave and endure the desert. But to shun the oasis is to reject the gift from God's other hand. Our goal is to *be* close to God, not to *feel* close to God. But if God wants to give us a sublime sense of his presence? To turn our backs on that just strikes me as rude.

Mystical experience, whether it feels good or painful, calls for discernment, not rejection. But why does God give it in the first place? In the Scriptures, an encounter with God is always followed by a call. Moses met God in the burning bush and was commissioned to lead Israel out of slavery in Egypt (see Exod 3:1-12). The prophet Ezekiel opens his book with an account of a wild vision featuring wheels, jewels, fire, a dome, fantastic winged creatures, and "something that seemed like a human form." He sums it up as "the appearance of the likeness of the glory of the Lord," adding that "[w]hen I saw it, I fell on my face, and I heard the voice of someone speaking." And what is he told? "Mortal, I am sending you . . . " (Ezek 1:1–2:3). It's a recurring pattern, and it turns up again in the New Testament, when Saul of Tarsus has a spectacular, life-changing vision of the risen Christ. Jesus tells him, "[G]et up and enter the city, and you will be told what you are to do" (Acts 9:6).

Mystical experience is not given for the sake of the recipient alone. Even if that experience is simply a whispered encouragement

5. John of the Cross, *Spiritual Canticle* I.8, trans. Kieran Kavanaugh and Otilio Rodriguez, rev. ed. (Washington, DC: ICS Publications, 2010 [1973]).

rather than winged seraphim, the visitation is ultimately meant to benefit the community. It's easy to see this when a Moses—or for that matter, a Martin Luther King Jr. ("I've been to the mountain-top")—is going to lead his people to freedom. But what of the mystic who simply lives with a deep sense of the overwhelming fullness of God's love? I know a mystic who lives immersed in the lavish grace and love of God. Despite a pretty rocky start in life, she is simply the most serene person I've ever met. A contemplative who lives simply and quietly, she's not leading any movements. But her whole being serves a purpose that I think is common to many mystics: her total certainty of God's great love is based on what she's experienced herself. It's not secondhand, not something she's read or heard about; she knows it for herself, as certainly as she knows anything.

A person like that is like a light on a garden path: when it's dark, they help us see a little of what's ahead so that we can keep going. When Moses came down from Sinai carrying the tablets of the covenant, "the skin of his face shone because he had been talking with God" (Exod 34:29). The Scriptures often use light to represent the holy: think of Jesus' transfiguration, in which "[h]is clothes became shining, exceedingly white, like snow," adding, with a charming domestic touch, "such as no launderer on earth can whiten them" (Mark 9:3 NKJV). After his resurrection, when the women go to the tomb of Jesus, they find there a pair of angels: "[S]uddenly two men in dazzling clothes stood beside them" (Luke 24:4). In the conversion of St. Paul, we hear that while he was heading to Damascus, "suddenly a light from heaven flashed around him" (Acts 9:3). And when the Lord appeared to John on Patmos, "his head and his hair were white as white wool, white as snow; his eyes were like a flame of fire, his feet were like burnished bronze, refined as in a furnace . . . " (Rev 1:14-15).

In Genesis, light is God's first creation: God projects something of the divine nature into the created order, and before it's over, projects that nature into it yet again by making humans in that same image and likeness. Mirroring God, humans try to bring the divine Light into their own creations. In iconography, that "uncreated" light is represented with gold leaf and is meant to serve as a window into the radiant presence of God. In art, saints, angels, and Christ himself are depicted with a halo representing the luminous quality of holiness. A mystic has experienced that light somehow, perhaps as a sublime radiance or perhaps, as John of the Cross suggested, a "radiant darkness": a light so dazzling that we're left seeing nothing at all. Mystical experience can take a variety of forms, but all are given, like all spiritual gifts, "so that the church may be built up" (1 Cor 14:5).

Mystics give us a glimpse of the great beauty of what we're all hoping for, of the sublime reality that awaits us, but that most of us can only squint at from this side of the veil. Like the high priests in the Jerusalem Temple, they've been invited past it to the side where God's presence is on at full volume. It's an experience that tends to overwhelm the senses: the word "ecstasy" comes from the Greek *ekstasis*, which means "standing outside oneself," outside the state of being in which one ordinarily lives. But the purpose of the gift is never a private spiritual buzz. *Charismata* are given to light the way forward for the whole church, not just the one to whom they're given.

Mystics as Sites of Charismatic Authority

Unfortunately, the church has not always welcomed these gifts. In a community that takes God seriously and needs, at times urgently, to know what God wants, having experience that suggests the ability to communicate directly with God does confer a degree of authority—*charismatic authority*, in Weber's terms. It doesn't take much imagination to envision scenarios where that kind of claim might not be appreciated. Institutional functionaries who have all the credentials and the impressive résumés can easily see mystics—like prophets—as upstarts and interlopers, whose novel messages threaten to overturn their tables and scatter their coins.

Medieval Europe, which did take God and the discernment of God's will seriously, produced a larger-than-historically-average crop of mystics. But it was also a time and place of competing factions: not only the constant skirmishes between rival political units, but also, at the top, the ongoing dispute over whether popes or emperors should have the last word. The emperors figured the popes' job was to stand back and pray while they got on with the business of ruling. Popes argued that as the heavens were higher than the earth, so their authority was higher than that of mere earthly rulers. In this contest over authority, over who had a legitimate right to be heard and obeyed, both sides would have been tempted to dismiss a third party entering the fray with an entirely different claim to authority.

This pattern would hold at all political and ecclesial levels, not just the top. The twelfth-century mystic St. Hildegard of Bingen ran afoul of diocesan authorities when she insisted that a revolutionary, who had previously been excommunicated, should be buried in consecrated ground. Hildegard's authority had earlier been ratified by St. Bernard of Clairvaux, whose own authority as abbot, scholar, and mystic was well established. Diocesan officials wanted the dead man exhumed and moved to unconsecrated ground, but Hildegard defied them, claiming, based on a vision, that he'd died with his sins forgiven. The clergy were unconvinced, and Hildegard's abbey was placed under interdict (no singing of the offices, no Masses, no sacraments). Hildegard stood firm, however, and she finally won the day when she threatened that those who forbid the praising of God on earth will end up in the place where there is no music.[6] When someone, even a woman, with that kind of connection to God made threats, powerful men with different agendas nevertheless felt obliged to listen.

6. Robert McClory, "Hildegard of Bingen: No Ordinary Saint," May 24, 2012, accessed February 3, 2025, https://www.ncronline.org/blogs/ncr-today/hildegard-bingen-no-ordinary-saint; Emily Kittell-Queller, "The Interdict at Rupertsberg," January 8, 2014, accessed February 3, 2025, https://emilykq.weebly.com/blog/the-interdict-at-rupertsberg.

Hildegard was a woman of rare intellectual and spiritual gifts, and she had friends in high places. She's a good example, though, of how charismatic authority can be a challenge to institutional authority within the church context, a theme developed by Hayley Pangle.[7] Pangle notes that in the twelfth and thirteenth centuries, widespread lay experimentation with mystical experience was reasonably well tolerated by the church. The Franciscans and Beguines both got their start during this phase, while Hildegard lived nearer the beginning of it.

By the fourteenth century, an "age of intolerance and repression,"[8] the church tried to seize control of movements associated with mysticism and even eliminate them completely. Pangle identifies three aspects of medieval mysticism that explain the church's unease. First, the fact that mystics felt free to interpret Scripture in creative and unauthorized ways, coupled with their lack of institution-based training and certification, left ecclesial authorities nervous about the potential for heresy. In our time, people often see the whole idea of heresy as something of a joke. But the Enlightenment was still centuries away, and for medievals, like the ancient pagans, orthodoxy was a matter of public security. If heretics could bring on the wrath of God, and that wrath might result in a famine or plague, then heretics were something like terrorists. With this in mind, the church's intolerance becomes easier to understand, but it still created considerable hardship for many of those mystics, who later proved to be entirely orthodox.

The second thing that brought mystics into tension with the institutional church was their claim to visionary and other supernatural experience. It didn't help that the visions reported by

7. Hayley E. Pangle, "Christian Mysticism as a Threat to Papal Traditions," *Grand Valley Journal of History* 11, no. 3 (2012), accessed February 3, 2025, https://scholarworks.gvsu.edu/gvjh/vol1/iss1/3/.

8. Steven Fanning, *Mystics of the Christian Tradition* (New York: Routledge, 2006), 1, quoted in Pangle, "Christian Mysticism as a Threat."

many female mystics of this period had erotic undertones. The fourteenth century saw the beginning of the repression of Beguine communities, but one female visionary who acquired considerable political influence during that century was the Dominican tertiary St. Catherine of Siena.

Catherine came from a large but otherwise ordinary family, though she was anything but ordinary herself. Catherine's visions began at age five or six, and she dedicated her life to God on the spot. Later on, determined not to marry, she went on an extreme fast and cut off her hair. She was using the same strategy Clare of Assisi had more than a century before: a woman with short hair in that society was simply not marriage material, and losing her locks bought her the freedom she craved.

Catherine's piety was troubling to her parents: among other things, she kept giving away food, clothes, and other possessions without bothering to ask anyone's permission. But they did allow her to withdraw to a room in the house that became her "cell." Here she experienced a growing intimacy with Christ that culminated, privately, in the mystical marriage. There was a wedding. There was an exchange of hearts. And there was a ring which, depending on the account you read, consisted of either conventional jewelry or Christ's own foreskin; regardless, it was always invisible to everyone but Catherine. While there have been many accounts of a mystical marriage taking place between a soul and Christ, I don't know that any others have been sealed in quite that form. Somehow I can't really see the risen and glorified body of Christ coming with a supply of extra foreskins. In any case, nuptial imagery made the church uneasy: what to do with all these sworn celibates who seemed to be desiring God with an almost erotic fervor? And it wasn't just the squeamishness that we might feel today; it was also a theological matter: the joining of two in marriage created "one flesh." Could a human becoming "one" with God not lead to trouble? Again, concerns for heresy loomed.

The third reason Pangle suggests for why mysticism was threatening to the medieval church is that the authority women acquired based on mystical experience resulted in an inversion, even a perversion, of gender norms. Conventional gender roles required men to lead and women to follow, passively and demurely. Yet in her short thirty-three years, Catherine of Siena rose from obscurity to become famous, first locally as a visionary and holy woman, and then throughout Europe as one who succeeded in pressuring the pope to return from Avignon to Rome. Catherine's public political influence was certainly not part of the conventional feminine repertoire, but her authority came precisely from her mystical experience.

So, a half-century later, did Joan of Arc's. Once the English got hold of Joan, it was not only her leadership of the French army or her possibly being a heretic or a witch that forced them to execute her. As the record of her trial notes, "The report has now become well known in many places that this woman, utterly disregarding what is honourable in the female sex, breaking the bounds of modesty, and forgetting all female decency, has disgracefully put on the clothing of the male sex, a striking and vile monstrosity."[9] The nerve of the girl.

Joan of Arc was obviously a remarkable case, but there were plenty of women mystics in this era whose holiness, like that of Catherine of Siena, attracted male disciples as well as female. Angela of Foligno (1248–1309) lived near Assisi and became a Franciscan tertiary. Famous for her spiritual revelations, she attracted a community of followers, both men and women. And yet the scribe who recorded her account of her spiritual journey is known to us only as "Brother A." Woman in the limelight, man in the shadows? For many medieval clerics, this just didn't seem right.

For all these reasons, mystics and the authority that comes with their gifts can pose a challenge to those whose authority is conferred by the institution. Charismatic authority is the authority of the poor, of those who don't have the credentials, the titles, and

9. Helen Castor, *Joan of Arc: A History* (New York: Harper, 2015), quoted in Lesley Kennedy, "Why Was Joan of Arc Burned at the Stake?," April 16, 2019, accessed March 31, 2020, https://www.history.com/news/joan-arc-burned-stake.

the weight of institutional culture, traditions, and more tangible resources behind them. (They may in certain circumstances *acquire* those institutional resources, but if so, they get them because of their charismatic gifts.) It's the authority that, like the Spirit, "blows where it chooses, and you hear the sound of it, but you do not know where it comes from or where it goes" (John 3:8). Sometimes that wind is a refreshing breeze, but sometimes it can blow the roof off.

Charismatic and rational-legal authority don't always play well together, and with the material resources mostly on the institution's side, it's easy to see how a mystic like Joan of Arc could end up at the stake. Medieval women, like others on the margins of power, could be rich in spiritual gifts but relatively poor in worldly resources (one of which was "being male"), while their enemies were, as Jesus said, "those who store up treasure for themselves but are not rich toward God" (Luke 12:21). Yet despite their poverty, even in a time of intolerance and repression, many women mystics of that era did manage to find a voice. God found ways to amplify voices that others would have silenced, and as examples of this, I'd like now to introduce a small group of women who show both the tension between charismatic and institutional authority and how, in their very poverty as women, they knew the gracious provision of their God.

The Mystics of Helfta

During the same period of religious revival that saw the beginnings of the Franciscans in Italy and the Beguines in northern Europe, there was a remarkable community of women in the German town of Helfta, just outside Eisleben where Martin Luther would be born. The nuns of Helfta were a Benedictine community; founded around 1229, they'd had a couple of homes before coming to rest at Helfta in 1258 in a monastery given them by two brothers of Gertrude of Hackeborn, the first abbess. By the end of the century, there would be over a hundred nuns at Helfta, most of whom came from noble, wealthy families, and many of whom were very well educated. The house was amply provided for materially; no poverty of the sort Clare was fighting for. It was also a center of intellectual and spiritual activity, with not only a library but also a handful of women highly regarded for their mystical gifts.

The cast of characters can be confusing, because there are two Gertrudes and two Mechtilds. Gertrude of Hackeborn (1223 or 1232–1291/92) entered the monastery at age five, became abbess at nineteen, and remained in that position throughout her life.[10] A pious woman, she experienced a few mystical revelations but was most notable for the way she encouraged the nuns in her care in their learning and their exploration of the spiritual depths. Gertrude's sister, St. Mechtild of Hackeborn (1240/41–1298/99), was really the family mystic. She also entered the cloister as a child—age seven—and while she served the community as cantor, she held no other official position. In middle age, she finally consented to confide an account of her spiritual experiences to two other nuns, who recorded them in Latin as the *Book of Special Grace.*

Mechtild's visions gave special attention to the Sacred Heart of Christ, which she portrayed in lyrical terms:

> As a rose, the Sacred Heart issued streams of fragrant perfume; as a fountain, it flowed with purifying water; as a harp, it resounded with sweet music to the honor of God.[11]

Along with nuptial imagery, in which the soul is the bride of Christ, this was the time when feminine piety especially was focusing on the heart of Christ as well as his wounds. Fiery furnace, bridal chamber, seat of mystical union—the heart was a powerful symbol and center of medieval devotion, as we've seen.

10. "Gertrude of Hackeborn," *New Advent Catholic Encyclopedia*, accessed April 8, 2020, https://www.newadvent.org/cathen/06533b.htm.

11. Jeffrey Hamburger and Susan Marti, eds., *Crown and Veil: Female Monasticism from the Fifth to the Fifteenth Centuries*, trans. Dietlinde Hamburger (New York: Columbia University Press, 2008), 161.

Saint Gertrude of Helfta ("Gertrude the Great," 1256–1301/02) was another who came to the cloister at age five. Like Mechtild, she was known as one of the earliest to write of a devotion to the Sacred Heart:

> O adorable Heart of my Jesus, furnace of Divine Love, receive my soul into the wound
> of Thy most Sacred Passion, that in this school of charity I may learn to make
> a return of love to that God Who hast given me such wonderful proofs of His love.[12]

Gertrude is also famous for her text *The Herald of Divine Love* (also known as the *Revelations*). This includes, among other things, an account of Gertrude's spiritual journey, composed by herself in Latin.

Gertrude served alongside Mechtild as second cantor, and the two were close friends and confidantes, consulting and supporting one another in a relationship that brings to mind the Celtic tradition of the *anamchara* or "soul friend." On one occasion Gertrude, full of wonder at the graces given to her and not wanting her unworthiness to tempt her to doubt, consulted her friend. She asked Mechtild to pray about these great gifts, and Mechtild was granted a vision in which the Lord assured her, "Everything in this soul is green and flourishing."[13] The two friends also served, unofficially, as the principal spiritual advisors to the other nuns at Helfta, and in that role they also served Dominican friars and laypeople.

Finally, Mechtild of Magdeburg (ca. 1207–1282/94) came late to the monastery at Helfta. She'd become a Beguine in Magdeburg in her twenties, and she didn't join the sisters at Helfta until she

12. "Prayers to and by Saint Gertrude the Great," accessed April 21, 2020, https://www.piercedhearts.org/treasures/devotions/to_saints/prayers_st_gertrude.htm.

13. Gertrude of Helfta, *The Herald of Divine Love*, quoted in Wendy M. Wright, *Sacred Heart: Gateway to God* (Maryknoll, NY: Orbis, 2001), 29.

was over sixty years old and in declining health, seeking refuge in a safe community when the Beguines began to come under fire. Most of Mechtild's works, gathered in a text called *The Flowing Light of the Godhead*, were written by her in low German before she came to Helfta. I particularly love the way she moves from the heights of mystical theology to an unpretentious charm:

> Now my German fails me; I do not know Latin. If there is something of merit here, it is not my doing; for there never was a dog so nasty that it would not come if its master coaxed it with a white breakfast roll.[14]

Mechtild's writings were subsequently rearranged and translated into Latin during her lifetime, and later into high German. As you can see from their dates, Mechtild of Magdeburg was at least a full generation older than the other Helfta mystics, and, having spent much of her life as a Beguine, with one foot "in the world," her spirituality differed from theirs. But she was much loved and greatly admired by her sisters, and was cared for by them until her death.

Helfta, then, was a spiritual powerhouse in which a few exceptionally gifted women, who occupied no formal administrative positions, nevertheless emerged as inspiring, charismatic leaders. Their spiritual "styles" differed in some particulars, which we'll explore shortly. But all of them were part of the emerging spirituality of the time, which was lavish, lush, emotionally expressive, and ardently in pursuit of the fullest mystical union with Christ. They found that union both objectively and reliably in the Eucharist, and subjectively in visionary encounters with the divine Bridegroom. As I mentioned earlier, this was a time of emphasis on Christ's humanity, particularly his wounded humanity. Sacramentally, we see this in the Eucharist's increasing centrality in this period.

14. Mechthild of Magdeburg, *The Flowing Light of the Godhead*, translated and introduced by Frank Tobin (Mahwah, NJ: Paulist Press, 1998), 72.

Under Abbess Gertrude, whose own devotion to the Eucharist was intense, the Helfta community received communion often. This practice had not been common before, but it reflected the longing for oneness with Christ that was characteristic of the age.

The piety of the High Middle Ages placed a new emphasis on Christ's suffering, and the desire to be united with that human, suffering Christ could express itself in dramatic ways: St. Francis and the stigmata, St. Catherine and the mystical marriage. And it is in the union of divinity with humanity in Christ, himself the marriage of heaven and earth, that salvation lies. As Carolyn Walker Bynum aptly summarizes it:

> The point of Christ's humanity is that Christ *is* what we are: our humanity is in him and in him it is joined with divinity. We encounter this humanity-divinity of Christ in the eucharist and in mystical union, *each of which is an analogue for the other.* It is symbolized especially in the Sacred Heart. We take refuge in it, drown in it, eat or drink it. It is a lake, a stream, an ocean, a chalice, a cave in the rocks, a nest. The humanity of Christ means that the work of salvation is already accomplished; we need only to unite with (eat or drown in) a union of divine and human that already is.[15]

Eucharist and mystical union are mutually analogous: that is, in both of these, union with Christ occurs. But participating in that union by receiving Communion is a choice, and we can receive as often as we choose—assuming it's available and we're suitably prepared. When we do, we have the church's assurance that we are one with Christ, so that whether we "feel" anything or not, we can trust that assurance. For many mystics, including those at Helfta, the Eucharist also served as the most common setting for ecstatic experiences of union. But those are given at the divine discretion:

15. Carolyn Walker Bynum, *Jesus as Mother: Studies in the Spirituality of the High Middle Ages*, vol. 16 (Berkeley: University of California Press, 1984), 191; emphasis added.

you can't just put "10:30 a.m.: mystical union" on your calendar, and even if something does happen, exactly what happens is a matter for discernment. Still, the "mutually analogous" nature of Eucharist and mystical union explains why, at a time when hunger and thirst for union with the Divine were acute, Eucharistic devotion took on such a central role.

Charismatic Authority at Helfta

The Helfta mystics' experiences of union with Christ, both objective and subjective, were the basis of their authority. Abbess Gertrude was the only one who occupied any church office, and her role was mainly to provide a supportive context in which the others could exercise their gifts. Gertrude of Helfta, Mechtild of Hackeborn, and the elder Mechtild of Magdeburg served in no official capacity, yet all had widely acknowledged spiritual authority, both within the cloister and well beyond it. Did their charismatic authority threaten the rational-legal authority of the clergy? Perhaps, but in significant ways it also supported it. Even more importantly for our purposes, what effect did the relative poverty of their gender have on these women's ability to exercise their authority? Did the church try to silence their voices, and if so, were there ways in which they were amplified in a kind of divine override?

To answer these questions, we're going to need to distinguish between the two younger nuns of Helfta, both of whom entered the monastery as young children, and the Beguine refugee, Mechtild of Magdeburg. The latter was over sixty years old when she came to Helfta, and she had entered the Beguine community at Magdeburg at age twenty-four. And since Beguines followed no universal rule, made no lifelong vows, and were not cloistered, Mechtild's formation was far more influenced by "the world" than was either of the others'. An important result, as Bynum points out, was that Mechtild had absorbed far more of the larger society's conventions regarding gender roles, including stereotypes of women as docile, passive, and weaker physically and morally as well as intellectually, and so on.

These had important consequences for Mechtild's sense of self, as well as her conception of her own vocation and the authority that came with it.

Mechtild left family and friends behind and sought out the Beguine community in Magdeburg precisely because she knew only one person there. She worried that even that one friendship might prove a distraction.[16] She had a strongly penitential bent, and she sought to have her spirit trained toward the suffering Christ like a vine on a trellis, through being lonely, misunderstood, and rejected. There are traces of lowliness and subservience in her sense of herself as a woman that we don't see in the other two. Gertrude of Helfta and Mechtild of Hackeborn were at peace with their roles as spiritual leaders and with the wielding of authority, even to the extent of assuming some aspects of the priestly role such as teaching and counseling. They don't see women as inferior to men, and they don't tend to think of aspects of vocations, such as nurturing souls or meting out discipline, in gendered terms. And while nuptial imagery features in both of these women's writings, they each reign serenely alongside Christ as "beloved queen,"[17] whereas Mechtild of Magdeburg, in her feminine weakness, is a bride who oscillates between tortured insecurity and ecstatic union.

As one to whom Christ speaks, the elder Mechtild has authority, but she doesn't conceive of her own authority in priestly terms. More prophet than priest, Mechtild is plenty willing to criticize the clergy for their corruption and to defend herself against their attacks. She once described a vision in which John the Baptist celebrated the Mass,[18] and was told this could not be true because the Baptist was a layman. In her defense, she suggests that her accuser ("my Pharisee") is a little slow on the spiritual uptake. Painstakingly reviewing John's credentials, she concludes:

16. Carol Lee Flinders, *Enduring Grace: Living Portraits of Seven Women Mystics* (New York: HarperOne, 1993), 47.

17. Bynum, *Jesus as Mother*, 253.

18. Mechthild of Magdeburg, *Flowing Light*, bk. 2, chap. 4, p. 73.

> Was this man really a layman? Prove me wrong, you who are blind! Your lies and your hate shall never be forgiven you without punishment![19]

Mechtild is well aware of the kind of reception she is courting here:

> I was warned against writing this book.
> People said:
> If one did not watch out,
> It could be burned.

God, taking the book from her, offers this reassurance:

> My dear One, do not be overly troubled.
> No one can burn the truth.
> For someone to take this book out of my hand,
> He must be mightier than I.[20]

Mechtild knows that as a woman, and especially one who is so much on her own, she is vulnerable to attack. She finds some security in religious structure and rules, even as she transcends them. But Mechtild's mysticism is like a trapeze act, high and daring:

> Ah, Lord, love me passionately, love me often, and love me long. For the more passionately you love me, the purer I shall become. The more often you love me, the more beautiful I shall become. The longer you love me, the holier I shall become here on earth.[21]

This is perhaps not the voice of someone who's been in the cloister since childhood. But Mechtild knows that the higher you fly, the harder you fall:

19. Mechthild of Magdeburg, p. 262.
20. Mechthild, bk. 2, chap. 26, p. 96.
21. Mechthild, bk. 1, chap. 23, p. 52.

> Now the time has come when some people, who have the appearance of being religious, torment the bodies of God's children and martyr their spirits. For he wants them to resemble his beloved Son who was tormented in body and soul.[22]

When you fall, your suffering unites you to the tormented Christ. This Mechtild wants above all else because she's counting on the poor in spirit being blessed—so she wants to be dirt-poor. The imagery of Gertrude the Great, by contrast, also features nuptial themes but stresses the soul's regal nature and the beauty of creation. Even her devotion to the wounds of Christ is less about suffering and sacrifice than about intimacy and union.[23] Mechtild of Hackeborn also imagines the soul as bride of Christ, and in one vision Mary, as her mother-in-law, scoots over to make a place for Mechtild next to Jesus. No tortured lover here; Mechtild, like Gertrude, reigns with her spouse and is secure in her role not only as bride of Christ but as spiritual advisor to others.[24]

Both of the younger Helfta nuns have a sure-footedness about them; their style is serene and confident, whereas the elder Mechtild is passionate in her ups and downs, a difference that Bynum connects to their biographies. The Helfta nuns had the security of living from earliest childhood in an established, financially and politically secure female community. Here gender stereotypes from the outside culture could be beaten back by highborn women of exceptional learning. Mechtild of Magdeburg grew up in the world. As a Beguine, she lived half in and half out of it in a quasi-religious way of life that was always unprotected and came under increasing suspicion and attack over the course of her lifetime.

Further, Mechtild, in common with other Beguines, intentionally sought out poverty and vulnerability. Where the younger mys-

22. Mechthild, bk. 1, chap. 25, p. 52.
23. Bynum, *Jesus as Mother*, 191–92.
24. Bynum, 213.

tics confidently took what they saw as their rightful place reigning at Christ's side, Mechtild of Magdeburg was a "mere woman," but in fact her lowly status and desolation were the very reasons Christ chose her. As bride of the King, she was more ardent than regal, more passionate than serene. But she was chosen, not in spite of her poverty, but because of it. Her sense was that the vocation of women was actually superior in one respect: precisely because women *are* different, are "other," their call is to be God's spouse. The "otherness" of women may be their poverty, in that it bars them from serving as priests. But it is also their treasure, in that it suits them for the complementarity that Mechtild would have seen as characteristic of the married state. That state of union with Christ is blessed beyond measure in itself, but it also gave her the authority to call out male clerics when they failed in their own role. This, she knew, put her in danger. When the danger became too great, she found safety in a community of "mere women" whose own authority was based not in church offices but in the strength of their charismatic gifts.

Gender, Poverty, and the Mystic's Authority

The thirteenth century was a time of intense religious fervor in western Europe, but it was also a time of growing clericalism within the church. More and more women were seeking a life of total dedication to Christ, but they found that opportunities for living out that dedication were not keeping pace with the demand. Options for a traditional religious vocation were dwindling, and in any case were mostly reserved for women who could bring a handsome dowry with them. For those with gifts of preaching, teaching, and the "cure of souls," clerical status was where the action was. Since that status was closed off to women, those who otherwise would have made effective spiritual leaders found themselves spiritually "dressed up" with no place to go.

And yet, God makes a path in the desert. As Bynum puts it: "[T]hese nuns derive their authority vis-à-vis others not from office but from their mystical union with Christ."[25] Precisely at a time when "office" was becoming increasingly important, an alternative way opened up. Bynum continues:

> [M]en and women were coming to value more and more certain religious roles and activities that women were more and more unable to fill. For the nuns of Helfta, Christ himself solved the dilemma. He gave them an authorization to do and be much of what contemporaries understood by evangelism, and his authorization was far more direct and final than any office or tradition could be.[26]

All three of our Helfta mystics accepted their God-given authority, which was also accepted as legitimate by others, at a time when men had a near-monopoly on both authority and power. Gender was normally a liability for women seeking influence in both ecclesial and secular settings. In short, their lack of access to rational-legal authority was their *poverty*. As women, they were shunted to the margins and their voices muffled by cultures and institutions that were formed by patriarchal assumptions. The sisters at Helfta overcame their impoverished status in part because they had other resources: education, noble family origins and ties, and the solidity of a community of women organized around a traditional monastic rule. Our Beguine was pretty well educated, but she had none of the rest of these advantages and indeed sought poverty for its own sake.

For all of the Helfta mystics, however, gender was a form of poverty. Yet it was also their advantage, because the Spirit provided another authority based in mystical union, union of a kind that was more commonly given to women at that time. Their very poverty itself was blessed in that, as Jesus had promised, theirs was the kingdom of heaven. It was theirs because the King had made each of them his bride, his beloved, in a union "more de-

25. Bynum, 249.
26. Bynum, 251.

lightful than priesthood."[27] This was saying a lot at a time when the sacraments, particularly confession and the Eucharist, were increasing in importance, because these made the priesthood more important. Did the authority of our women mystics pose a threat to clerical authority?

The potential was there—otherwise, Mechtild of Magdeburg would not have needed to defend herself against "blind Pharisees" and would not have needed to seek the safety of Helfta in the first place. The church was worried about heresy, particularly heresy coming from women, who might fall into it through either depravity or ignorance. Our Helfta nuns largely evaded this problem, and eventually became "*Saint* Gertrude the Great," and "*Saint* Mechtild of Hackeborn. Mechtild of Magdeburg lived more on the edge and dared, on the strength of her charismatic authority, to denounce corrupt clerics. She was never canonized, and her writings never became part of the "canon" of mystical texts—though perhaps with renewed attention in our day, they might be.[28] Her poverty was deeper, and her threat to institutional authority was greater.

In fact, all three mystics were orthodox to the marrow. The spirituality of all three was deeply rooted in the sacraments, especially the Eucharist, which meant they could hardly dispense with the institutional church or its functionaries. Even when Mechtild of Magdeburg chastised corrupt priests she did so because, like the younger nuns, she held the priesthood in such high regard. It pained her to see anyone who functioned *in persona Christi* dishonoring such a noble call.

The mystics who spent their lives in the Helfta cloister grew up in a community of women, led by women, where women were scholars and intellectuals as well as mystics. As nuns, their withdrawal from the world shielded them to a degree from the world's disdain for women and its interest in silencing their voices. Yet as

27. Bynum, 209.

28. Flinders, *Enduring Grace*, 45–56.

Elaine Heath argues,[29] the church has always spoken most authentically from the margins, and at times even the church itself has recognized this. The church is a human institution, full of flawed people with their own agendas. Yet the heart of Christian teaching is a rejection of worldly values, and because of this, sometimes those who speak from the margins—from their poverty—find an audience. When their voices are amplified by gifts that are the fruit of union with Christ, of unmediated experience of God, then those on the margins, whether because of gender, race, social class, disability, or any other status, can find themselves with an authority that simply blows in on the breath of the Spirit, and can no more be stopped than the wind.

29. Elaine Heath, *The Mystic Way of Evangelism: A Contemplative Vision for Christian Outreach* (Ada, MI: Baker Academic, 2017).

Chapter 6

Racism

The Poverty of Peoples

People know about the Klan and the overt racism, but the killing of one's soul little by little, day after day, is a lot worse than someone coming in your house and lynching you.

Samuel L. Jackson

In 1992 political scientist Andrew Hacker wrote of *Two Nations: Black and White, Separate, Hostile, Unequal*,[1] and it seems that today, more than thirty years later, that is still an apt description of American society. We live with such dramatically divergent perceptions of the world around us that they constitute fully different realities. For example, an NPR/Ipsos poll conducted in August 2020 found that while over 80 percent of Black Americans believe that white people enjoy advantages over others in the United States,

1. Andrew Hacker, *Two Nations: Black and White, Separate, Hostile, Unequal* (New York: Scribner, 2003).

only 49 percent of white Americans agree.[2] A 2011 study[3] even found that 30 percent of whites believe they've been the victim of racial discrimination, and that as discrimination against Blacks has declined, it has been overtaken by discrimination against whites.

Are they right? Let's take a look at how Blacks and whites are faring in the United States. There are obviously many other groups within and outside the US with histories of racial conflict. But I'm going to focus on the situation of African Americans for several reasons. First, because one chapter in one book cannot possibly say anything meaningful about, or do justice to the experiences of, multiple racial groups in multiple settings. Second, the Black/white divide is so old, so deep, and so intense that it forms a defining feature of American history and culture. Third, at nearly 14 percent, African Americans are exceeded only by Hispanics and whites in their share of the US population.[4] Further, the fact that Blacks are a heavily urban/suburban population makes them highly visible and, for many white Americans, threatening.

Finally, one of the key institutions that has helped African Americans endure and survive the overwhelming poverty of racism through the centuries has been the Black church.[5] As Cornel West has argued,[6] the Black church was one of the most important "buffer institutions" that prevented African Americans from slipping into nihilism and despair. The church also served as a key resource and institutional network during the Civil Rights Move-

2. Ipsos, "White and Black Americans Far Apart on Racial Issues," August 27, 2020, accessed April 6, 2023, https://www.ipsos.com/en-us/news-polls/npr-racial-inequality-issues.

3. Michael I. Norton and Samuel R. Sommers, "Whites See Racism as a Zero-Sum Game That They Are Now Losing," *Perspectives on Psychological Science* 6, no. 3 (May 2011).

4. US Census Bureau, "Quick Facts," accessed April 29, 2023, https://www.census.gov/quickfacts/fact/table/US/PST045221.

5. Henry Louis Gates Jr., *The Black Church: This Is Our Story, This Is Our Song* (New York: Penguin, 2022).

6. Cornel West, *Race Matters* (New York: Vintage, 1994).

ment of the 1950s and '60s, and West shows how the decline of the church has been a loss to Black communities. But out of the *poverty* imposed by white supremacy has come a soul-preserving *theology of Black liberation* which, in the words of its founder James Cone, "sees God as concerned with the poor and the weak."[7] In short, it affirms their belovedness. In this theology, voices that might have been silenced speak authoritatively from within Black experience; they are speaking truth to power. They bring the authentic gospel, not only to African Americans themselves, but to all of us—especially those of us whose vision of Christ's teaching has been distorted by years of white supremacy.

I don't want to be misunderstood here. In no way am I saying "It's just as well that Black people have been oppressed, because something good came out of it for the rest of us." No amount of good could ever justify the suffering that African Americans have endured. Nothing can ever make it "just as well." But God is infinitely powerful and brings healing where no healing is possible, or even imaginable. As the risen Christ shows us, even one who triumphs over injustice, torture, humiliation, and a hideous death comes back . . . but with scars. Nothing will ever erase or efface these scars, nor will anything ever undo the cruelties and injustices inflicted on those whose blackness reflects the image of God. But Black liberation theology speaks the truth about them, and that is a step toward healing and a sign of indomitable spirit, even in the face of the worst of human malice, evil, and indifference.

The Steps Ahead

In this chapter, I want to show how the experience of living with centuries of systemic racism, which continues to this day, is a form of *collective poverty* experienced by African Americans—and not

7. "Black Liberation Theology, In Its Founder's Words," NPR's *Fresh Air*, March 31, 2008, accessed April 30, 2023, https://www.npr.org/2008/03/31/89236116/black-liberation-theology-in-its-founders-words.

just material poverty, but poverty broadly defined. I'll begin by showing how I can justify saying racism "continues to this day," and what white supremacy, which is often misunderstood, actually means. Next we'll look at how Black liberation theology, as well as womanist theology, which focuses on the experience and perspectives of Black women in particular, appeared in this context. In these theological movements, we'll see once again the paradox of poverty: how a crushing poverty of spirit can motivate people to struggle, both as individuals and communities, to find in God their belovedness and the promised kingdom. A fruit of that struggle has been restoring the true gospel to the whole church.

A church that ignores racism proclaims a false, distorted gospel, which has been heard in too many white churches for too long. Thankfully, Black liberation theology has articulated, out of an agony nothing can justify, the gospel Christ himself preached in his hometown of Nazareth. It's the gospel in which he has come to liberate the oppressed, to unleash the captives, to announce God's special care for the poor and afflicted.

One other word before we begin. It's not my intention to provide a comprehensive look at either racism and its effects or Black liberation/womanist theology. Such an ambitious agenda would require not just a full book but a series, at least. Instead, I'm going to attempt to provide a taste of the evidence of ongoing racism in the US, and draw upon a few key scholars to give a sense of how Black theologies have brought us a truer gospel. Readers who would like to explore these issues in greater depth will be able to keep themselves busy for a long, long time.

Triangles, Pyramids, and Systems of White Supremacy

I spoke of a "crushing system of white supremacy" just now, and I'd like to describe two conceptual frameworks that can help us understand it. Oddly enough, both of them are represented as triangles. Once we've done the conceptual work, we'll look briefly at some of the evidence that racism is still at work in US society.

The first of the triangles is Johan Galtung's "Conflict" or "Violence Triangle,"[8] which shows how inequalities in different social dimensions produce systems of white supremacy and periodic outbreaks of violence.

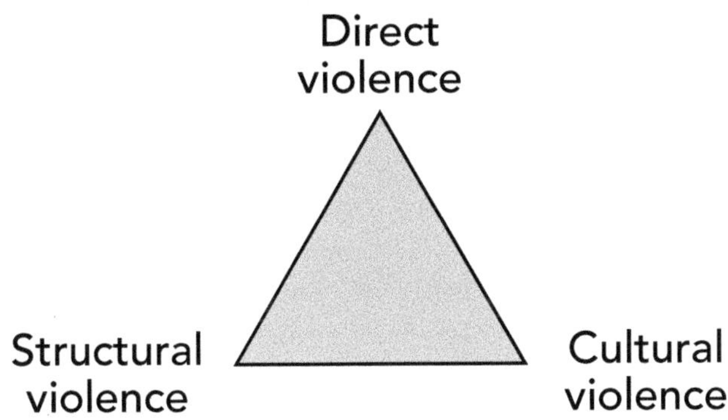

Galtung's Violence Triangle

In the triangle, each angle represents a form of conflict or violence (the two can be used interchangeably here). Let's begin with "direct violence." This is what most people think of when they hear the word "violence": people hurting one another's bodies. Shootings, lynchings, bombings, coshing people over the head, sinking a blade into them. Simple enough.

"Cultural violence" is another angle, and includes all the ways in which the "other" is dehumanized, stereotyped, seen as inferior, lazy, threatening, or otherwise undesirable and offensive. This is where prejudice comes in: all the negative images and attitudes about other groups that stir our distaste, fear, and contempt for those who differ from us. It's where we see politicians, journalists, clergy, and other leaders manipulating existing fears and creating new ones: the group, whether immigrants/refugees or even Indigenous people,

8. Johan Galtung, "Violence, Peace and Peace Research," *Journal of Peace Research* 6, no. 3 (1969): 167–91.

are reaching frightening numbers, making demands, threatening to change "our" way of life, to turn "us" into a minority, committing crime, threatening "our women," and otherwise creating chaos. They're "rats" (Nazi Germany), "cockroaches" (1990s Rwanda), "illegal aliens" (contemporary US). When people dehumanize the other, direct violence is often on the horizon. After all, extermination is a legitimate response to infestation. In short, cultural violence often paves the way for and justifies direct violence.

Finally, "structural violence" is everything in a society that prevents members of some groups within it from achieving their full potential. In the United States, for example, neighborhood racial segregation means that in "high-poverty elementary schools" (those in which 75 percent or more students are eligible for free or reduced-price meals), 80 percent of students are Black or Brown; in high-poverty high schools, it's 82 percent. The fact that significant shares of public school funding are based on property taxes means that schools in poor areas are chronically underfunded, and those students who need the most support usually end up getting the least. These inequalities continue when it comes to high school graduation rates, college enrollment and graduation rates, and participation in the labor and housing markets, where the cycle will begin anew with their children.

The three angles of cultural, structural, and direct violence are interconnected. It's easy to see that people who are viewed as inferior—stupid, lazy, threatening—might not have the best chances in the job market. But the effect goes both ways: people who are chronically unemployed or underemployed are likely to be seen as inferior: all those stereotypes of them as "stupid" or "unqualified" get reinforced. If they're also seen as criminals, they may have more run-ins with the police, higher arrest rates, and higher incarceration rates. All of which further reinforce their negative image and their difficulty securing stable employment. If they get fed up enough, or if some spark ignites frustrations—say, a verdict that seems unjust, or a police or civilian shooting of an unarmed member of the group (itself an example of direct violence)—then rioting may break out. More direct violence.

All of this may seem very simple and obvious, but we often miss the connections. When incidents of direct violence such as riots or rowdy protests are covered in the news, we typically don't see them accompanied by in-depth analyses of the grievances that provoked them. Airtime is expensive, space and attention spans are limited, and many consumers of news are not schooled in the analysis of social issues. That analysis may be available somewhere, especially online, but it will likely take extra effort to find it, an effort that many of us are not motivated to expend.

Even if there isn't deliberate "spin" going on, the ordinary conventions of journalism can contribute to the problem. Journalists are often trained to look for individuals who can comment on the story and provide a "sound bite." Videos may show looters carrying away TVs, or rioters throwing rocks and bottles, but how do you film the desperation born of years, of generations, of limited opportunity? If you need video to accompany your story, you're going to go for the dramatic and instantly recognizable, not complex social-historical situations that require a lot of background and explanation.

All of this reinforces the notion that it's *individual actors* who are responsible for the situation that's unfolding. There must be people who can be connected to what's happening, some place to lay the blame. The cognitive work required to understand patterns of history linked to present-day institutions and the interplay of cultures, not to mention the imaginative challenge of putting ourselves in the shoes of people with whom we likely have little contact and even less shared perspective, is more than most news consumers are prepared for. And journalism's definition of what's "newsworthy" (riots) and what isn't (ongoing structural conditions) means that even well-intentioned journalists can unwittingly feed the problem.

When we see only the "fire" and the "spark" that ignited it, what we miss is the slow and quiet accumulation of fuel over a period of decades, even centuries. The impression news consumers are left with can be that the outburst of direct violence was essentially unprovoked. It happened because group members are violent by nature, further reinforcing the image (cultural violence) of the group as crime-prone and menacing. This in turn may lead to police crackdowns, with more arrests and incarcerations, which take group members out of school and the labor force (structural violence).

The value of the conflict triangle is that when we stop people from shooting at each other but don't deal with the negative views they have of each other, or the inequality in their opportunities for a decent life, there can be no real peace. There can only be a temporary cease-fire, and circumstances that will continue heating up until the direct violence is ignited again.

How many times have we seen this? In April 2023, the United States was reeling from the story of Andrew Lester, an 84-year-old white resident of Kansas City. Ralph Yarl, a Black 16-year-old, was trying to pick up his siblings and went to Lester's address by mistake. When Yarl rang the bell, Lester shot him in the head and arm, right through the glass door, no words exchanged. Yarl survived; Lester was facing felony charges, but died days after entering into a plea agreement. Their story illustrates how direct violence can seem to appear out of nowhere. But nothing comes out of nowhere, and Lester undoubtedly had spent years seeing young Black men as dangerous, an image that is a strong component of American culture and cultural violence.

I find Galtung's triangle useful because it helps take the focus off of bigoted individuals and shows that the problem of racism is institutional, cultural, pervasive, and self-reinforcing throughout society. In other words, it helps us see white supremacy as a *system*, with multiple parts that move and work together to produce the outcome of racial inequality, denigration, and violence.

Yet even in a racist system, racism is carried out by *people*—who may or may not have racist intentions. What roles do different social actors play in perpetuating racism? In many, if not most, white people's view, "racism" is primarily a matter of individual extremist attitudes and actions, which is why many white people are so afraid of being identified with it. For a person of color to raise the specter of racism in a situation in which white people are involved often makes them feel personally attacked as immoral, unfeeling bigots. They often respond by pointing out that they were not responsible for slavery or any of the other outrages perpetrated against Blacks and others before their time.

In short, they become defensive, and the person who raised the issue likely becomes frustrated, knowing that none of this is the point. The point, as has often been said, is not that white people personally planted the tree of racism but that, if they're not actively working to cut it down, they continue to live on its fruits. My own upbringing is an example of this. My father (who was white) served in the Navy in World War II, working on an aircraft carrier, where he became a cook after the war ended. He then came home and went to work as a mechanic. He was smart and hardworking, spent his entire career at Lockheed, and rose through the ranks to become a high-level executive. We had a penthouse apartment in Rome with a pool on the terrace and another on the grounds below. My mother had lots of help with the housework, and I attended an excellent international school and three weeks of summer camp in Switzerland.

I never met the man who would have been my father-in-law, as he died long before I met my husband. But he too was a Navy cook; he too was smart and hardworking. But he was a Black man who worked in the steel mills outside of Pittsburgh, and he had no outlet for his talents. With nothing better to look forward to, he drank heavily and died in his early fifties. How things might have been different if he'd been in my father's shoes.

I had nothing to do with creating the circumstances that made for a great life for my father, and a short one for my husband's father. My dad, a mechanic and the son of a mechanic, experienced dramatic upward mobility, in part because he never had to compete with hardworking, gifted Black men like my husband's dad. That was not my doing (or his either, for that matter); it was all in place long before I was ever thought of. Still, I benefited from it, going to much better schools than my husband had the luxury of attending, getting second chances after every stupid decision I made. My husband also experienced dramatic upward mobility: from the projects in Pittsburgh to a Vanderbilt PhD and a successful academic career. But every step along the way was harder for him, and he had to be better than I, had to prove himself constantly to doubters and gatekeepers. And unlike me, most of his childhood companions ended up in dead-end careers, in prison, or in the ground.

With this "tale of two fathers" in mind, I'd like to turn to the second conceptual framework, a pyramid that speaks to the different social actors in a racist society and the roles they play. I learned about this framework in a workshop put on in Belfast by an organization called Mediation Northern Ireland, and it shows in simple, intuitive terms how people who think they have nothing to do with one another can actually be cooperating in perpetuating a sectarian (or racist) social system.

Sectarianism as a Social Pyramid

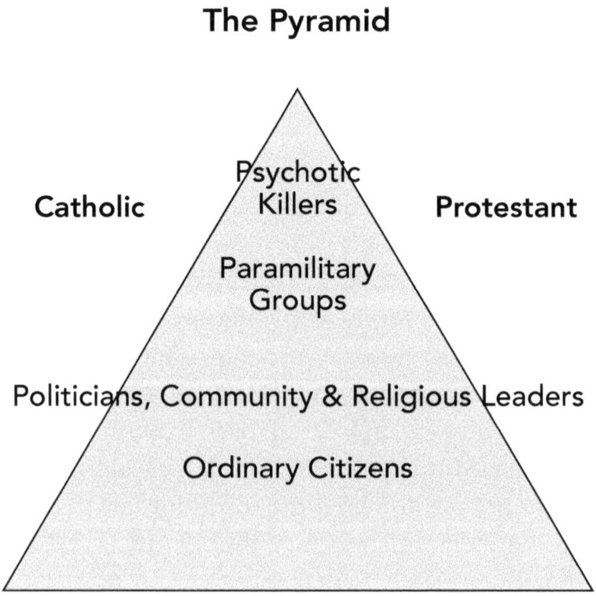

The Pyramid

Catholic

Psychotic Killers

Protestant

Paramilitary Groups

Politicians, Community & Religious Leaders

Ordinary Citizens

Source: Mediation Northern Ireland

In the context of the "Troubles" in Northern Ireland, the two sides of the conflict are the Catholics and the Protestants. But in this context, these are not so much religious terms as ethnic terms. The conflict was not really about religion; it's just that the Irish are majority Catholic and the British are mostly Protestant or Anglican, so the denominational terms are a kind of shorthand. The combatants were worried about politics, not doctrines: the Irish wanted the North to be part of the Republic of Ireland, and the British wanted to remain loyal to the UK.

During the decades of active fighting, there were always those who genuinely enjoyed the violence. They appear at the top of the pyramid as the "psychotic killers." They didn't see the conflict as tragic but as an occasion to take sadistic pleasure in hurting and intimidating others, issuing the orders that would keep the violence going. Fortunately, their numbers were few, but they were still powerful. More numerous were members of the paramilitary organizations on both sides, those who did most of the actual work of planting bombs, throwing Molotov cocktails, and policing segregated neighborhoods to make sure no one crossed a border without paying for it in blood. Incidentally, Northern Ireland was long known as one of the best places in the world for knee surgery, because of the tendency of paramilitaries to punish people by shooting out their knees. Their orthopedic surgeons had plenty of practice.

Under the paramilitaries in the pyramid, and more numerous still, are the politicians and community and religious leaders. These are the people who would certainly never throw a petrol bomb, but they have a public voice. One of the most famous examples is Ian Paisley (1926–2014), minister of his own fundamentalist, breakaway Presbyterian sect and longtime leader of the right-wing Democratic Unionist Party, which he founded. He co-led the opposition to the Sunningdale Agreement of 1973, a power-sharing plan that called for cooperation between the governments of Northern Ireland (Protestant, Unionist) and the Republic of Ireland. Baron Arthur Faulkner, head of the less extreme Ulster Unionist Party who served briefly as Prime Minister of Northern

Ireland, had brokered the alliance, but it was not popular with Unionists and split his party. Ian Paisley's comment on the Agreement was in his usual rhetorical style: "Mr Faulkner says it's 'hands across the border' to Dublin. I say if they don't behave themselves in the South, it will be shots across the border!" A few months later, four car bombs exploded in Dublin, killing thirty-three people.[9]

Leaders like Paisley would certainly find it indecorous and distasteful to carry out actual, direct violence, and they would deny any intention to participate in it. Their weapon is their voice, which they use to demonize the opposing side (cultural violence) in ways that encourage others on their side to participate. The boots-on-the-ground paramilitary members take both inspiration and permission from public figures and know that the speeches they give will serve as powerful propaganda, garnering support for their own work among the public.

On the bottom of the pyramid we have ordinary citizens. These are not involved in the violence either, but a word or a joke uttered at the pub, after church, "among friends," contributes to the sense of solidarity in the group and the prejudices they share. Ordinary citizens read the paper, watch the news, attend church, belong to ethnically exclusive clubs, and no doubt consume online content, which easily becomes an echo chamber. This makes them ignorant of perspectives on the other side of the conflict, and extreme segregation in Northern Ireland made it unlikely that these impressions would be countered by personal experience with the Other.

The lesson of the pyramid is that while each level disavows the "extremism" of those above it, each level also depends on the tacit permission and support of those below it. Politicians and clergy may make speeches against the use of violence by paramilitaries or other hate groups. But they will also make inflammatory statements that motivate and legitimate that violence. When ordinary

9. "Shots Across the Border," *Broadsheet*, January 10, 2014, accessed April 25, 2023, https://www.broadsheet.ie/2014/01/10/shots-across-the-border/.

citizens decide to tolerate that kind of speech, they keep those leaders in office, in print, on the air, in power.

To summarize: racist conflict and violence come in multiple forms in a society, forms that drive and strengthen one another. And those within the society may criticize the most inflammatory language and the most violent actions, but if we're not actively opposing racism, then we are playing our part to support it, whether we're honest or informed enough to recognize it or not. Just as the different forms of conflict in a society reinforce one another, the different actors each play their role in maintaining the conflict. And it's no good trying to just opt out of it all. In a conflict-ridden society, silence is also speech.

Where Integrity Lies

So what's the answer? How can a person who's not a target of racism live with integrity in a society suffused with racism? How can a white person go, as Ibram X. Kendi would say, from thinking it's enough to be non-racist to becoming antiracist? How do white people step out of their place in the sectarian/racist pyramid and refuse to play their part, however quiet and passive it might be, in keeping white supremacy alive?

Well, it's love, of course; that is the answer. But before you roll your eyes and slam this book shut, let me say a bit more about what love is, and what it isn't. Love, as I'm hardly the first to point out, is not primarily an emotion. It may bring emotions with it, but love doesn't consist of warm, affectionate feelings toward the other. Those can come from a nice dinner, a great day at the beach, a spectacular sunset. I'm told they can come from tequila shots. They can well up within us when we find someone who makes us feel good: makes us feel attractive, desirable, valued. The thing is, with this kind of "love," we value the other mainly for how they make *us* feel. When we hit a rocky or boring stretch in the relationship, this love is often revealed for what it is: a pleasurable sensation that we can move on from as soon as we stop enjoying it.

Thomas Aquinas had a deeper definition of love: love is willing the good of the other, *as other*—that is, without reference to oneself. It's self-less. With this kind of love, I can even renounce my beloved if it's for their best, even knowing that it will leave me grief-stricken. This kind of love is what Jesus spoke of: the love that will lay down its life for a friend. Jesus both taught and lived this kind of love, and it's the example we're called to follow. It's not a fleeting emotion, but an act of the will. It's why we can promise to love someone until death parts us, and why we can love people we don't even like, or have never met.

Love at this level isn't automatic or easy. It doesn't just happen; if it did, it'd be a lot more common. So how do we get there? In one of Cornel West's early books, *Prophetic Reflections* (1993), I see a process that can lead us to an authentic, divinely driven love. I should point out that I'm building on, rather than exactly reproducing, West's vision. This shows us what love as Aquinas defined it, love that is a selfless act of will, looks like on the ground. It consists of three steps.

The first step is to see and honor the *imago dei* in the other. As followers of Christ, our love begins here, because this is the basis of human dignity: we are all—no matter how common, contemptible, wicked or boring—bearers of the divine image.[10] This is non-negotiable, unchanging, and the reason we can love people without stopping to determine if they are worthy. As C. S. Lewis famously said, "There are no *ordinary* people. You have never talked to a mere mortal. . . . Next to the Blessed Sacrament itself, your neighbor is the holiest object presented to your senses."[11] The Sacrament and our neighbor are holy for precisely the same

10. I'm not saying that atheists do not love, even profoundly and selflessly. Their love might begin with a radical commitment to the equality and rights of all people. But for Christians, as well as Jews and Muslims, the belief that we all bear the image of God is the natural starting point.

11. C. S. Lewis, *The Weight of Glory and Other Addresses* (New York: Simon and Schuster, 1975), 39–40. While not all Christian traditions are sacramental, all value holiness.

reason: they both bring us into the presence of God. Yet how often do we show the same reverence to our neighbor that we show to the divine Presence, however we understand it? What would it look like if we did?

You might think it would look like taking action to help our neighbors when they suffer. That's true, but it's not the next step, and much harm has been done by the assumption that it is. Rushing in to "help" before we know what help, if any, is wanted or needed betrays a paternalistic, colonialist mindset, the attitude that approaches the Other with a "civilizing mission." "Trust me," it says, "I know what's best for you. I'll show you what to do. In fact, I'll do it for you." Earnest and well-meaning white people have a sad reputation for taking over other people's movements. One of the worst examples is the way many white feminists have claimed to address the problems of "women," without realizing that, for women of color, white women themselves are often the problem—an issue we'll return to later.

This is not how love works. It's not how God works. Have you noticed how rare it is for God to barge into human affairs and take over? Notice how Jesus treats the blind man Bartimaeus (see Mark 10:46-52). He kept calling out to Jesus as he passed: "Jesus, Son of David, have mercy on me!" When they brought Bartimaeus before him, Jesus did a funny thing: he asked Bartimaeus, "What do you want me to do for you?" I can imagine people in the crowd thinking, "Well duh, he wants to see. Get on with it." But Jesus didn't make that assumption, and he certainly didn't just start healing him. He asked. He listened. He gave Bartimaeus the precious gift of recognizing his agency, his dignity. Jesus respected his autonomy, though many people even today don't show that kind of courtesy to people with disabilities.

But this is the way of love: it listens, it waits until we're ready; then it's available to work with us, even to serve us. Between honoring the *imago dei* and taking action on behalf of our neighbor, this crucial middle step is often overlooked in our rush to action. Cornel West calls it "analysis," but at its most basic, it's *listening.*

Let's make this concrete. Think of someone you know you love, beyond any doubt. Now imagine that person's experienced a great loss: they've flunked out of school, got fired, got divorced, had a terrible diagnosis. You already see the *imago dei* in them; the more dear people are to us, the easier that part is. If they come to you in pain, and you immediately start suggesting things that should be done—"take them to the cleaners," "smear them on social media," "go to Kazakhstan for the secret cure"—you are just going to annoy them. And you know that, though you'd be surprised at how many people don't. So what would you do instead?

You'd sit with them and listen. You'd let them tell you the story, as many times as they need to. You'd let them voice their questions without trying to give them the answers. You might educate yourself about the situation, do a little research to see if their industry is in a freefall and everyone's on the chopping block, not just them. You'd let them cry if they want, and you wouldn't tell them to calm down. In other words, you wouldn't tone police, gaslight, minimize, deflect, or tell them they're oversensitive or overreacting. You wouldn't add to their pain by focusing on how it's not your fault, and you had nothing to do with it so your conscience, at least, is clear. And you wouldn't engage in one-upmanship: "You think raising two kids alone is hard? Try four." If you really love them, you'll let it be about them and not make it about you.

In short, when we love another person who's in pain, we hear them. We see them. When Hagar was alone and desperate in the desert and the angel came and gave her new hope, she called God *El-Roi*, "God who sees me." And the angel told her to name her son *Ishmael*, "God hears" (see Gen 16:13, 11). Isn't this what we all want: to be seen, to be heard? Isn't this why people fall at the feet of celebrities, and hope for "likes" on social media? It's as if we fear that if we live and die in obscurity, our lives will have had no meaning. But God's eye is on the sparrow, and no one lives or dies without God's eye on them. Love *notices*. Love pays *attention*. That's analysis, and without it any action we take is likely to be premature and ineffective.

But we must come to action eventually. Just as faith without works is dead, analysis without action is sterile. There are people whose primary action is prayer, and while that may be hard for some of us to understand and accept, it is a form of action. For most of us, however, action means getting out into the world and pushing for change, maybe even making some noise and getting into some good trouble, as John Lewis said. Or perhaps, as Brian Stokes Mitchell suggests, "[our] sword could be a sermon, or the power of the pen."[12] Action must be discerned carefully—that's what the "analysis" stage is for, plus plenty of prayer—but once we've heard our call, we must respond to it faithfully and courageously. If we simply close our eyes to racism, as too many white people do, we will be like the religious authorities to whom Jesus said, "If you were blind, you would not have sin. But now that you say, 'We see,' your sin remains" (John 9:41).

Is Racism Still a Thing?

I think it's fair to say that blindness and denial are the most common forms of racism in the United States today, though overt racism seems to be making a resurgence of late. Many white Americans think of racism as something that is part of our history, that we passed anti-discrimination legislation in the 1960s and did away with all that. Further, we had decades of affirmative action, so everyone has now had an equal chance to compete on a level playing field. But the legislation we have targets only the most simple and obvious forms of discrimination, and affirmative action, even before recent rollbacks, only helped those group members who were already doing relatively well. For example, affirmative action in college admissions only helps those who've graduated from high school. Affirmative action did help to build the Black middle class, but it's done little to raise up the Black poor. It's complicated, and if we don't understand the nuances and complexities, perhaps we haven't loved enough to listen.

12. Brian Stokes Mitchell, "Make Them Hear You," *Ragtime: The Musical*, by Lynn Ahrens and Stephen Charles Flaherty (1996).

White supremacy, as we have seen, is a mix of individuals, images, and institutions, all working together to maintain the racially unequal status quo. Many white people tend to equate "white supremacy" with white supremacist *organizations*, which together form the white supremacist *movement*. So we hear "white supremacy" and envision the Klan, the neo-Nazis, the Proud Boys, and others sadly too numerous to name. These are the American version of the "psychotic killers" and "paramilitaries" from the sectarian pyramid, and they're responsible for much direct violence as well as a considerable amount of cultural violence.

But when we speak of a white supremacy *system*, or of racism as *systemic*, we're not speaking primarily of prejudiced individuals, whether alone or in groups. Galtung's violence triangle does a good job of getting at what we mean: a system in which institutional practices, cultural perceptions, and personal "violence" (physical, but also hostility and intimidation) all work together to maintain the subordination of one or more groups within it. But for a more detailed description of systemic racism, let me turn to sociologists Joe Feagin and Kimberley Ducey:

> Systemic racism includes the complex array of antiblack practices, the unjustly-gained political-economic power of whites, the continuing economic and other resource inequalities along racial lines, and the white racist attitudes created to maintain and rationalize white privilege and power. Systemic here means that the core racist realities are manifested in each of society's major parts . . . —the economy, politics, education, religion, the family—[reflecting] the fundamental reality of systemic racism.[13]

13. Joe Feagin and Kimberley Ducey, *Racist America* (New York: Routledge, 2018), quoted in Paula A. Braveman et al., "Systemic and Structural Racism: Definitions, Examples, Health Damages, and Approaches to Dismantling," *Health Affairs* 41, no. 2 (February 2022), accessed May 2, 2023, https://www.healthaffairs.org/doi/10.1377/hlthaff.2021.01394.

So is the United States this kind of system, or is this picture an exaggeration, a fictional view of a society that was guilty of racism in the past but has moved beyond it? This is a question that can easily take a full semester or even years to answer, but I'd like to provide a few quick examples of social patterns that are hard to explain if racism is no longer operating routinely (i.e., not as occasional exceptions) in the United States. I know numbers can cause some people's eyes to glaze over, and I won't linger long over them. But there are some numbers we need to face, because they tell us inescapable truths about the state of race in America.

Let's begin at the most basic levels of life and health. According to the National Institutes of Health, as of 2019, life expectancy for Blacks lagged over three years behind that of whites. Only the American Indian and Alaska Native populations were behind Blacks.[14] Between 2017 and 2019, infant deaths were over twice as high for Black babies as for white. African American women are over three times as likely to die during the pregnancy-postpartum period than are white women.[15] In 2019, Blacks were 30 percent more likely than whites to die from heart disease,[16] and nearly twice as many Blacks as whites have diabetes.[17] Further, while the American Psychiatric Association reports that rates of depression are higher in whites than in Blacks, they also note that underdiagnosis and

14. National Institutes of Health, "Life Expectancy in the U.S. Increased between 2000–2019, but Widespread Gaps among Racial and Ethnic Groups Exist," June 16, 2022, accessed May 2, 2023, https://www.nih.gov/news-events/news-releases/life-expectancy-us-increased-between-2000-2019-widespread-gaps-among-racial-ethnic-groups-exist.

15. PRB, "Maternal Death among U.S. Black Women," March 9, 2023, accessed May 2, 2023, https://www.prb.org/resources/maternal-death-among-u-s-black-women/.

16. US Department of Health and Human Services, Office of Minority Health, "Heart Disease and African Americans," March 9, 2023, accessed May 2, 2023, https://minorityhealth.hhs.gov/omh/browse.aspx?lvl=4&lvlid=19.

17. American Diabetes Association, "Statistics about Diabetes," July 28, 2022, accessed May 2, 2023, https://diabetes.org/about-us/statistics/about-diabetes.

misdiagnosis are more common among racial/ethnic minorities. One trend for minority youth is particularly chilling: when they have behavioral health problems, they are more likely to be referred to the juvenile justice system than to appropriate health care providers, compared to white youth.[18]

Black unemployment rates have been roughly twice those of whites for many years. Yet there are two things we should remember about this. First, "unemployed" is a category that includes only those who are jobless *and* seeking work. Those who have given up trying to find work are not included in these statistics, and that will include many more African Americans than whites. If we included everyone who's capable of working but not in fact working, the gap would be considerably larger.

Second, data on unemployment, and most of the other indicators of how well Blacks and others are doing, are typically collected on the "non-institutional civilian population." In the age of mass incarceration, this distorts the position of African Americans.[19] The imprisonment rate (prisoners per 100,000 population) is 181 for whites, 901 for Blacks. Black men are about five times more likely to be imprisoned than white men, and in the 18- to 19-year age range, that difference rises to nearly thirteen times.

All of this means that very large numbers of Blacks, especially Black men, who are worse off in American society in terms of education, employment, income, mental and physical health, and so on, are *not included in the statistics*. This means the statistics give an overly optimistic view of how well African Americans are doing. Even so, they are twice as likely to be unemployed as whites.

Consequently, over twice as many African Americans as whites live in poverty. Per capita income for whites is 1.6 times greater

18. "Mental Health Disparities: Diverse Populations," December 19, 2017, accessed May 2, 2023, https://www.psychiatry.org/File%20Library/Psychiatrists/Cultural-Competency/Mental-Health-Disparities/Mental-Health-Facts-for-Diverse-Populations.pdf.

19. Becky Pettit, *Invisible Men: Mass Incarceration and the Myth of Black Progress* (New York: Russell Sage, 2012).

than that of Blacks. And we see the most striking differences when we look at wealth—that is, at assets held by families. White families' average net wealth is between $100,000 and $200,000, while Black households' average is between $10,000 and $20,000. So the net worth of white families is about *ten times that of Black families*, a number Harvard sociologist Alexandra Killewald calls "staggeringly large."[20] Wealth matters because it can serve as a cushion during times of adversity: lose your job and it is your wealth that keeps you off the street. Wealth also matters because, unlike income, it can be passed down to the next generation so that your children don't have to start from the bottom.

As I mentioned earlier, neighborhood residence affects the schools children attend, which sets in motion so many other things. If we look at the kinds of courses that prepare students for college, we see a racial gap: while 40 percent of white high school students take Advanced Placement (AP) or International Baccalaureate courses, only 23 percent of Black students do. And even those figures mask differences, because not only do schools with majority Black/Brown student bodies offer fewer AP courses, but their content is also much less challenging, meaning that even students who do enroll in college aren't as prepared to thrive there. Predictably, only 28 percent of Black students leave college with a degree, while nearly 40 percent of white students do.

Remember the Black/white gap in life expectancy? Were you thinking it's because Blacks experience higher rates of poverty than whites? It is that, but not only that; it's also the product of documented racial differences in health care. A 2005 study concluded that even when comparing only Blacks and whites with the same insurance status, the same age, income, and so on, Blacks are still more likely to receive lower quality care. When it comes to cardiac care, kidney dialysis and transplants, care for patients with HIV/AIDS, cancer, strokes, or psychiatric disorders, even when

20. Liz Mineo, "Wealth Gap May Be a Key to Other Inequities," *Harvard Gazette*, June 3, 2021, accessed May 3, 2023, https://news.harvard.edu/gazette/story/2021/06/racial-wealth-gap-may-be-a-key-to-other-inequities/.

subjects are matched on social class and other relevant factors, Black patients receive inferior care compared to whites. Research has even shown that Black children seen in emergency rooms for abdominal pain are significantly less likely to receive pain medication than their white counterparts.[21]

I could go on like this for a really long time. In every dimension of life in the United States, from neighborhood residence and its effects on education, occupation, and income, to political power, exposure to environmental pollutants, stereotypical portrayals in film and television, even having one's natural hair defined as "unprofessional," racism is a toxic smoke that seeps into every corner of American life. Yet one place where it doesn't so much "seep" as blow through like a tornado is the criminal justice system. Let me take a brief moment to give some examples.

Race and Criminal Justice

Years ago I had occasion to visit a men's prison. As our group moved through it, I thought you could make a kind of parlor game of it: "Find a white prisoner." Having co-authored research on race and imprisonment, I wasn't surprised by the demographics of the place. But to know about it is one thing; to see in person a sea of almost exclusively Black and Brown faces was a gut-punch.

Welcome to the age of mass incarceration, where for white men the lifetime likelihood of imprisonment is one in eleven, while for Black men it's one in *three*.[22] Women's participation in crime has always been lower, and the reasons for this have been debated for some time. But among women, too, the gap exists: lifetime likeli-

21. Monika K. Goyal et al., "Racial Disparities in Pain Management of Children with Appendicitis in Emergency Departments," *JAMA Pediatrics* 169, no. 11 (November 2015): 996–1002.

22. Thomas P. Bonczar, "Prevalence of Imprisonment in the US Population, 1974–2001," Washington, DC, Bureau of Justice Statistics, August 2003, https://bjs.ojp.gov/content/pub/pdf/piusp01.pdf.

hood of imprisonment for white women is one in one hundred eleven, while for Black women it's one in eighteen. Think of the ripple effects of these numbers on Black and white communities. I have already spoken of the consequences of Blacks being absent from the data we use to gauge Black progress. But the absence of the people themselves means spouses, partners, prospective partners, parents, workers, voters, role models and more, who *aren't there.*

Why are so many more African Americans incarcerated than whites? The simplest place to look for an answer is Black rates of participation in crime. But there is nothing simple about this problem. Let me just suggest a few of the complexities. First, how do we know how much crime is being committed, and by whom? We can look at arrest data, but these can easily be affected by bias in policing practices. Also, some crimes, such as sexual assault, are severely underreported. While victimization surveys ("Have you ever been a victim of. . . ?") can help with this, they're obviously not much help with homicide, or with so-called "victimless" crimes like illicit drug use, or with crimes people may not even be aware of, such as identity theft. There's no source of data that's perfect, and that's part of the complexity.

What we really want to know when we ask "Is the criminal justice system perpetuating racism?" is what proportion of the racial differences in imprisonment is justified by Black crime rates, and what part is unjustified, and at least potentially the product of discrimination. There are some types of crime for which we can say with confidence that Black participation rates are higher, most notably homicide. When there are bodies, when not only crime statistics but vital statistics are kept, when there is less police discretion about whether a crime occurred and whether to investigate it, we can be more sure of the accuracy of our picture. We can be less certain about other violent crimes, and still less about property crimes. Policing practices such as racial profiling, for example, might net a higher level of arrests of Black suspects than is warranted by their criminal activity. And then any step through the whole process, from arrest to trial, conviction, sentencing, and serving time, can be affected by practices that place Blacks at a disadvantage. These practices can vary between jurisdictions as well, so that state or national averages can mask a lot of variation. Complexity.

But it's in drug-related offenses that we know with certainty that Black imprisonment rates *cannot be justified* by higher involvement in either possession or sales. African Americans both use and sell drugs at lower rates than whites, but since President Reagan, like Nixon before him, declared a "war on drugs," Black arrest rates have been as high as six times those of whites. And the penalties are not racially neutral. For a long time the penalties for crack cocaine, used predominantly by Black and Brown people, were as much as a hundred times more severe as those imposed for the use of powder cocaine, favored by whites.[23] Legislation passed by the Obama administration reduced the gap from 100:1 to 18:1,[24] and further reforms have followed in the Trump and Biden administrations.

Some part of the difference in Black and white imprisonment rates is due to differences in Blacks' participation in crime. Where is that coming from? No serious scholar today believes that members of any racial group are inherently crime prone. In fact, the scientific consensus today is that, biologically speaking, "race" does not exist. It's a figment of the European colonial imagination and a product of history. There is nothing in the superficial differences in our appearance that's related to criminality. But the structural, cultural, and direct forms of violence African Americans live with all their lives—these are criminogenic. That is, they

23. Deborah J. Vagins and Jesselyn McCurdy, "Cracks in the System: 20 Years of the Unjust Federal Crack Cocaine Law," American Civil Liberties Union, October 26, 2006, accessed May 9, 2023, https://www.aclu.org/other/cracks-system-20-years-unjust-federal-crack-cocaine-law.

24. American Civil Liberties Union, "President Obama Signs Bill Reducing Cocaine Sentencing Disparity," August 3, 2010, accessed May 9, 2023, https://www.aclu.org/press-releases/president-obama-signs-bill-reducing-cocaine-sentencing-disparity.

generate criminal behavior, though the ways they do so are complicated and the subject of ongoing research.

Images of Blacks as criminal have been shown to create cycles in which innocent people can become targets of police activity. "Stop and frisk" is a "proactive" police practice in which motorists and pedestrians who alert police suspicions can be stopped, questioned, and patted down for weapons. Officers may also use physical force at their discretion. The criteria for being able to stop and frisk are "more than whimsy but less than probable cause."[25] Stop and frisk has by no means been confined to New York City, but it was a "signature policy" of Michael Bloomberg's three terms as mayor, from 2002 to 2013.

At its peak in 2011, nearly 700,000 stops occurred: 55 percent of those stopped were Black, another 32 percent were Latino, and only 10 percent were white. The most telling figure, however, is that 88 percent of those stopped and frisked—again, primarily Black and Brown people—were innocent of wrongdoing. The stops resulted in no arrest and no summons.[26] This is consistent with other racial profiling studies, in which stops of Black motorists yielded fewer arrests than those of whites, suggesting that whites are stopped only when the police have good reason to think something suspicious is going on (probable cause), but many Blacks are stopped on a flimsy pretext.

A large 2014 study[27] examined the effects of stop and frisk experiences on the mental health of young men in New York City. Eighty-five percent of subjects reported having been stopped at

25. US Department of Justice, "Stop and Frisk," n.d., accessed May 10, 2023, https://www.ojp.gov/ncjrs/virtual-library/abstracts/stop-and-frisk-0.

26. NYCLU (ACLU of New York), "Stop and Frisk Data," May 23, 2017, accessed May 10, 2023, https://www.nyclu.org/en/stop-and-frisk-data.

27. Amanda Geller et al., "Aggressive Policing and the Mental Health of Young Urban Men," *American Journal of Public Health* 104, no. 12 (December 2014), accessed May 10, 2023, https://ajph.aphapublications.org/doi/full/10.2105/AJPH.2014.302046. See also https://www.nyu.edu/about/news-publications/news/2014/october/stop-and-frisk-linked-with-trauma-and-stress-sociology-study-finds.html.

least once in their life, and 46 percent had been stopped in the past year. The men were asked to describe their encounters with police, and they were also asked about symptoms of stress, anxiety, and trauma. The researchers found that the most severe mental health symptoms were associated with those whose encounters were felt to be unfair, aggressive, or involved the use of racially charged language. Yet even those whose encounters were less antagonistic reported feeling stress, anxiety, and trauma, and Black respondents reported these feelings more than others did.

The consequences are chilling. Hundreds of thousands of innocent people, nearly 90 percent of them Black and Brown, have been traumatized by stop and frisk policing without having engaged in crime. Imagine the result of that trauma. Picture a young Black man who's never committed a crime but is dealing with trauma symptoms from previous experiences of this aggressive form of policing. See him on a city street, approached by police officers who are looking for "suspicious" behavior. The young man is already experiencing anxiety, perhaps post-traumatic stress, and he begins to tense up. The more he does, the more suspicious he looks, and a feedback circle has been set in motion that will likely condemn him to more police confrontations in the future.

This is a good example of how cultural violence (the image of young Black men as crime prone) feeds direct violence ("frisking"). And it's easy to imagine that as the mental health consequences of these experiences accumulate, the men affected may become less and less able to hold down steady employment. How hard is it to imagine men like this ending up falling into criminal behavior—particularly when you set this one phenomenon in the context of neighborhood segregation, poor quality education, unemployment and underemployment, and all the rest?

The fact is that *racism is criminogenic*, in two main ways: first, Black people are treated differently, from initial police contact all the way through incarceration and reentry into society. Second, pervasive inequality creates patterns of higher Black involvement in crime. Reviewing these patterns, criminologist Robert Crutchfield concludes that "a large portion of racial disproportionality in imprisonment that appears to be accounted for by arrest rate differences is likely instead to be the effects of structural racism that affect people in ways that produce differential rates of involvement in crime."[28]

This means that even when arrest data show higher rates of criminal behavior by African Americans, we cannot draw conclusions about Black criminality without setting it in a context of historical, ongoing, and pervasive racism. This is American history: slave patrols and plantation owners administered "justice" during the days of slavery, and afterward, the "Black Codes," laws that only applied to Black people, condemned many to lethal forms of hard labor for the most trivial infractions. The terrorizing of Black communities by the Klan and others, plus lynchings and other forms of violence, were common during the days of Jim Crow segregation. But as Michelle Alexander argues in her widely acclaimed book *The New Jim Crow*, through the "war on drugs" and mass incarceration, the control of African Americans through the criminal justice system continues. This is American history, but now there are those who want to make it illegal to teach that history, want whole generations of young people—including young Black people—to grow up knowing nothing of what Black people in this country have endured and survived.

How have they endured it all? How have they survived? When Cornel West speaks of the "threat of nihilism" facing Black Americans, it rings true. The temptation to think of life as meaningless, of struggle as pointless, is hard to measure but is no doubt part of the story I've been telling here. West argues that the Black church has long served as an "institutional buffer" against nihilism, but he worries that in an increasingly secular and consumerist society, that buffer is eroding fast. Yet out of that tradition has come a theology of Black liberation, a theology that calls people of all races back

28. Robert Crutchfield, "The Peculiar Journey: Race, Racism, and Imprisonment in American History," *Crime and Justice* 51 (2022): 22.

to the roots and essentials of Christian faith: that God is intensely interested in, even identifies with, the poor, that poverty and suffering of every kind has meaning, and that every tear shed by even the most insignificant and unvalued person stings the eyes of God too.

In the rest of this chapter, I'd like to examine this theological tradition and show how it has flowered amid the most grotesque oppression and violence. Remember how the slave Hagar gave the Lord a name, a powerful, beautiful, sacred name: *El-Roi*, "the God who sees me." This is a name for all who have known affliction, and the theology of Black liberation bears witness to the fact that the poor in spirit are always seen and fiercely loved by God.

A Theology of Black Liberation

Black liberation theology came out of the later days of what we know as the Civil Rights Movement of the 1950s and '60s. African Americans had fought in segregated units for their country in World War II, as loyal and patriotic as their white comrades. And those who served in Europe, in particular, had the refreshing experience of escaping for a while from the suffocating atmosphere of Jim Crow—whether explicit, as in the South, or de facto, as in the North. Coming home, however, they faced the disappointment of a society that still treated them as pariahs rather than heroes. They watched as white veterans benefited from the GI Bill, low-cost mortgages, and improved housing in the suburbs—benefits that were closed off to them. The glacial pace of change was maddening, and what patience they'd had was running out. As activist Fannie Lou Hamer would say of the struggle for voting rights, "We been waitin' all our lives, and still gettin' killed, still gettin' hung, still gettin' beat to death. Now we're tired waitin'!"[29]

29. Quoted in Jerry DeMuth, "Fannie Lou Hamer: Tired of Being Sick and Tired," *Nation*, April 2, 2009, accessed July 14, 2023, https://web.archive.org/web/20180131081604/https://www.thenation.com/article/fannie-lou-hamer-tired-being-sick-and-tired/.

Additionally, as I mentioned earlier in my "tale of two fathers," there was a lot of upward job mobility created by changes in the American occupational structure that essentially sucked large numbers of working-class white men into white-collar jobs. But discrimination kept Black men out of these jobs, their "dream deferred," as Langston Hughes put it. Many Black women found work as domestics, which made them the breadwinners of their families and created a gender reversal that could be tough for couples to navigate. Further, it was still the heyday of lynching (1880s to 1960s), when even the aspirations of Black people to improve their social standing or "better themselves" was interpreted by many whites as an affront: "uppity" and offensive. Far from loving their Black neighbors according to the commandment, whites were so offended by their presence that nearly five thousand Black men, women, and children were lynched during that era.

The combination of rising expectations and vicious suppression created a moment in which Blacks in large numbers were prepared to risk what they had to seek justice for themselves and their children. But Black thinking is not monolithic, and there were multiple views on the form their response should take.

How tempting it must have been to take up the challenge issued by the poet Claude McKay in 1919:

> O kinsmen! We must meet the common foe!
> Though far outnumbered let us show us brave,
> And for their thousand blows deal one death-blow!
> What though before us lies the open grave?
> Like men we'll face the murderous cowardly pack,
> Pressed to the wall, dying, but fighting back![30]

Yet Blacks were not only "far outnumbered" but even further outgunned, and such an uprising would've been suicidal. Instead,

30. Quoted in James H. Cone, *The Cross and the Lynching Tree* (Maryknoll, NY: Orbis, 2011), 50.

inspired by Gandhi and the gospel, many civil rights activists engaged in nonviolent direct action as a way of dramatizing to the nation the brutality of white racism. Narrating that drama with powerful speeches and writings, Martin Luther King Jr. "appeal[ed] to the conscience of the larger community, in an effort to create a *beloved* community."[31] Ralph Abernathy said that "violence is the weapon of the weak and nonviolence is the weapon of the strong."[32] And countless protesters put their bodies in harm's way, armed only with the weapon of the strong.

Other civil rights leaders didn't necessarily share the conviction that facing down white opposition armed solely with the love of Christ would be enough. Charles F. McDew, one of the leaders of the Student Nonviolent Coordinating Committee (SNCC), spoke for many:

> "Gandhi used, in India, the tactic of having people lay down on railroad tracks to protest . . . and it worked. . . . But if a group of black people lay down on railroad tracks here, in South Carolina, Georgia, Alabama, Mississippi, Texas, Louisiana, any of these Southern states, a train would run you over and back up to make certain you're dead. You cannot make a moral appeal in the midst of an amoral society. . . . And so, [to Dr. King,] 'Thank you, but no thanks.' "[33]

Voting rights activist Fannie Lou Hamer declared that she loved segregationists simply to avoid entertaining the toxicity of hatred in her own heart. But she had her limits: "I keep a shotgun in

31. Dara T. Mathis, "King's Message of Nonviolence Has Been Distorted," *Atlantic*, April 3, 2018, accessed July 14, 2023, https://www.theatlantic.com/politics/archive/2018/04/kings-message-of-nonviolence-has-been-distorted/557021/ (emphasis added).

32. "Ralph David Abernathy," n.d., accessed July 14, 2023, https://law.jrank.org/pages/3894/Abernathy-Ralph-David.html.

33. Library of Congress Civil Rights History Project, "Nonviolence Philosophy and Self Defense," https://www.loc.gov/collections/civil-rights-history-project/articles-and-essays/nonviolent-philosophy-and-self-defense/.

every corner of my bedroom and the first cracker even look like he wants to throw some dynamite on my porch won't write his mama again."[34]

As time and the struggle went on, there were gains: the Civil Rights Act of 1964, the Voting Rights Act of 1965, and the Fair Housing Act of 1968, while the desegregation of schools following the Supreme Court's decision in *Brown v. Board of Education* (1954) was inching along, with plenty of reversals, bitterness, and violence. And once again, rising expectations and the glacial pace of change left a lot of African Americans fed up. The Nation of Islam and its adherent-turned-detractor, the charismatic Malcolm X, along with the Black Panther Party and others, were uninterested in campaigns to desegregate the South. They wanted to address the inequality and powerlessness of northern, urban Blacks.

Indeed, Dr. King himself was moving in this direction before his assassination, asking "What good is having the right to sit at a lunch counter if you can't afford to buy a hamburger?" King named and opposed the violent consequences of capitalism, questioned the legitimacy of the Vietnam War, and called for racial and economic justice. He ended up dead, as he knew he would, and the center of gravity of the Black push against racism moved from civil rights to nationalism, self-sufficiency, self-determination, Black liberation, and Black Power. Black theologians, too, began asking harder, more provocative questions, speaking—in love—truths that the white churches and white society urgently needed to hear.

The Black Church and Resistance

Racism has been called "America's original sin," and the struggle against it over the centuries has been our greatest moral challenge. In facing that challenge, white America has too often rejected the chance of redemption. So the question arises: while African

34. Quoted in Mathis, "King's Message of Nonviolence."

Americans were putting themselves on the line in the fight for a more perfect union, where was the church?

It depends, of course, on which church you mean. The Black church[35] has long been the institutional network that connected African Americans across long distances, and it has been a vital resource in the struggle against racism. Henry Louis Gates Jr. is worth quoting in full on this point:

> The Black Church has a long and noble history in relation to Black political action, dating back at least to the late eighteenth century. . . . The church fueled slave rebellions, nurtured and sustained the Underground Railroad, and was the training ground for the orators of the abolitionist movement. . . . It powered antilynching campaigns and economic boycotts, and formed the backbone and meeting place for the civil rights movement. Rooted in the fundamental belief in equality between Black and white, human dignity, earthly and heavenly freedom, and sisterly and brotherly love, the Black Church and the religion practiced within its embrace acted as the engine driving social transformation in America, from the antebellum abolitionist movement through the various phases of the fight against Jim Crow, and now, in our current century, to Black Lives Matter.[36]

The Black church had always been a place where Black life mattered: Black suffering and oppression, Black creativity and joy, Black cries from the heart, and Black laboring for justice. But it was in the context of the struggle for Black Power that a theology of Black liberation was born. On July 31, 1966, fifty-one Black pastors took out a full-page ad in *The New York Times* calling for more serious action toward eradicating racism. This statement was preceded by

35. The "Black church" is not a monolith, any more than the "white church" is. But Black churches were united in their opposition to slavery, Jim Crow, and the oppression and devaluation of Black people.

36. Gates, *Black Church*, xix.

the 1964 publication of Joseph R. Washington's book *Black Religion.* Washington argued that because of segregation, white Christians in America carried the tradition of Christian faith inherited from Europe, and Black churches—because of their separation and "faith" that was less in Jesus than in things like justice—did not have an authentic connection to church tradition. Therefore, he concluded, there was no such thing as Black theology.[37]

This kind of reasoning, from an African American religious leader and scholar, cried out for refutation—and got it. In the context of the Cold War, the struggle of developing nations for liberation, and the emerging global and pan-Africanist consciousness, Jesus in Black theology came to be identified with the movement to decolonize and liberate those whom Franz Fanon called "the wretched of the earth" (*les damnės de la terre*). When Stokely Carmichael called for "Black Power," a multivalent term encompassing economic self-determination, political rights and influence, and a cultural revaluation of all things African and Black, a number of Black clerics and academics began to explore its theological implications. James Cone, considered the founder of Black liberation theology, published *Black Theology and Black Power* in 1969. In it, he proposed that the mission of Jesus was, like that of Black Power, the liberation of the oppressed.

Dwight Hopkins, a student of Cone, affirmed that "as a product of the African-American struggle, Cone's book gave liberation theology to the world."[38] Of course, enslaved African Americans had always connected their hopes with the exodus story of the liberation of God's people from slavery in Egypt. Many "Negro spirituals" are based on this link, which formed a key theme of Black liberation theology:

37. Dwight N. Hopkins and Edward P. Antonio, eds., *The Cambridge Companion to Black Theology* (New York: Cambridge University Press, 2012), 9.

38. Quoted in Arthur Fournier, "Black Theology of Liberation: Hopkins Educates Church Leaders, Expands Scope of Scholarship," *The University of Chicago Chronicle*, March 16, 2000, accessed July 18, 2023, https://chronicle.uchicago.edu/000316/hopkins.shtml.

Go down, Moses,
'Way, down to Egypt land
And tell old Pharaoh to let my people go.

The Ohio River, the boundary between the slave-holding South and the free North, finds its way into many spirituals as the "Jordan," crossed by Moses and the children of Israel:

Deep river,
My home is over Jordan,
Deep river, Lord,
I want to cross over into campground.

The children of Israel had been freed from slavery by a God who *saw* them: "I have surely seen the oppression of My people who are in Egypt, and have heard their cry because of their taskmasters, for I know their sorrows" (Exod 3:7 NKJV). God promises to deliver them and to bring them to a good land, a land flowing with milk and honey. This was the God of the Black church, the God who saw and felt the affliction of the oppressed, who would crush the power of the mighty and bring justice and freedom.

The Scriptures have for centuries been an important source of inspiration for Black struggle, and this was no less true by the time of the Civil Rights Movement. Martin Luther King Jr. is not typically thought of as a theologian, but as a Christian pastor, his passion for justice came both from the suffering of his people and from his reading of the Bible. King was particularly drawn to the prophet Amos, who famously castigated Israel for its punctilious observation of religious rituals while the wealthy ignored the suffering of the poor. God was not impressed with Israel's feast days and sacrifices, Amos said; only a genuine commitment to justice for the poor would cut it. King quoted from Amos in his speech at the March on Washington: "But let justice roll down like waters, and righteousness like an ever-flowing stream" (Amos 5:24).

It's a tradition that continues. In a speech given before the Martin Luther King Jr. holiday in 2021, Baptist pastor and Georgia's first Black US Senator Raphael Warnock cited the police killings of Eric Garner and George Floyd. But he preached a message of hope to those experiencing "spiritual exhaustion":

> In God's vision for the land, not only is there equity, not only is there integrity, not only is there possibility in God's vision for the land, there is inclusivity. In God's economy, there's a place for everybody—red, yellow, Brown, Black and White.[39]

The Black church has, throughout African American history and up to the present, conveyed a message of hope, a message of meaning and purpose in the present, and justice to come. Amos, Isaiah, and other prophets of the Hebrew Scriptures have been a rich source of that hope.

But of course, it doesn't end there. Cone and later Black theologians would find inspiration too in the *Magnificat*, Mary's song of liberation:

> He has put down the mighty from their thrones,
> And exalted the lowly.
> He has filled the hungry with good things,
> And the rich He has sent away empty. (Luke 1:52-53 NKJV)

Did Jesus hear this song at his mother's knee? Certainly his teachings were consistent with her theological perspective. In his parable of the sheep and the goats, Jesus warns his listeners that whatever they do to the most insignificant and forgotten people around them, he will consider done to himself. Plenty for Black theologians—not to mention white people—to contemplate there.

But perhaps it's in Jesus' inaugural address in the synagogue at Nazareth that liberation theology in general, and Black liberation

39. Quoted in Nicole Chavez, "Sen.-elect Warnock Says 'the Soul of Our Nation Hangs in the Balance' in Sermon Ahead of MLK Day," *CNN*, January 17, 2021, accessed November 21, 2023, https://www.cnn.com/2021/01/17/us/warnock-mlk-ebenezer-church-sermon/index.html.

theology in particular, find their greatest inspiration. Using the words of Isaiah (see Isa 61:1-2), Jesus announces his mission as liberator of the oppressed:

> The Spirit of the Lord is upon me,
> because he has anointed me
> to bring good news to the poor.
> He has sent me to proclaim release to the captives
> and recovery of sight to the blind,
> to let the oppressed go free,
> to proclaim the year of the Lord's favor. (Luke 4:18-19)

Cone's student Hopkins observes that "Jesus says my mission is to eradicate poverty and to bring about freedom and liberation for the oppressed. And most Christian pastors in America skip over that part of the book."[40] Cone showed that indeed, clergy and theologians, even those as preoccupied with social justice as the influential Reinhold Niebuhr, either ignored racism altogether or remained comfortable with a moderate, gradualist approach to it:

> Niebuhr had "eyes to see" black suffering, but I believe he lacked the "heart to feel" it as his own. Although he wrote many essays about race, commenting on a variety of racial issues in America and in Africa and Asia, the problem of race was never one of his central theological or political concerns.

Cone maintained that white supremacy was "America's central *theological* problem."[41] Yet white theologians, who had taken on issues of class, gender, and anti-Semitism, were mostly silent on the subject of race. When called upon to notice the theological implications of racism, they tried, as Marxist analysts would also

40. Quoted in Fournier, "Black Theology of Liberation."

41. James H. Cone, "Theology's Great Sin: Silence in the Face of White Supremacy," chap. 10 in *Cambridge Companion to Black Theology*, 146; original emphasis.

do, to reduce race to class—that is, to insist that racial inequalities were all the product of class inequalities, and when the latter were eliminated, the former would be too. Yet it only takes a moment's thought to see through this. If every Black person in America were suddenly middle class or higher, would all their troubles disappear? Would the police not profile them? Would whites welcome them as neighbors? In *The Rage of a Privileged Class: Why Are Middle-Class Blacks Angry? Why Should America Care?* journalist Ellis Cose tells story after story of how middle-class Blacks experience racism on a daily basis. Clearly, race is its own problem, not reducible to class, and it's a big one. Perhaps *the* big one. So why would white theologians be silent on it?

For a number of reasons, Cone says,[42] the first of which is that they *can*. Theology is no exception to the general rule that while people of color must understand whites and their ways to survive, whites can afford to ignore the experiences, needs, and concerns of people of color. Just as Canadians tend to know a lot about the United States, and most people in the US know very little about Canada, it's the eight-hundred-pound gorilla on your doorstep that must be watched carefully if you're going to survive. Gnats, on the other hand, can be swatted away as needed. (Note: I am definitely not calling Canada a gnat.) Cone's observation here is apt: "Powerful people do not talk, except on their own terms and almost never at the behest of others. All the powerless can do is to disrupt—make life uncomfortable for the ruling elites."[43]

A second set of reasons for white theology's silence on racism is guilt and denial. Whites know that they are not on the moral high ground on matters of race, though they like to think that they've earned their positions in society fairly, not because of historical colonization, slavery, and discrimination. But as I mentioned earlier, this is largely because white people tend to think in individualistic terms. Not having deliberately defrauded

42. Cone, "Theology's Great Sin," 147–52.

43. Cone, 147.

anyone themselves, they tend to be blind to the defrauding their *group* has done, and how they continue to benefit from it on the basis of their *group* membership.

Third, white theologians have tended to avoid issues of race for fear of stirring up Black emotions. Cone notes that it's difficult for African Americans not to be angry about the long history of living under white supremacy, and difficult also not to let that anger affect the ways they talk about it. White people who do engage in interracial conversation have to get used to passionate expressions of anger and sorrow and being reminded of how fully justified they are. There are two modern terms for what people do when they're unwilling to empathize in this situation. The first is *gaslighting*, where they challenge the person's hold on reality: "They didn't mean it"; "You're just oversensitive"; "I don't think that was about race at all." The second is *tone policing*: "Calm down; we're just trying to have a conversation here"; "There's no need to be so aggressive about it"; "Your tone is unprofessional."

Comparing the heated rhetoric of Malcolm X with the more conciliatory speech of Dr. King, Cone observed that Malcolm was not interested in sparing white feelings, believing they needed to know how Black people really felt. Cone adds that the tone of Black liberation theology was more consistent with that of Black Power, which made white theologians less than eager to engage them: "I must admit I was pretty hard on them and that partly accounts for their silence. But I was not going to pamper privileged whites."[44] Indeed, how could a theology that claims any sort of connection to the heart of God be spoken without passion? In *A Black Theology of Liberation*, Cone speaks to this point:

> Because black theology is survival theology, it must speak with a passion consistent with the depths of the wounds of the oppressed. . . . Christian theology cannot afford to be an abstract, dispassionate discourse on the nature of God in relation

44. Cone, 50.

> to humankind; such an analysis has no ethical implications for the contemporary forms of oppression in our society.[45]

For mystical theology in particular, to speak of the wounds of the oppressed is to speak of the wounds of Christ himself, and to speak of the passion is to speak passionately. Christ's wounds contain all wounds. So deep is his identification with humankind, especially with the poor and marginalized, that those given special clarity of vision will of necessity speak "the language of commitment." When you see the face of Christ in every face, no face can be forgotten, and indifference is not an option.

Finally, white theologians have tended to avoid taking on racial justice because, like whites in general, Cone says, they are "not prepared for a radical redistribution of wealth and power."[46] Power doesn't make concessions willingly. Yet whites must break their silence, he insists, and work actively on an antiracist theology as part of a larger antiracist struggle. Analyzing ecclesial institutional structures to identify ways they support racism, making space for the voices of people of color—these are among the suggestions Cone has for the kinds of fruits that might be worthy of repentance.

There have been exceptions among white theologians, including the truly exceptional South African Dominican priest and anti-apartheid activist Albert Nolan (1934–2022). Influenced by the Black Consciousness movement started by Steven Biko and by liberation theologian Gustavo Gutierrez, Nolan preached, taught, and published—sometimes at great personal risk—a combination of Black and liberation theology, while also serving as chaplain and mentor to white university students. He likely was one of the (anonymous) authors of the 1985 *Kairos Document*, a statement by mostly Black religious leaders calling for South African churches to engage in nonviolent resistance to apartheid.

45. Quoted in Dennis W. Wiley, "God," chap. 6 in *Cambridge Companion to Black Theology*, 77.

46. Cone, "Theology's Great Sin," 152.

In his book *God in South Africa: The Challenge of the Gospel*, Nolan argues that while the white churches have claimed to preach the "gospel," in fact, they often don't. The message of the church will not be the gospel if it is not good news—and not a generic message called "good news," but genuine good news for a specific people in a specific time and place:

> There is a definite shape, certain definite characteristics, that any message would have to have in order to qualify as a true gospel, as the gospel of Jesus Christ for a particular people at a particular time.[47]

In the white churches of South Africa, what the church was preaching (the core doctrines of Christianity) was hardly news. Further, as we saw earlier, when Jesus announced his mission, he said his news was "good" *specifically for the poor*. Nolan points out that, especially in a divided society, what's good news for the poor and weak is not likely to be good news for the rich and powerful. But the poor and weak, as we learn in the parable of the sheep and goats, are precisely the criteria that matter.

So there can be, in Nolan's view, no generic gospel: "[A] timeless gospel of timeless truths . . . is simply not the gospel; it does not even have the shape of news, let alone good news."[48] We are not called to repeat Jesus' life or his message to first-century Jews, Nolan says, but to bring good news, as Jesus did, to our specific time and place, news that brings hope to the "least" among us. We need to speak to the issues of our time in the same spirit in which Jesus spoke to the issues of his time. Can anyone deny that racial injustice is one of the chief issues of our time? If our "news" doesn't bring about meaningful change and inspire hope in those who suffer, is it good news?

47. Albert Nolan, OP, *God in South Africa* (Grand Rapids, MI: Eerdmans, 1988), 8.

48. Nolan, *God in South Africa*, 15.

Black liberation theologians have been accused of presenting a "new" or even "false" gospel. Yet Nolan and others show us that it is in the crucible of Black suffering, whether in South Africa or the United States or elsewhere, that the true gospel, the real "good news," has been restored to us. Once again, I want to emphasize that I'm not saying this somehow makes the whole tragic history of racism worthwhile. What I'm saying is simply this: if we want to have any sense of what Jesus has to say to us today, the prophetic voices of Black liberation theology are voices we need to hear. If we are to obey the commandment to love our neighbor, it is our obligation to *listen*. It is the very least we can do.

Strange Fruit

One of the most striking examples of white theologians' failure to engage Black issues is their silence on the realities of white supremacy in general, and lynching in particular. Lynching was only one part of a multipronged strategy for enforcing white supremacy. But it was a particularly ugly part.

Technically, lynching is any extra-legal punishment enacted by a crowd. It probably predates the American Civil War, but its heyday in the United States began in the post-Reconstruction period. For about a decade after the war, Federal troops remained in the South to ensure that, among other things, the rights of emancipated Blacks were protected. African Americans made remarkable strides during this time, investing in education for their children, exercising their right to vote, even holding political office.

But this honeymoon period was short-lived. By 1877, Federal troops were withdrawing from the South, a result, in part, of a waning interest in and commitment to racial equality. This gave southern whites a free hand, which they used to establish a new system of quasi-slavery in the region. Several pieces fit together to accomplish whites' two primary objectives. The first of these was to *control* a newly freed population which, they assumed, had every reason to be angry and potentially violent. Despite all the imagery that depicted Blacks as happy Sambos and loyal Mammies content to serve, whites who lived close to slavery knew this was far from the truth. And their understandable fear that Blacks might use their new freedom to slaughter their former masters in their beds meant that Priority One was to keep Blacks under control. Priority Two was to maintain access to Black *labor*, so simply running them out of the South was not an option.

Whites found all kinds of pretexts for lynching Black men, women, and children. But nothing could whip up an angry mob like an allegation that a Black man had made sexual overtures toward a white woman. The lynching of fourteen-year-old Mississippi resident Emmett Till showed that even the rumor of offending behavior, even by a boy, could bring on the most savage violence. Many white people today likely think of a lynching as the loose, vigilante-conducted equivalent of a hanging by the state: a noose, a jerk of the neck, and it's over. But lynchings could involve unimaginable sadism and contempt. Victims weren't just hanged, but burned, hunted down, and subjected to torture in front of a jeering throng before being finished off, possibly in front of their own families. I've read of victims being castrated and forced to eat their own testicles.

And while some of these acts occurred in hidden away places, it was not unknown for a lynching to become a public spectacle. Men would bring their wives, and even children, for a day's entertainment. There might be a picnic. Years ago, my husband and I saw an exhibition on lynching called *Without Sanctuary* at the Andy Warhol Museum in Pittsburgh. The exhibition featured nearly a hundred postcards of lynchings, with victims being "whipped, beaten, stoned, stripped, gouged, burned, mutilated, shot, and then hanged by their necks from trees, from lampposts, from bridge railings," while crowds looked on, grinning in "a carnival atmosphere."[49]

49. Jim Davidson, "Without Sanctuary," n.d., accessed November 18, 2023, https://www.heinz.org/UserFiles/Library/h-W02-WithoutSanctuary.pdf.

Think of it: these are *postcards*. These aren't photos of crimes surreptitiously taken by appalled witnesses. These were vehicles for a message of "Having a wonderful time; wish you were here." And each of these victims was pulled from safety, denied justice, tortured, jeered at by the crowd, and executed. Does this sound familiar?

It did to James Cone. Writing in *The Cross and the Lynching Tree*, the founder of Black liberation theology is worth quoting at length:

> Both the cross and the lynching tree were symbols of terror, instruments of torture and execution, reserved primarily for slaves, criminals, and insurrectionists—the lowest of the low in society. Both Jesus and blacks were publicly humiliated, subjected to the utmost indignity and cruelty. They were stripped, in order to be deprived of dignity, then paraded, mocked and whipped, pierced, derided and spat upon, tortured for hours in the presence of jeering crowds for popular entertainment. In both cases, the purpose was to strike terror in the subject community. It was to let people know that the same thing would happen to them if they did not stay in their place.[50]

White clergy and theologians who neglected to speak out on racism, particularly on this most extreme manifestation, utterly failed to see Christ in "the least of these"—even when the parallel was almost impossible to miss. Albert Nolan said that the gospel *must apply to our own time and place, or it is not the true gospel.* "Can one really," Cone asks, "understand the theological meaning of Jesus on a Roman cross without seeing him first through the image of blacks on the lynching tree?"[51]

How did African Americans survive the horrors of this time and place? Not by meeting violence with violence; that was a fight they would never win. But not by being passive victims either. Cone observes that southern Blacks were sustained by their music and

50. Cone, *Cross and the Lynching Tree*, 31.
51. Cone, 31.

their faith. Both were an expression of life and hope in the face of nihilism and despair. In *The Spirituals and the Blues*, Cone shows that the blues were a defiant affirmation of Black humanity and value in the face of grief and loss, a "liberating catharsis."[52] Then the church assured them each week of their value, that their humanity was created and cherished by God, and that they were part of a community that inverted the values of the white world.

Cone sees in "slave songs," precursors to the blues, a deep tradition of Black prayer that was foundational for the rejection of the idolatrous, heretical white church's belief and worship. A white savior who did not identify with the "least" of these, a white god who mistakenly put "inferior" Blacks into a creation he'd declared "very good," these were the false god and false beliefs of too many, though not all, white Christians, which the Black church stood against as doing violence to the true image of God in Black people.

The lynching tree is a reminder of racist contempt for Black life. Yet viewed through the lens of Black theology, it becomes—like the cross—a powerful, paradoxical symbol of how the apparent victory of dark forces is ultimately overcome by the light, which "shines in the darkness, and the darkness does not overcome it." Because just as the suffering One on the cross had been called "My Beloved, in whom I am well pleased," God says the same of every victim of the lynching tree—and everyone who knows they could be next. Black lives matter to God—today, as in the heyday of lynching, and always. When we see in every act of police or civilian brutality against Black victims the crucifixion anew of Christ, when we understand that what's done to them is done to him, we've grasped the fundamental message of Black liberation theology. And the gospel, the *true* gospel, is being restored to us through it.

But Where Are the Women?

Every example of racism I've mentioned so far has affected Black women as well as men. But in Black liberation theology, as in

52. Cone, 12.

white feminist theology, the experiences and perspectives of Black women have not been the focus of attention; indeed, at times they are all but invisible. Earlier I quoted Elaine Heath as saying that the church has always spoken most authentically from the margins—as opposed to those times when it's sat comfortably at the center, seduced by worldly wealth and power. Using this principle, I believe the gospel is most authentically preached by those at the margins, and Black women—trebly marginalized by race, gender, and (often) class—have much to say to us of the true gospel of Jesus Christ.

Womanist theology centers the experiences of Black, often African American, women within gendered hierarchies in the church, the academy, the family, and beyond. Emerging some twenty years after Black liberation theology, womanist theologians began to critique the failures of both it and white feminist theology to include their social and spiritual experience. Stephanie Y. Mitchem gives us a definition with which to begin:

> Simply put, womanist theology is the systematic, faith-based exploration of the many facets of African American women's religiosity. Womanist theology is based on the complex realities of black women's lives.[53]

Notice the emphasis on Black women's *lives*. In womanist theology, knowledge is not pursued primarily for its own sake, and research is not conducted for the sake of expanding knowledge: "Theories were intended to empower and influence other people, certainly beyond the academy."[54] Patricia Hill Collins asks three questions of any social theory: "Does [it] speak the truth to people about the reality of their lives? . . . Does [it] equip people to resist oppression? . . . Does [it] move people to struggle?"[55] This is an approach that is uninterested in the more abstract concerns of typical

53. Stephanie Y. Mitchem, *Introducing Womanist Theology* (Maryknoll, NY: Orbis, 2002), 73–83 Kindle.

54. Mitchem, *Introducing Womanist Theology*, 73.

55. Quoted in Mitchem, 74.

academic research, even theology, even Black liberation theology. A womanist, in the words of Alice Walker, who gave us the term,

> Loves music. Loves dance. Loves the moon. *Loves* the Spirit. Loves love and food and roundness. Loves struggle. *Loves* the Folk. Loves herself. *Regardless.*[56]

In Walker's words we can hear the insistence on Black women's belovedness, on their essential goodness, despite every force that tries to see them differently.

Mitchem notes that the founding discipline of womanist theology is ethics, but it makes extensive use of other academic disciplines such as history and sociology, as well as biblical studies and other forms of theology-related scholarship. This sometimes creates problems of communication, as interdisciplinary studies often do: when womanist scholars speak of "theory," for example, they don't mean a set of axioms generating hypotheses that can be tested with empirical data to explain and predict social phenomena. This is the way I, trained as a sociologist, think of theory.

In womanist theology, as in other forms of liberation theology, the central priority is different: to understand the lives of marginalized people—in this case, Black women—and how their spirituality and religious practice sustains them and their communities. So rather than, for example, analyzing the mechanisms that create conditions that cause suffering in Black communities, as a social scientist might do, womanist theologians might start with that suffering, and ask: How do women in those communities endure it? How does their faith sustain them? How does their spirituality help them create a supportive, life-giving community in the face of these challenges?

Delores S. Williams, one of the founders of womanist theology, shows why the concerns of Black women could not simply be

56. Alice Walker, *In Search of Our Mothers' Gardens* (San Diego: Harcourt Brace Jovanovich, 1983), xi.

subsumed under feminist theology:[57] First, and perhaps most glaringly, Black women's experience has often simply been left out of feminist analyses, with race not included among "women's issues." White feminists were inclined to see patriarchy as the root of all evil. But when men are conceived as the enemy, one effect is to divide the Black community.[58] In womanist theology, gender is *a* problem, but it's not *the* problem.

Black women know that sometimes white women are themselves the problem: think of the countless Black women who have labored as domestics for white women, underpaid and often mistreated—sometimes subtly, sometimes blatantly. It's a situation captured memorably in the 2011 film *The Help*. But the tension between Black and white women has other historical roots. White suffragists, for example, made the strategic decision that their cause would be more likely to succeed if they pressed only for votes for white women, throwing their Black sisters under the political bus. Living and working close to these kinds of realities, womanist theologians have not divorced their work from the context of Black women's everyday lives and struggles.

Indeed, Williams maintains that two of the central concerns of womanist theology are survival and community building and maintenance.[59] Family roles of mothering and nurturing, of teaching the next generation their belovedness—often enough in the absence of fathers—place a special burden on Black women, whose energies and other resources must at times reach to extended family and fictive kin. But the problems I discussed earlier in this chapter threaten the entire African American community: poverty, unemployment, inadequate housing and health care, police brutality, mass incarceration, drug trafficking and interpersonal violence—racism's ripple effects are experienced by Black men,

57. Delores S. Williams, "Black Theology and Womanist Theology," chap. 5 in *Cambridge Companion to Black Theology*, 60–62.

58. Mitchem, *Introducing Womanist Theology*, 56.

59. Williams, "Black Theology and Womanist Theology," 59.

women, and children. When white supremacy causes huge numbers of Black men to die or disappear into prison, the women are left to hold families and communities together. For these reasons and many more, the experiences of African American women are unique, and cannot be reduced to some generic "Black" experience, any more than they can be reduced to a "female" experience.

Prophetic Voices

There is no way, in such a short space, to do justice to the problem of white supremacy or to the responses of Black liberation and womanist theologians to the suffering it has caused. And I want to emphasize again that I am *not* saying that the richness of Black or womanist theology somehow makes the suffering that's necessitated them worthwhile. Nothing could do that. Only God can heal those wounds, and only God can and will untangle the knots that racism has wound in our society. That is the Christian hope. But for now, we need the voices of prophets from the margins to speak truth to us. For white people, that truth will not always be pleasant to hear. But we need to be clear that it *is* the gospel. A gospel that disregards the suffering of Black people, and how that has affected Black individuals and communities through history and in the present, is at best an incomplete gospel. At worst, it's a false gospel, and it's a gospel that has all too often been at its worst.

The voices of Black men and women who speak of Christ as liberator, of the good news as the release of the captives and the oppressed—these bring news that may not be good for those who are invested in the status quo. It was the same when Jesus was preaching. Jesus had uncomfortable words for those who'd ignored him in "the least of these": "You that are accursed, depart from me into the eternal fire prepared for the devil and his angels" (Matt 25:41). I don't know exactly what that means; I suspect we all have our own ways of imagining it. But it can't be good news for the recipients.

There can be no news of true importance that's good for everyone, at least in the short term. Even something as universally beneficial as the reversal of climate change would be bad news for those who oppose measures to bring that about, because they benefit right now from our destruction of the earth. Similarly, truths spoken by the Black prophets of history and today are good news in that they bring long-neglected aspects of the gospel back to us: concerns for justice, equality, integrity, and love in our dealings with our neighbors. When white people fail to recognize the *imago dei* in their Black neighbors, they are ultimately falling into idolatry: worshiping a God who is not also Black, Brown, yellow, and red. Worshiping a God who does not declare the whole human race to be "very good," to be beloved. Instead, they are worshiping a god of their own making. But the prophetic voices of Black liberation and womanist theology are, if we are listening, speaking a true gospel, one that can save us from ourselves.

PART FOUR

A Poverty Tradition of Our Time

Chapter 7

"Hitting Bottom"

Poverty in the 12-Step Tradition

God enters through the wound.

Carl Jung

Our look at poverty traditions has taken us well back into history: to ancient history with the Scriptures and the desert hermits; to the Middle Ages with the Franciscans and the Helfta mystics; and into the Early Modern age with the growth of devotion to the Sacred Heart. In looking at racism we have, regrettably, come right up to the present; as we have seen, racism continues to impoverish both its victims and its beneficiaries in the present day, as it has for centuries. It shows no sign of disappearing, and the creative and deeply spiritual ways people have found to survive and thrive in the face of it are ever evolving.

In this chapter, I want to examine a tradition that has a relatively short history and is going strong in the present day, one in which poverty is of central, explicit, importance. Alcoholics

Anonymous (AA), mother of all 12-step programs, was founded in the 1930s, and has generated many other programs based on the same model to bring drug addicts, overeaters, gamblers, and more to sobriety. It must be said at the outset that AA has plenty of critics: it's too religious; it's a cult; it requires complete abstinence, which may not be necessary; and its effectiveness compared to evidence-based methods of treatment is either discouraging or difficult to determine. We will hear these critiques in more detail later in this chapter, but I'm bringing them up now to emphasize that adjudicating between 12-step and other modes of treatment is not the point of this chapter. Nor will we be particularly bothered by the spiritual dimension of the 12-step tradition, since this is, after all, a book in which spirituality is pretty much the point. We will pay attention to those AA detractors too. But having done so, we'll then take as given the idea that pointing people toward a "higher power" is not a bad thing—mindful that we part company with many researchers, clinicians, and addicts as we do so.

The aim of this chapter, then, is to acquaint ourselves with a poverty tradition that is entirely of our own age—the twentieth and twenty-first centuries—and one in which poverty of spirit is of central importance. In the 12-step tradition, poverty is spoken of as being "powerless over alcohol," as "hitting rock bottom," and this is believed to be precisely the point where, for most addicts, healing can begin. The idea in brief is that an addict who is still maintaining a semblance (or perhaps a delusion) of control over their life and their substance use can remain in denial about the damage their addiction is causing, both to themselves and to their families, friends, and coworkers. As a result, they will be unmotivated to seek help or do the hard work of becoming sober. As we'll see, this denial and the rationalizations that come with it are not a purely psychological problem; the neuroscience of addiction has shown how our brains become complicit in maintaining dependence.

The agenda of this chapter, then, is first to provide a brief and accessible overview of the neurobiology of addiction as it is currently understood. We'll then consider a spirituality of addiction:

what are the spiritual causes and consequences of addiction, and how has addiction been understood in Christian thought, over the centuries and today? For example, what insights can we glean from St. John of the Cross' idea of attachment that could be applied to addiction? After this, we'll trace the history of AA and the 12-step tradition, hearing from both its adherents and its detractors. All of this will prepare us to focus in specifically on how the 12-step tradition has placed a premium on poverty of spirit, a poverty many recovering addicts have looked back on and called it "blessed."

The Neuroscience of Addiction

We are dopamine-seeking creatures. Dopamine is a chemical in the nervous system that acts as a messenger, conveying messages between nerve cells. In more technical terms, it's a *neurotransmitter*, and it plays a critical role in the body's reward system because it affects how we experience pleasure. "Pleasure" must be understood broadly here: not just sex and birthday cake, but enough positive feelings to enable us to get out of bed in the morning, or appreciate holding a grandchild. Dopamine is important to motivation, whether to help a stranger or make a friend, to perform well on the job or to pursue a hobby we enjoy. Without enough dopamine, we aren't motivated to make plans, to work on achieving goals, or to work at all. At the most basic level, without enough dopamine, we won't seek food, water, or procreation. So dopamine is essential to our survival—both individually and as a species. To seek it is hardwired into us.

Our bodies are meant to function within a range of dopamine values, roughly 50–100 nanograms/deciliter of blood.[1] Fifty would be where you'd be, say, on an ordinary morning looking ahead to a day of work: 50 ng/dL will get you to your coffee and out the door. On a really bad day, where everything goes wrong and you just

1. R. Corey Waller, "Addiction Neuroscience 101," *YouTube*, April 4, 2018, accessed February 28, 2025, https://www.youtube.com/watch?v=bwZcPwlRRcc.

want to knock off early, get in your PJs, and sit in front of the TV with a pint of Ben and Jerry's, you're at about 40 ng/dL. Favorite foods, sex, and other "normal" pleasures take us into the 90s. Best day ever? The one where you've just gotten a promotion and a raise, your kids bring home terrific grades, and you're headed out to dinner with your beloved? Add a winning lottery ticket, and that will take you up to about 100 ng/dL. Our brains can take the amount of ecstasy represented by that number, but they're not really meant to go any higher.

What happens when recreational drugs hit the system? Alcohol, marijuana, and heroin will push the dopamine level into the high hundreds, while methamphetamine will take it as high as 1,100 ng/dL—over ten times our natural limit. It's a dopamine blast so large that our bodies are overwhelmed.

But our bodies don't appreciate being overwhelmed and will take steps to restore equilibrium. This is true whether we're talking about core temperature, levels of fluids, blood sugar, oxygen/carbon dioxide ratio—or dopamine. With dopamine, long-term use of a substance like methamphetamine will start by taking the person up to 1,100 ng/dL; subsequent doses will take them to 900, then 600, and so on. Eventually that same dose will be required to get up to the normal level of 50. If the drug is removed, the person's dopamine level can sink to 10 ng/dL, inching up to 20 on their *best* day. This is why the process of addiction takes a person from experiencing a "high" from the drug to needing the drug just to avoid feeling miserable. Ten ng/dL isn't enough to get out of bed and do anything—even the basics like personal hygiene or caring for one's children.

The one motivation we don't lose at that level is survival. When dopamine levels sink this low, the body craves it. This is lizard brain stuff: when we reach this point, we don't care what's moral or ethical. We'll sell our kid sister to get the drug that will free us from this wretchedness. Our drive to survive is unthinkably powerful. This is why people driven to the point of starvation have resorted to some pretty unsavory problem-solving methods, like feeding *on* their children instead of feeding them. In fact, the craving for a drug to which a person is addicted is considerably more powerful than the craving for food or water. Studies using functional MRIs (MRI videos rather than still shots, so you can apply stimuli and see how the brain changes in response) have shown that in a person deprived of water for several days, the brain's reaction to hearing a waterfall, having water sprinkled on their feet, and so on is dramatically less than we'd see in an addict hearing or talking about their drug of choice. The same is true for descriptions of food, or the smell or taste of a favorite food, in people deprived of food for five days. For an addict, the craving for their drug is not about pleasure—it's about survival.[2]

The reason addicts build up tolerance (the need for increasing doses to get the same effect) and dependence (the feeling that one cannot function without the drug) is that when the massive dopamine hit from the drug overwhelms the body, the body works to restore equilibrium. It does this in part by "pruning" back dopamine receptors so that the extra dopamine has, you might say, no place to land. And if the drug is removed, or if the dose is postponed, the dopamine that is manufactured by the body also has fewer places to "land," so the person's experience is of a very low dopamine level. The distress symptoms of withdrawal ensue.

There's a lot more complexity to the neuroscience of addiction than I've been able to represent here. For example, environmental cues play a role in signaling to the brain that it may shortly expect a dose of the drug. An interesting example of this is the way college students drink when on their home campuses compared to when they are studying abroad. (Having led eight study abroad programs, I've found this research both fascinating and worrying.) Say a college student typically drinks at fraternity parties, or at a pub just off campus. Alcohol is a central nervous system (CNS) depressant, and when the student enters that place (the frat house or pub) which their brain associates with a dose of alcohol,

2. Research cited in Waller, "Addiction Neuroscience 101."

it offers protection by sending out a CNS stimulant. Then the dose of alcohol will take them to baseline, or something within a manageable distance of it.

But when students go abroad, they often drink—and heavily—in situations where they've never drunk before. Different settings, new companions, unfamiliar types of alcohol—all of these can prevent the brain from realizing that a hit of CNS depressant is coming. When there's no anticipatory hit of a CNS stimulant, students can find themselves far more intoxicated, and much more quickly, than they expect. There have been cases in which students were taken to an emergency department with the suspicion that they've been unknowingly drugged, and nothing but alcohol turned up in their system, at lower levels than expected based on their level of intoxication.[3]

Other complexities are turning up in research all the time. Experimental research (on animals, not humans) has even found that brains that have experienced cocaine addiction show changes in gene expression.[4] These complexities are fascinating but need not detain us here. For our purposes, this basic understanding of how addiction affects the body will suffice; from here, we will move to considering how addiction affects the spirit.

Addiction and Our Souls: Insatiable Thirst

In chapter 2, I called Photini, the Samaritan woman Jesus meets at Jacob's well, "a picture of addiction, of turning again and again to something that promises satisfaction but never quite delivers." Photini's thirst is insatiable, can only, in fact, be sated by water that

3. Jason Kilmer, PhD, Lecture to groups of study abroad students at the University of Washington, 2013.

4. National Institutes of Health, "Dopamine Found to Play Unexpected Role in Cocaine Withdrawal," *National Institute on Drug Abuse*, April 13, 2020, accessed January 30, 2023, https://nida.nih.gov/news-events/science-highlight/dopamine-found-to-play-unexpected-role-in-cocaine-withdrawal.

is living, infinite, eternal. Jesus offers her this water and Photini—humbled by stigma, lonely from working outside the community, worn out by returning again and again to seek water that doesn't satisfy—Photini accepts Jesus' gift and is transformed by it. Jesus, remember, has met her on level ground: he is thirsty himself, and has no way to draw water from such a deep well except to ask this Samaritan woman for help. He is not offering judgment from on high; he displays his own need while offering to fulfill her greatest need.

What makes this scene so powerful is how relatable it is: we have all been Photini at some point in our lives, though some of us more than others. What is this need that drives her to return again and again to a source of water that cannot ultimately satisfy? Haven't we all been there? Some addictions are more destructive than others: I tend to self-soothe with chocolate, and that's never going to land me face-down in the gutter, cost me my family, or send me to jail. But whether it's chocolate or heroin (or even working out, in case you're thinking you're immune to all this), we have all looked for relief in places that were never designed to provide it. And in the process, we've fashioned idols for ourselves as surely as the children of Israel did with the golden calf in the desert, when they needed something that was not God to make them feel better about where they were.

So what is this need, and where does it come from? The seventeenth-century French philosopher Blaise Pascal called it an "infinite abyss" within us. Let's hear this in context:

> What else does this craving, and this helplessness, proclaim but that there was once in man a true happiness, of which all that now remains is the empty print and trace? This he tries in vain to fill with everything around him, seeking in things that are not there the help he cannot find in those that are, though none can help, since this infinite abyss can be filled only with an infinite and immutable object; in other words by God himself.[5]

5. Blaise Pascal, *Pensées* (New York: Penguin, 1966), 75.

Just like Photini, right? And like the rest of us, if we're honest. Saint Augustine, whom we can thank (or blame) for the concept of "original sin," famously said, "You made us for yourself, Lord, and our hearts are restless until they rest in you." So in some way we were created incomplete, in need, impoverished, because God wants to be what completes us. We were never meant to be self-sufficient; we were created for community—with other humans, to be sure, but we were also created to be drawn into the community that is God.

The idea of "original sin" is unpopular these days, but Augustine wasn't stupid. It's probably more useful to think of it as an original wound; I tend to think of it as an "original kink" in our nature. In his book *Addiction and Grace*, the late psychiatrist and spiritual teacher Gerald May gives us a different take on the story of Eden and the "fall" from grace. He sees the primal parents not as willful and rebellious so much as naïve and gullible. They didn't eat the fruit as an act of defiance, but because it looked attractive, and they made the mistake of believing the serpent when it told them it was good and they wouldn't die. What was "death" to them, after all?

And so they immediately find themselves in a downward spiral of shame, denial, mental gymnastics, and rationalizations. In other words, they talk and act exactly like addicts, and God, who will not "enable" further self-destructive behavior (there is, after all, still one forbidden tree to eat from), allows them to suffer the consequences. God lays out some boundaries, which he allows an angel with a flaming sword to enforce. In banishing them from the garden, May says, God is not so much punishing Adam and Eve as protecting them, showing them some "tough love."

But the scar from that original wound has been etched on the human soul, and we carry it still. Life is hard, at times unbearable, and we do all kinds of unhelpful things as we try to bear it. We cover that "infinite abyss" within us with all manner of trash and rubble; it disappears from view, and we can forget its existence until the divine Archaeologist excavates it for us. This excavation, this divine "dig," is the process of kenosis which we encountered in Paul's letter to the Philippians. It takes this uncovering to find the original structure of our souls. In short, it takes poverty.

But oh, when we find it. Recall Thomas Merton's description of the *point vierge*, the Eden point, in our souls: "This little point of nothingness and of absolute poverty is the pure glory of God in us. . . . It is like a pure diamond, blazing with the invisible light of heaven."[6] It is this abyss of beauty, built into every human soul, that we clutter up with things that were never meant to fill it. As a young teen, I once stood with my family and some other travelers on a roadside in Switzerland, all of us gazing in awe at the pristine alpine meadow before us. And then I gazed in horror as one of those travelers crumpled up a candy wrapper and tossed it on the ground. This is the same bone-headed spirit in which we drop litter around the *point vierge*, which God created as the meeting place in our souls. It exists for God alone, or for God-with-us, and it is there that God waits for us until we are ready for an encounter that will change us at our very core.

A Spirituality of Addiction

In spite of the junk we throw over and around it, the still point itself remains pristine, always. Kenosis declutters the space so we can get to it and God can commune there with us. And that space isn't just sitting there; it has a kind of vacuum effect, which creates desire. Gerald May calls it an "inborn desire for God," and he describes this desire as "our deepest longing and our most precious treasure."[7] Of course it would be: it's this desire that was implanted within us to pull us back to our belovedness, back to our place as heirs of the kingdom. A precious treasure indeed.

6. Thomas Merton, *Conjectures of a Guilty Bystander* (New York: Bantam Doubleday Dell, 1994), 158.

7. Gerald G. May, *Addiction and Grace: Love and Spirituality in the Healing of Addictions* (New York: HarperOne, 1988), 1.

But because of the clutter, we don't seek God or even human love with a pure and passionate heart. Love can be glorious, but love also hurts; sometimes love hurts a lot. We love our parents and grow up to realize how human and flawed they are, and we grieve. Then we lose them, and grieve all over again. We love siblings and friends, only to become estranged from them. We fall in love and are snubbed, or invisible, and our hearts break. Or our love is returned, and we lose our beloved to sickness, dementia, death. We look for love from God at times like that, and God can seem a million miles away: snubbed again. It takes real courage and optimism to get up from the dust and choose vulnerability again after an experience like that. Most of us, until grace has worked on us for a while, will swear that we'll never fall for that trap again.

But the longing is still there, like it or not. And when we feel this vulnerable, we don't like it; we'll just do without love, thank you very much. We *repress* our desire, pushing it down within us, but desire is like matter: it doesn't go away, it just changes form or location. So we stuff it deep into our subconscious, hoping to bury it for good, only to have it squirt out the sides in unhealthy behaviors. Or we *displace* our desire onto other things, deciding (probably not consciously) that, after all, shopping is a pretty good substitute for a relationship. Either way, we have not dealt with the problem of our unfulfilled desire, our longing to know our primal identity: *Beloved*. In one way or another, that longing will come back to haunt us.

Repression, May says, was thought for generations to be the source of most all self-destructive behavior, including addiction. But he argues that *attachment* is a different and even more sinister process which, instead of pushing our desire out of sight, instead fixes it onto some object, person, or behavior, creating a need, an obsession, an addiction. Recall that we need to be within a certain range of dopamine to function, and our bodies work hard to keep us in equilibrium. When that equilibrium is disrupted by stress, or perhaps more accurately, when disequilibrium *creates* stress, anything that draws us back into equilibrium and reduces the stress is noted by our nerve cells as the means to a "new normal." This path to a new normal is called adaptation, which is another word for attachment. We become attached, May argues, to anything that makes things normal for us, and with that attachment, a new addiction is born. The process of *tolerance* means that in time, as our nerve cells prune away dopamine receptors, it will take more and more of the object of attachment to get us to equilibrium, and eventually it may not work at all, as we saw earlier.

Once an attachment is formed we are enslaved, virtually powerless to resist the thing that makes life enjoyable or at least tolerable. This powerlessness, incidentally, is where the 12-step process begins, and we'll return to it shortly. For now, the point is that the desire we were born with, which was meant to draw us to the place of interior communion with God, has been hijacked by the object of our attachment, along with the *eros* or psychic energy that was given to fuel our quest for God. In its place is the oscillation between craving and lethargy, a cycle from which free will is not enough to escape. As May says,

> Psychologically, addiction *uses up* desire. It is like a psychic malignancy, sucking our life energy into specific obsessions and compulsions, leaving less and less energy available for other people and other pursuits. Spiritually, addiction is a deep-seated form of idolatry. The objects of our addictions become our false gods. These are what we worship, what we attend to, where we give our time and energy, instead of love.[8]

Perhaps we think we are too spiritually mature to fall into this trap? The apostle Paul was pretty grown up, and yet:

> I do not understand my own actions. For I do not do what I want, but I do the very thing I hate. . . . I can will what is right, but I cannot do it. For I do not do the good I want, but the evil I do not want is what I do. . . . So I find it to

8. May, *Addiction and Grace*, 13; original emphasis.

> be a law that when I want to do what is good, evil lies close at hand. For I delight in the law of God in my inmost self [note his awareness of what I've been calling the "abyss" at the center of his being], but I see in my members [i.e., his limbs, farther from the core] another law at war with the law of my mind, making me captive to the law of sin that dwells in my members. Wretched man that I am! Who will rescue me from this body of death? (Rom 7:15, 18b-19, 21-24)

These processes, whether they bring us to what people usually think of as "rock bottom" or not, do bring us face-to-face with our poverty. The first thing we must give up on is salvation by willpower, which Paul has already done or he would not be looking to be rescued. Most of us have to fail at overcoming our attachments and addictions again and again before we'll give up on our own strength of will. When we can no longer pretend to be self-sufficient, when we realize we need to be "rescued" from a living death, we have a choice: we can despair, or we can accept our poverty and submit to the rescue. Perhaps the saving agent will be entirely secular: the National Institute on Drug Abuse lists medications, behavioral interventions, and digital therapeutics as "safe, effective, and desirable treatment strategies for substance abuse and overdose."[9] These are evidence-based approaches that we can take to be sound and trustworthy, and they are in no way incompatible with the spiritual "rescue" I am pointing to here.

But as an answer to our inner poverty, they are incomplete. In spiritual terms, they can dig away at the top layers of rubble covering the still point of our soul, but that will only bring us to the levels of attachment experienced by most people around us. It will never bring us to the true freedom for which Christ has set us free (see Gal 5:1). A person who quits drinking but doesn't deal with the problems that caused the drinking in the first place can

9. National Institutes of Health, "Treatment," *National Institute on Drug Abuse*, n.d., accessed February 13, 2023, https://nida.nih.gov/research-topics/treatment.

become what AA calls a "dry drunk," substituting a new addiction (coffee, cigarettes, exercise) for the old one. A dry drunk still carries a lot of misery, which can show itself in anxiety, depression, chronic victimhood, and more.[10] I once knew one who'd moved to coffee; he was known by name in every Starbucks in our neighborhood, and in Seattle, that's a lot. One evening when I wasn't ready for a drink, I asked him for a cup of coffee. He didn't have decaf, which is my usual jam, but I figured I could handle one cup of regular. The guy made me a quadruple shot without bothering to tell me, which made for a very short party and a long night in the emergency room.

Dry drunks can clear out a good bit of rubble by moving from mere sobriety to actual recovery, which in AA means working the steps. But real freedom is a work of grace, and since all of us have multiple attachments, we all need a lot of this grace. Wretched people that we are! And yet, Gerald May argues that we were actually created, presumably deliberately, with a capacity for forming attachments. It is, as they say, not a bug, but a feature. Given the amount of suffering and enslavement attachments can cause, why would God build this into us?

Since this is God, we can start with an assumption of love. For May, it goes back to our innate longing for God. We have a deep desire to be united with God, but we are what social theorists call *rational actors*. "Rational" here does not mean the opposite of "insane"; it means that we seek to maximize benefits to ourselves while minimizing costs. So if we have a goal, we seek the cheapest and easiest way to achieve that goal; that's the "rational" choice.

On the journey to knowing our belovedness in God, attachments are like shortcuts. Finding and attaining union with God is not easy; this is why spiritual traditions have compared it to things like climbing a mountain. When we're standing at base camp and

10. "What to Know about Dry Drunk Syndrome," *WebMD*, July 8, 2023, accessed February 8, 2025, https://www.webmd.com/mental-health/addiction/what-to-know-dry-drunk-syndrome.

the summit of the mountain is thousands of feet above us hidden by clouds, and we know that a long slog over slippery glaciers and deep crevasses lies between us and that summit, the temptation to buy a ticket and take the gondola can be pretty fierce. Most of us have bought a lot of those tickets in the course of our journeys. The problem is that the gondolas don't go to the summit; they go to dead ends, where we end up stranded and cold. Then we just stare numbly at that ticket, like the person described by Isaiah:

> Such a person feeds on ashes; a deluded heart misleads him;
> he cannot save himself, or say,
> "Is not this thing in my right hand a lie?" (Isa 44:20, New International Version)

It seems like God has duped us, allowed this exercise in futility, knowing full well that we'd seek the easier way to the top. Why doesn't God just outlaw gondolas? Why does God allow deception and fraud in the first place, knowing that we're gullible and lazy? These are reasonable questions, but what is the alternative? If the longing for God is what will finally draw us into union, into deeply knowing ourselves as beloved, we can see that this longing is critical to our soul's ultimate well-being. Fine so far. But why couldn't God just make all the dead ends and blind alleys disappear? Why not simply show us that there is only one way to the summit, and that it'll be so rewarding that we may as well start up the trail?

This is what people are usually asking for when they say, "Why doesn't God just show himself? Why all this coy peek-a-boo, where we get glimpses, but then we lose sight of them until it's hard to remember or believe that God even exists?" The next step is from questioning to demand: "If You exist, show yourself or I am *done*." And if God did show up? In full, radiant, divine glory, without any real searching on our part? May argues, correctly I believe, that this would make love impossible: "We would experience a kind of love, to be sure, but it would be love like a reflex."[11] The "love" we'd

11. May, *Addiction and Grace*, 94.

return to God would be forced out of us, not freely chosen. And there is no love that is not freely chosen. God refuses to become another attachment or addiction. We must choose out of freedom, or not at all.

In the Bible, when people do "see" God as it were face-to-face, they have usually gone through some preparatory process first. Often enough, it actually is a tough climb up a mountain: think of Moses on Mount Sinai and the three disciples on Mount Tabor during the transfiguration. And then they're profoundly changed: Moses' face, we're told, shone so brightly that he had to veil it when he returned to the people (see Exod 34:29-35). Jesus' three disciples were terrified as the cloud enveloped them, and he strictly charged them to say nothing of the experience until he was raised from the dead (see Mark 9:9). Can you imagine keeping a secret like that from your closest friends? After the resurrection, though, Peter spoke up. Assuring his readers that he was an eyewitness to Christ's glory, he continues:

> [Jesus] received honor and glory from God the Father when that voice was conveyed to him by the Majestic Glory, saying, "This is my Son, my Beloved, with whom I am well pleased." We ourselves heard this voice come from heaven, while we were with him on the holy mountain. (2 Pet 1:17-18)

Wild as this experience must have been, the three disciples had already been through a lot with Jesus by the time it occurred. They had freely chosen him, had given up everything to follow him. Imagine if they'd experienced the transfiguration on the first day they met him? There would have been no choosing, just helpless submission.

And God wants, longs, even, to be chosen by us. If we have tasted nothing else in our lives, if we have not known other delicacies, how could we "taste and see that the Lord is good" (Ps 34:8)? We would have nothing to compare God to. We could not choose God over and above all else if we had no experience of anything else. It would hardly be a compliment to me if my husband chose me without ever having met another woman. And the fact that in choosing me he chose against all the rest makes the choice a sacrifice (some days more than others), just as the choice for God is always a sacrifice, always to some extent painful. The cross is always there, because it must be. There is no real love without it. There is no one-sided coin, no passion with only the melody of desire and no counterpoint in suffering. We are bought with a price (1 Cor 6:20)—and so is God. We don't have the price, to be sure, but that is where grace comes in.

To recap our journey: We are created with a deep, sacred space within us, a *point vierge*, placed in our souls by God to be a pristine point of meeting, of communion, of union. This is where we can always know ourselves as God's beloved. But life is hard, and we form attachments and addictions that heap rubble on this sacred space. We may try to excavate it ourselves, but we're soon brought up against our powerlessness, our poverty. Willpower will fail us again and again, until we give up and submit to the divine "rescue." We may even "succeed" in mastering our addictions by displacing them onto other things, becoming "dry drunks." And we may genuinely succeed in recovering from addiction through secular treatment alone. But the spiritual problem goes deeper; excavating the *point vierge* is a work of grace, but to really uncover it, we have to exhaust the illusory solutions and *choose* God. It's a painful process, but as saints and mystics have testified through the ages, the path to loving union always, at some point, takes us through dark and desert places.

Alcoholics Anonymous: The Original 12-Step Movement

Alcoholics Anonymous (AA) had its origins in 1935 in a meeting in Akron, Ohio, between two "hopeless alcoholics."[12] These were Bill W., a stockbroker from New York, and Bob S., a surgeon local

12. Alcoholics Anonymous, "The Start and Growth of A.A.," n.d., accessed February 14, 2023, https://www.aa.org/the-start-and-growth-of-aa. I am greatly indebted to this source for the history recounted in this section.

to Akron. Both men had been influenced by the Oxford Group, an English Christian movement with nondenominational roots that emphasized a personal experience of conversion and practices that would generate spiritual and moral depth. The Oxford Group was not oriented toward alcoholism, but taught spiritual disciplines that would exert a profound influence on the founders of AA and on its approach to recovery. For instance, the Oxford Group had little in the way of institutional structure: no hierarchy, no membership lists, no buildings, and no paid employees. All of these would become, in time and with experimentation, principles of AA.

But back to our story. The Oxford Group and a longtime friend, Ebby T., had helped Bill become sober, and he had maintained his sobriety by working—not very successfully at first—with other alcoholics. Dr. Bob, in contrast, had not been able to stay sober until he met Bill. Ironically it was Bill, a medical layman, who introduced Dr. Bob to the idea of alcoholism as a disease. With this approach, and the inspiration of Bill's example, Dr. Bob never drank again. This marks the birth of Alcoholics Anonymous, though the name would come later. But the pair immediately began working with alcoholics at City Hospital in Akron and quickly had their first success.

Months later, a second group formed in New York, and by 1939, a third in Cleveland. The twelve steps began to take shape in a book (*The Big Book*) published by Bill with input from members. Publicity and allyship from the likes of John D. Rockefeller Jr. spurred rapid growth, which is hardly surprising given that AA was really the only hope of a large, if hidden, group of suffering and desperate people. By the end of 1939, membership was already at 2,000; two years later, it had grown to 6,000; and by 1950, it was up to 100,000. The next decade would be challenging, as the fledgling organization tried to figure out how to get such a large and diverse group of people, each of whom had a major mental health problem, to get along and work together. Still, over the course of the decade, AA was finding its way as a movement, and by 1950, the principles on which it stood had proved to be stabilizing and successful.

Dr. Bob, along with the dedicated and much loved Sister Ignatia, worked with hospitalized alcoholics until his death in 1950. Sister Ignatia carried on the work after his death, and was recognized for her efforts by multiple entities, including the White House. By 1955, the now-international fellowship of AA had a board of trustees and called its second General Service Conference in St. Louis, Missouri, at which Bill, who would die in 1971, turned the care of the organization over to the trustees. "At this moment, the Fellowship went on its own—A.A. had come of age."[13]

Today, AA exists in approximately 180 countries, and while it's difficult to say with certainty how many people have achieved sobriety through it (it is, after all, anonymous), it has served as a template for numerous other 12-step groups, as well as support groups (such as Al-Anon) for people affected by a loved one's addiction. Participation in AA or other relevant groups is often mandated by the courts, and because it's free, it's a resource recommended by health care and social service personnel for those who can't get access to residential and other costly treatment programs.

Is AA the Only Way?

Alcoholics Anonymous and other 12-step groups have drawn criticism on multiple points, two of which I'll describe here. First, they are abstinence-based, when critics maintain that a "harm reduction" model is effective and doesn't require renouncing alcohol completely. Second, because 12-step programs require members to rely on a "higher power," critics argue that they push people to adopt religious views and practices that may not be welcome to many addicts, or necessary.

While AA is the most widely known abstinence-based approach, the Minnesota Model, founded shortly after AA, shares most of AA's assumptions (such as alcoholism being a disease), and it is often used in conjunction with AA membership. But the

13. Alcoholics Anonymous, "Start and Growth of A.A."

Minnesota Model involves both inpatient and outpatient treatment involving a multidisciplinary team of treatment professionals. This approach is famously employed at the Hazelden Betty Ford Foundation, among many others.

In its earliest days, AA was the first, and for a time the only, semi-successful treatment for alcoholics. It offered hope to countless desperate people who had no other recourse, and it saved lives. But how many, and at what cost? The abstinence and spiritual requirements of AA were unacceptable to some addicts, and unnecessary in the view of some treatment professionals and researchers. The harm reduction alternative arose from these concerns, and this approach has two different emphases. The first seeks to reduce the personal and social harm associated with alcohol or drug use without trying to reduce substance use itself. Needle exchanges, developed in the context of the HIV/AIDS pandemic, are a well-known example of this. The second and more contested harm reduction approach does aim to reduce the use of alcohol and drugs to safer, more moderate levels. This approach uses meetings and other in-person and online peer support, which are meant to hold the addict accountable for their use.

The critical question, of course, concerns the relative effectiveness of abstinence vs. harm reduction models. Gauging the effectiveness of AA is challenging, not only because members are anonymous, but also because addicts often live unstable lives and may be hard to trace over a long period of time. On top of that, addicts often lie. In fact, Audrey Kishline, who in 1994 founded the harm reduction organization Moderation Management, was touting her program while drinking on the sly herself. In 2000 she announced that after all she was going to need to follow an abstinence regimen, but her story was a tragic one: an accident just a few months later resulted in two deaths, and a prison term for Kishline. This was followed by a divorce and finally, in 2014, her suicide.[14]

14. Amy Girvan, "The Next AA? Welcome to Moderation Management, Where Abstinence from Alcohol Isn't the Answer," *The Guardian*, March 16, 2015,

Kishline's story is not exactly an advertisement for the harm reduction approach, but although hers was a high-profile case, it was just one case. How effective is harm reduction relative to AA? Is either of them highly effective? How much do we know?

Given the stigma attached to alcoholism and drug abuse, it's no surprise that addicts aren't always forthcoming about their using, but it does make it difficult to judge how effective different programs are. And that's true for abstinence-only approaches, where at least we know what we mean by "success" (though we might quibble about the time period we use to gauge it). With harm reduction programs, in which the goal is for people to drink "in moderation," how do we judge whether a person has succeeded or failed? Are they succeeding if they avoid binge drinking? If they drink without exceeding a certain blood alcohol limit? If they drink without getting into trouble? Criteria for success will of necessity be somewhat arbitrary, which means that consensus on effectiveness is likely to be elusive.

Addiction is a complex phenomenon, and it's likely that multiple factors will affect which form of treatment will be most successful for which addict. Without going deep into the existing research, it seems safe to say that more studies using more sophisticated methods and designs can only help us get closer to that goal. But in the meantime, Bill W. himself acknowledged the complexity of both addicted individuals' experience and the means needed to treat their addiction: "We took the position that A.A. was not the final word on treatment; that it might be only the first word. For us, it became perfectly safe to tell people they could experiment with our therapy in any way they liked."[15]

---

accessed February 27, 2025, https://www.theguardian.com/society/2015/mar/16/the-next-aa-moderation-management-abstinence-alcohol-isnt-the-answer.

15. Ernest Kurtz and Katherine Ketcham, *The Spirituality of Imperfection: Storytelling and the Search for Meaning* (New York: Bantam, 1992), 130.

Working the Program

Alcoholics Anonymous calls itself a *fellowship*, which exists to help people achieve sobriety. Membership is free and open to all, regardless of age; the only requirement is that a person desire to stop drinking. They needn't even have stopped when they attend, and people have been known to show up drunk. But they must have the desire, and they must be willing to "work the program." AA is a culture that has a lot of sayings—you might call them proverbs—and one of them is, "The program works if you work it." The program is based on the following twelve steps:[16]

1. We admitted we were powerless over alcohol—that our lives had become unmanageable.
2. Came to believe that a Power greater than ourselves could restore us to sanity.
3. Made a decision to turn our will and our lives over to the care of God as we understood Him.
4. Made a searching and fearless moral inventory of ourselves.
5. Admitted to God, to ourselves, and to another human being the exact nature of our wrongs.
6. Were entirely ready to have God remove all these defects of character.
7. Humbly asked Him to remove our shortcomings.
8. Made a list of all persons we had harmed, and became willing to make amends to them all.
9. Made direct amends to such people wherever possible, except when to do so would injure them or others.

16. Alcoholics Anonymous, "The Twelve Steps," n.d., accessed February 27, 2023, https://www.aa.org/the-twelve-steps.

10. Continued to take personal inventory and when we were wrong promptly admitted it.
11. Sought through prayer and meditation to improve our conscious contact with God as we understood Him, praying only for knowledge of His will for us and the power to carry that out.
12. Having had a spiritual awakening as the result of these Steps, we tried to carry this message to alcoholics, and to practice these principles in all our affairs.

This, Richard Rohr has said, is "the marrow of the Gospel."[17] In other words, it's a way of life that is just what Jesus was calling people to when he told them to "Repent, for the kingdom of God is near." It's a basic process of conversion: making a commitment to follow this program means believing and trusting in God; turning our life and will over to God; honest examination of conscience; a firm resolve to make amends where we have harmed our neighbor; and sharing this gift with others who need it. Is this not the basic pattern of the Christian life? Whether all alcoholics should be compelled to live "the Christian life" or indeed any religious way of life is, as we've seen, a point of contention, and many prefer not to.

Recovery is a "spiritual awakening," though, and requires those who enter into it to, in the words of John the Baptist, "Bear fruits worthy of repentance" (Matt 3:8 NKJV). Because we all become consummate bullshit artists when our addictions are at risk, the only fruits worthy of our repentance are unflinching honesty, with ourselves and others, and changed behavior. The 12 steps require this, and only the knowledge that their life is at stake and they're powerless to help themselves will motivate most people to undertake such a demanding discipline. For those of us whose addictions and attachments are less obvious, whose idolatry is more hidden, we can go our entire lives without being pushed to this kind of reckoning.

17. Richard Rohr, *Breathing Under Water: Spirituality and the Twelve Steps* (Cincinnati, OH: Franciscan Media, 2011), xii.

But it is *poverty* that will shatter our illusions, that will force us to face down the lies we live with, whether we're "addicts" in the conventional sense or not—lies about how we're in control, we can stop any time, we're making it work, there's no need to change. As long as we believe in our self-sufficiency, we will not be motivated to make the kind of radical change that true repentance and conversion require. Why change direction unless you realize you can't get where you want to go from here? This is why the first step is to accept and admit one's powerlessness. *Powerlessness* can be understood as a synonym for poverty, and in the 12-step tradition, healing doesn't begin until we own our poverty, even embrace it. Most of us who believe in our own power won't make radical, difficult changes because we aren't convinced we need to. It's hitting bottom that jolts sleepers awake to a painful recognition that their lives are out of control, and they can't do anything about it.

It must be acknowledged, however, that not everyone who decides to stop drinking has a "hitting bottom" experience, any more than everyone who decides to follow Christ has to turn away from a sensationally sinful past. Thérèse of Lisieux was raised in a family of saints, died at age 24 without having ever done much obvious sinning, and was canonized herself less than thirty years later. She was, spiritually speaking, a "quick study," and there are alcoholics who figure out that they need help long before they completely dismantle their lives.

But poverty comes in a multitude of forms: Thérèse experienced severe losses and grief at an early age, was bullied mercilessly at school, and suffered from extreme sensitivity, scrupulosity, and anxiety. In other words, her life certainly lacks the "thud" of a soul hitting bottom, but the cross found its way to her all the same. Just so, those who deal with physical or mental illness or disability, discrimination, stigma, and exclusion, because of race, gender, sexuality, or other reasons, often find that the "bottom" is pretty much where they begin. When this happens, it doesn't take years of dismantling the ego and hacking away at their self-sufficiency; they have precious little of this to begin with, and their journey will look different from those whose life includes years of substance abuse and hiding from the truth about their captivity.

Regardless of where it begins, this journey is going to take courage, and the addict will need companionship and support. Much of this comes from the meetings, which one can attend as often as needed. But additionally, in AA, as soon as one's poverty is accepted, the next step is to place one's trust in a power greater than oneself. This has been, as we've seen, one of the main points of criticism of the 12-step tradition from the earliest days. Bill W. and his collaborators addressed the issue in *The Big Book*, first published in 1939, in a chapter called "We Agnostics." The tone is accepting: readers are not disparaged for not believing in God, but the writers show how they themselves, beginning as agnostics or atheists, had come to believe in something they could call God. Step 3 reads: "Made a decision to turn our will and our lives over to the care of God *as we understood Him*" (emphasis added).

So members are urged to find some "higher power," something greater than themselves in which they can place their trust. This could be God, or it could be the group itself. One therapist has suggested nature, evolution, or Batman. Regardless, you have to trust something outside yourself.[18] People can't be at peace with their powerlessness unless someone or something else has power.

The Wound as Our Greatest Strength

The Swiss psychiatrist Carl Jung said, "God enters through the wound." Just five words, but their wisdom is powerful. Kurtz and Ketcham, in *The Spirituality of Imperfection*, elaborate on Jung's statement:

> The descent to the depths brings the realization that without help one is lost. The spirituality of imperfection is the spirituality of the weak and the broken, the poor and the humble. It

18. Illissa Ducoat, "A Higher Power for Those Who Don't Believe in a Higher Power," PsychCentral, July 26, 2016, accessed August 12, 2024, https://psychcentral.com/blog/a-higher-power-for-those-who-dont-believe-in-a-higher-power#1.

> is and always has been a spirituality for people with large and strong passions, with troubled pasts and uncertain futures, a spirituality both ordinary and unconventional.[19]

Remember that the resurrected Jesus approached his astonished disciples wounds-first: "Look at my hands and my feet; see that it is I myself. Touch me and see . . . " (Luke 24:39). Henri Nouwen wrote movingly of wounded healers, and the struggle to know our belovedness:

> Personally, as my struggle reveals, I don't often "feel" like a beloved child of God. But I know that that is my most primal identity and I know that I must choose it above and beyond my hesitations. . . . Choose now and continue to choose this incredible truth. As a spiritual practice claim and reclaim your primal identity as beloved daughter or son of a personal Creator.[20]

Richard Rohr, speaking of wounded healers, reminds us that "There is no other kind. In fact, *you are often most gifted to heal others precisely where you yourself were wounded, or wounded others.*"[21] It's a gift, and part of the blessedness of our poverty.

This resonates so deeply with me. I can trace back to childhood a belief that goes deep in my psyche that I am not enough, that I'm unworthy of approval and must work harder and harder to avoid letting people down. Knowing that this is the product in part of my early experiences is kind of reassuring. It does not, however, eradicate or even diminish the power of the belief itself, which led to decades of overwork that took a serious toll on my health.

That's my wound. Well, it's probably not the only one, but it's a big one. And yet, a result of this woundedness is that I have

19. Kurtz and Ketcham, *Spirituality of Imperfection*, 111.

20. Henri J. M. Nouwen, "You Are Beloved," January 4, in *You Are the Beloved* (New York: Random House, 2017).

21. Rohr, *Breathing Under Water*, 69.

a special gift for seeing the divine radiance in others, even and especially when they don't see it in themselves. As I described in *The Sacred Gaze*, like Thomas Merton, I've had those moments of not knowing how to tell people that they're "shining like the sun."[22]

In treating addiction, health care professionals can provide interventions that will help with the process of recovery. In other words, not all healers need to be wounded themselves, or not in the same ways as their clients. But there is a special bond that forms when a person on the bottom meets someone who's been there and found their way up to a new and fulfilling life. As we saw when Jesus met the woman at the well, the most powerful healing comes when the healer reaches not down, but across. Jesus came with his thirst, and he offered to give Photini "living water" for her thirst. One who reaches down *to* us is likely also to look down *on* us. We've all known religious leaders who've maintained a façade of invulnerability and control, and we've seen the condescending attitude that comes from that sense of self—until they, too, topple off their pedestal. But one who reaches across, from the position of their own need or their own similar experience—that is someone we can trust.

And it's their honesty that we come to trust. Poverty is fundamental to the human condition; whether we're addicts in the conventional sense or not, we all share the original wound, and it will gnaw away at our vitals whether we own it or not. We can spend a lifetime in denial, forcing it down until it squishes out the sides and splashes onto others. But it will appear somewhere, somehow. People who are pretending this isn't true cannot be trusted by people who know it is. And because AA and the 12-step tradition begin with the acknowledgment of this wound, of this powerlessness, it is a movement of our time in which poverty is not only understood but *prioritized*. This is indeed the marrow of the gospel, and wisdom we all need.

22. Susan R. Pitchford, *The Sacred Gaze: Contemplation and the Healing of the Self* (Collegeville, MN: Liturgical Press, 2014).

Chapter 8

Conclusion

The Paradox of Poverty

Precisely where I feel my poverty
is where I discover God's blessing.

Henri Nouwen

So many of the greatest and deepest spiritual truths are found in paradoxes. They come up time and again in Jesus' teachings: the last shall be first; good leaders are slaves to those they lead; those who love their life will lose it, and those who hate their life will live forever. Blessed are the poor in spirit, those who mourn, those who are rejected, slandered, persecuted. And the puzzles go back further in the Scriptures: in Job we see that the righteous suffer, and we are never told why. We are just reminded of our place in the creation, and that there is much that is, and will remain, mysterious to us.

God seems to delight in hiding nuggets of truth, like Easter eggs, within paradoxes. And why would we expect otherwise, when God's own self is a paradox? The mystery of the Trinity is like a Zen koan: you can't reason your way to a "solution"; you can only respond, and an appropriate response will change you. How can three be one, and one three? This is not a riddle, and there is no solution. There is only surrender, only allowing oneself to be swept into the current of love between Three that is so powerful that they are One. Love is everything, because love is God's own self.

So at the heart of the paradox of poverty is this truth: When Jesus said the poor in spirit are blessed, it's because of love. Not because only the poor in spirit are God's beloved; we all are. But because it's the poor in spirit who tend to abandon all other promises of happiness and fall face-down in the dust before the One who calls them Beloved. This is how most of us learn the glorious truth of our identity. As Henri Nouwen said, "One of the tragedies of life is that we keep forgetting who we are."[1] Poverty is the divine gift that keeps reminding us of our true identity, our true belovedness in God. That is blessedness indeed.

How have we seen that work? Let's take a quick look back and see how the different traditions we've examined have understood poverty (or not) and the role it plays in drawing us into that current of divine love.

The curse of Constantine was that once the early church achieved first acceptance and then dominance, poverty of any kind was the last thing on its agenda. Rather than demand, as Clare later would, the "privilege of poverty," the church by this time went for privilege, full stop. But there were always voices calling it back: the desert hermits spurned luxury and ease, and embraced a fierce asceticism that would keep their hearts pure and their souls close to the kingdom. But Constantine lives on. In our own time, we have seen over a century of Prosperity preaching, which rejects both material poverty and poverty of spirit ("I say to you, how dare you be poor!"). The church seems to be in a repeating cycle of succumbing to the seduction of worldly wealth and power, and then being called back by prophetic voices to the original vision, a pattern sociologists have referred to as the "secularization-revival cycle."

1. Henri J. M. Nouwen, *Here and Now: Living in the Spirit*, 10th anniversary ed. (New York: Crossroad, 2006), 36.

But what do the Scriptures say? We obviously haven't been able to do a thorough review of Scriptures dealing with poverty of spirit, but in the texts we have examined, a few central themes appear. From the very beginning, from Adam and Eve in the Garden, we see the foolish tendency of humans to grab from God rather than receiving what God desires to give. Even the Greeks understood this, as we see in the myth of Prometheus: stealing from the gods is never going to end well.

Jesus showed us a better way. If we want to prepare ourselves to receive all that our loving God has to give us, we need to submit ourselves to the process of being emptied out—kenosis—trusting that we are God's beloved, and that God will not withhold anything that's good for us. That's why Jesus said that the "kingdom of heaven"—every good thing you could possibly imagine or desire—belongs to the poor in spirit. Jesus showed us that the key to happiness ("blessedness") is to trust in the infinite love of the God who *is* love and who calls us Beloved, even when we feel that life is taking everything away. This is when, as St. Paul said, we see ourselves truthfully, "as having nothing, and yet possessing all things" (2 Cor 6:10 NKJV).

Francis and Clare of Assisi certainly understood the connection between poverty and belovedness. They were both, as I said, infatuated with poverty to a point that seems almost bizarre until you realize what poverty meant to them. Francis' courting of Lady Poverty, his swearing lifelong fidelity to her, was his way of saying that the poor Christ was everything to him. Clare said as much in her letters to Agnes, urging her to be true to her vocation as the poor spouse of the poor Christ, who is in fact the most noble and glorious of all. In her fourth letter, after urging Agnes to meditate on the poverty and vulnerability of Christ, from the infant in the manger to the sacrificial victim on the cross, she links it all to their belovedness:

> As you further contemplate His ineffable delights, eternal riches and honors, and sigh for them in the great desire and love of your heart, may you cry out:

Draw me after you,
We will run in the fragrance of your perfumes,
O heavenly Spouse!
I will run and not tire,
until You bring me into the wine-cellar,
Until Your left hand is under my head
And Your right hand will embrace me happily,
[and] You will kiss me with the happiest kiss of Your mouth.[2]

Probably the tradition that most explicitly connects poverty (understood as pain and suffering) with love is that of the Sacred Heart. A devotion that began by focusing on Jesus' wounds and grew in time to focus on his pierced (you could say, broken) heart is one in which suffering and love are impossible to separate. The medieval, early modern, and later mystics who have seen the heart of Christ as a place of refuge, a place where the beloved is invited to find shelter, saw in that heart unspeakable suffering motivated by an unfathomable love. What makes the Sacred Heart different from the other poverty traditions we've considered is that here it is Christ's suffering, not ours, that is the focus. Yet the invitation is there to bring our wounds to our wounded God, and to know them healed by his lavish, limitless love.

With the mystics of Helfta, we turned our attention from individual to collective poverty of spirit. Though anthropologists have revealed a few exceptional matriarchal cultures, the poverty of being not-male seems to have been a near constant across time and space. Societies have done better and worse jobs of recognizing the humanity and rights of women, transgender, and nonbinary people,[3] but it's safe to say that medieval Europe was not a place

2. Clare's fourth letter to Agnes of Prague, quoted in Claire Marie Ledoux, *Clare of Assisi: Her Spirituality Revealed in Her Letters*, trans. Colette Joly Dees (Cincinnati, OH: St. Anthony Messenger Press, 1997), 81.

3. In this chapter, I focused on the silencing of women, both to keep it simple and because there's been less known and written about LGBTQ+ people who

where women's voices were frequently heard by those in power. Excluded from holy orders, even high-born and well-educated women were not welcome at the tables where arguments were heard and decisions made.

Yet the Spirit had one ace up Her sleeve: the experiences and wisdom of mystics gave them a kind of authority—charismatic, rather than institutional—that did tend to be respected. That is, unless they were executed, which often depended on whether they had a male champion who was himself respected. But the value placed on mystical experience at that time meant that women such as those who gathered at Helfta, especially those like our two Mechtilds and two Gertrudes, authors of wonderful mystical texts, had their voices heard, even amplified. Helfta was a place where smart and devout women, who experienced themselves as deeply loved by God, flourished. Their contribution to the spiritual tradition was not devalued or discarded. It was a rare and beautiful moment indeed.

Coming closer to the present day, we also looked at racism as a form of collective poverty of spirit. When the white church has ignored the sin of racism, it has forsaken its mission to love our neighbor. While the church has mostly refrained from direct violence, at least lately (with white "Christian nationalism" being a notable contemporary exception), it has formed part of the institutional and cultural systems of violence. The church's leaders have played their part in upholding white supremacy. They have emboldened the extremists above them in the pyramid and allowed the people below them to turn a blind eye to their neighbor's suffering, to fail to recognize the *imago dei* in the other. Thus we have worshiped a partial god, and a partial god is a false god. We've failed to oppose the countless ways in which racism continues to afflict Black people and others. In short, we've preached a false

---

lived in that era. I think in our own time, we could see plenty of parallels to the dynamics revealed in the chapter.

gospel, taken God's name in vain. And "the LORD will not hold him guiltless who takes His name in vain" (Exod 20:7 NKJV).

But there is good news, if we're willing to hear it. The Black church has long been a space of loving support and freedom for those who suffer because of racism, and Black voices from within the church have for generations spoken truth to power. Black liberation theologians have offered a gospel that proclaims good news to the poor, release to the captives, freedom for the oppressed, and recovery of sight to the blind. This is the gospel Jesus proclaimed, and if white folks will lay down their defenses and hear it, they will indeed recover their vision. Further, as womanist theologians have expanded this vision to be more inclusive of Black women's experience, the gospel preached grows deeper and more authentic still.

Finally, in the 12-step tradition we have seen a poverty-focused movement that is very much of our own time. Alcoholics Anonymous and its offshoots place poverty squarely at the heart of recovery: Step 1 is the acknowledgment of one's own powerlessness over the object of their addiction. In this chapter, we looked at both the neuroscience and spirituality of addiction, the ways our bodies and souls deal with powerful attachments. It seems almost perverse that God created us with a capacity for attachments, but as we saw, this is poverty: we must see the idols for what they are before we can choose the true God in freedom. And God will not have us without freedom; of what use are slaves to a God who is love?

It's been quite a journey. In all these traditions, we have seen the people of God grappling with the knottiest of questions: how are the poor blessed? Or perhaps, why are the blessed ones poor? What did Jesus mean when he blessed the poor in spirit? Followers of Christ have been wrestling with this question for a couple of millennia, and there's been so much wisdom generated by their struggles. Let's not forget that God blessed Jacob when he wrestled with the angel. Sure, he ended up with an injury—a sign of his poverty—but God honored his struggle. I am convinced that God honors ours as well.

Poverty: The Way Home to God

Poverty is a paradox. It's a mystery, a koan. The problem is that the church has not really taught us how to deal with koans. As a result, when we feel our poverty, when we experience things that make us feel humbled and diminished, we're apt to jump to the wrong conclusions. We think God is disappointed in us, that we're all wrong and possibly damned. We can find ourselves sucked into a shame tornado instead of knowing in our bones how much God cherishes us. If we could only see our poverty for what it is, an invitation to take refuge in the heart of Jesus and know ourselves beloved, we could miss out on a lot of pain. There would still be pain, to be sure: the pain of the poverty itself. But for most of us, the worst suffering is the suffering that feels like it has no meaning, that seems like a pointless waste.

In God's economy, nothing is pointless; nothing is wasted. Think of Carl Jung and the shadow side of the person, the part of us we hide, reject, and repress. It is, as Jung taught us, that thing we have no wish to be. Yet the shadow is part of us, and if we confront and integrate it, we have a shot at wholeness and completion, of psychological well-being. We wouldn't be better off without it. It's not a pointless waste; it's just a mystery.

Similarly, in the traditions we've examined in this book, poverty is not something we'd be better off without; it is absolutely central to our spiritual wholeness and well-being. This is not because God delights in seeing us grovel. It's because, first, it's the reality of our condition, and God is never fond of our believing in lies. But it's also because it pushes us in God's direction. It seems fair to say that we all need that push, because falling back on our own cleverness and strength is a hard habit to break. It's part of the human condition, the temptation of pride to which we all fall prey. It's not that everyone has to have a spectacular story of conversion from an obviously disastrous life, but that even the most dedicated among us need daily to hear the words given to Zechariah: "Not by might, nor by power, but by my spirit, says the Lord of hosts" (Zech 4:6).

One tradition we didn't look at closely, because it's been so much discussed elsewhere, is John of the Cross and the "dark night of the soul." John correctly saw that times of spiritual darkness, even intense darkness, should not automatically be seen as signs that we've sinned or lost our way. They can actually be signs that we are progressing along the spiritual path, being invited to love God for God's own sake rather than the good feelings we may have unwittingly focused on before. Darkness can be a mark of spiritual depth, just as the crashes and falls of a toddler are happy evidence that the child is learning to walk.

What if the church taught us this? Not in the occasional sermon or class, as it does now, but intentionally and systematically? What if the church reached into the treasure it's accumulated over the centuries and, as Jesus advised, brought out "things new and old" (Matt 13:52 NKJV)? It's this treasure of the new and the old that we've examined here, the wisdom schools that have appeared over the centuries in which poverty is the curriculum and the knowledge of our belovedness the degree we earn upon graduation. I can imagine the commencement speech being given by Henri Nouwen:

> [A]ll I want to say to you is "You are the Beloved," and all I hope is that you can hear these words as spoken to you with all the tenderness and force that love can hold. My only desire is to make these words reverberate in every corner of your being—"You are the Beloved."[4]

"Blessed are the poor in spirit," Jesus said, because, as we've seen, they are quicker to give up on themselves and their own resources. It's the illusion of our self-sufficiency that keeps us from giving up on our own way, keeps us gritting our teeth and trying to have the willpower to become the people we want to be. The wealthier we

4. Henri J. M. Nouwen, *Life of the Beloved: Spiritual Living in a Secular World* (New York: Crossroad, 2002), 29–30 Kindle.

are, the longer we can play this game, and the greater the shock when we finally lose. And we will lose; it's inevitable. But we so often don't see it coming because we believe in our false self, the self with no shadow. It's this self that lives in a state of isolation, of the sense of separation from God and others and its own authentic being—that lives, in other words, in hell—because it cannot accept its own dependency.

But we have a choice; we never have to believe a lie. We can cling to our unreal, shadowless self, or we can take the exceptionally sound advice of Brennan Manning, who knew a thing or two about poverty:

> Define yourself radically as one beloved by God. This is the true self. Every other identity is illusion.[5]

God grant us the wisdom to see our poverty, as so many of our spiritual forebears have, as the path to this true self. It's the path that leads us through the wounds of Jesus into the depths of the heart of God. There is no safer refuge, no greater joy.

And God give us the grace to find there the courage and strength to fight the unholy poverty that afflicts our neighbor: to recognize in them the *imago dei*, to see and hear them with our full attention, and then to allow them to lead us to taking action that really helps. For this is the other face of love: it's not just about my own belovedness, but about taking my neighbor seriously—*really* seriously—as God's own beloved. If my poverty doesn't take me to this place, then I have missed the whole point and ended up in hell after all.

But if my poverty brings me to understand both myself and my neighbor as cherished by God, chosen and beloved, then the connectedness of us all is revealed. United, we are drawn together into the current of love flowing among the Persons of the Trinity, and the circle is complete.

5. Brennan Manning, *Abba's Child: The Cry of the Heart for Intimate Belonging* (Colorado Springs, CO: NavPress, 2015 [1994]), 42.